T0329459

THE MAGNIFICENT EMPEROR WU

THE MAGNIFICENT EMPEROR WU

CHINA'S HAN DYNASTY

Hing Ming Hung

Algora Publishing
New York

Library of Congress Cataloging-in-Publication Data

Names: Hung, Hing Ming, author.
Title: The Magnificent Emperor Wu : China's Han Dynasty / Hing Ming Hung.
Description: New York : Algora Publishing, [2020] | Includes
    bibliographical references. | Summary: "One of the greatest emperors in
    Chinese history, Liu Che (157 BC-87 BC) is known posthumously as Emperor
    Wu. Under his reign China expanded its territory dramatically. Liu Che
    consolidated China's power under a strong central government founded on
    Confucian principles. This book, based largely on the writings of
    China's ancient historian, Sima Qian, summarizes the development of the
    Han Dynasty and the reign of Emperor Wu"— Provided by publisher.
Identifiers: LCCN 2020003087 (print) | LCCN 2020003088 (ebook) | ISBN
    9781628944167 (trade paperback) | ISBN 9781628944174 (hardcover) | ISBN
    9781628944181 (pdf)
Subjects: LCSH: Han Wudi, Emperor of China, 156 B.C.-87 B.C. | China—Kings
    and rulers—Biography.
Classification: LCC DS748.16.H36 H86 2020 (print) | LCC DS748.16.H36
    (ebook) | DDC 931/.04092 [B]—dc23
LC record available at https://lccn.loc.gov/2020003087
LC ebook record available at https://lccn.loc.gov/2020003088

Printed in the United States

Table of Contents

INTRODUCTION

One of the greatest emperors in Chinese history was named Liu Che (157 BC–87 BC). The seventh emperor of the Han Dynasty, he is known posthumously as Emperor Wu. Under his reign China expanded its territory dramatically. Liu Che consolidated China's power under a strong central government founded on Confucian principles.

Where did he come from? The Western Han Dynasty was founded 100 earlier by Liu Bang (256 BC–195 BC), and it lasted 202 BC–AD 8. Liu Bang was on the throne for seven years, and when he passed away in 195 BC, his son Liu Ying succeeded him as emperor. Emperor Liu Ying also ruled for seven years, passing away in 188 BC at the age of twenty-three. After he died, power was left in the hands of his mother Lü Zhi. She acted according to her own will. She put a young son of Emperor Liu Ying on the throne but she made her brothers and her brothers' sons regional kings, so the members of the Lü family held great power. After her demise, the members of the Lü family fomented a rebellion. Premier Chen Ping and General Zhou Bo put down the Lü rebellion and invited Liu Heng, King of the State of Dai, to take the throne of the Han Dynasty. In 180 BC Liu Heng ascended to the throne. He ruled until 157 BC, when he passed away, to be succeeded by his son Liu Qi. Emperor Liu Qi was on the throne of the Han Dynasty for sixteen years and was succeeded by his son Liu Che in 141 BC.

The Huns lived in the grasslands of Mongolia. They were nomadic people, living on horseback. They often invaded the northern border areas of the Han Dynasty. One time when Emperor Liu Bang was in Pingcheng, in 201 BC, Modu, the King of the Huns, sent 400,000 elite soldiers who surrounded Emperor Liu Bang in Baideng for seven days. Emperor Liu Bang adopted one of Chen Ping's stratagems. He sent a secret envoy to present precious gifts to Modu's wife. Then Modu's wife persuaded Modu to let Liu Bang and his troops go. But still the Huns frequently invaded the territory of the Han Dynasty. The Han Dynasty sought to pacify them by marrying a princess of the royal clan to the king of the Huns.

When Liu Che ascended the throne, he was determined to defeat the Huns. In spring 129 BC, he sent General Wei Qing and other generals to march north to fight them. General Wei Qing battled the Huns in Longcheng, the place where the Huns held their ceremony of offering sacrifices to Heaven. He was triumphant; he won the first victory over the Huns for the Han Dynasty and from then on the Han troops won more victories over the Huns. In 119 BC Emperor Liu Che sent General Wei Qing and General Huo Qu Bing across the Gobi Desert to fight the Huns, and their King had to flee to the far north. General Huo Qu Bing commanded his troops to fight and pursuit them to Hanhai (now Lake Baikal, southern Siberia, Russia). They won a great victory.

Seeking to unite with the State of Yuezhi to attack the Huns, Emperor Liu Che sent Zhang Qian on a mission to the states in the Western Region. Zhang Qian started out from Chang'an (now Xi'an, in the south central part of Shaanxi Province). It was a long way: he went past what is nowadays Gansu Province of China, Inner Mongolia — an Autonomous Region of China, Mongolia, the Xinjiang Uygur Autonomous Region of China, and Kyrgyzstan, Kazakhstan, Uzbekistan and Afghanistan in Central Asia.

It was Zhang Qian who opened up the original "Silk Road". This important trade route united a huge region for commercial, cultural and administrative links for many centuries. In autumn 2013 the leader of the Chinese government proposed "One Belt One Road" when he was on a visit to the countries in Central Asia and Southeast Asia. "One Belt" means the Silk Road Economic Belt and "One Road" means the 21st – Century Maritime Silk Road.

The State of Nanyue (which covered the areas of today's Guangdong Province and Guangxi Zhuang Autonomous Region) would not submit to the Han Dynasty. In 111 BC Emperor Liu Che sent troops to attack the State of Nanyue and pacified it. So Emperor Liu Che made great contributions in the unification of China.

After Emperor Liu Che passed away, he was given the honorary title of Emperor Wu (Chinese character:), because he was powerful, valiant, intelligent and far-sighted.

Most of the materials used in writing this book are taken from the "Records of the Great Historian" (Chinese: 史記 or Shiji) by Sima Qian (145–85 BC) of the Former Han Dynasty. Some of the materials are taken from "History of the Former Han Dynasty" (Chinese: 前漢書 or qianhanshu) by Ban Gu (32–92) of the Later Han Dynasty. "A Comprehensive Mirror for the Aid of Government" (Chinese: 資治通鑒 or zizhitongjian) by Sima Guang (1019–1086) of the Song Dynasty is a chronicle. I use this book as a thread to link all the materials pulled from different sources.

Portrait of Liu Che, Emperor Wu of the Han Dynasty (157 BC–87 BC)

2.

A Map of Modern China

CHAPTER ONE: LIU BANG FOUNDS THE HAN DYNASTY

1. YING ZHENG UNIFIES CHINA AND BECOMES THE FIRST EMPEROR OF THE QIN DYNASTY

During the period of the Warring States (403 BC–221 BC), China was divided into seven states. They were: the State of Qi (now the most part of Shandong Province), the State of Chu (now the areas of Jiangsu Province, Anhui Province, Hubei Province and Hunan Province), the State of Zhao (now the southern part of Hebei Province and the northern part of Shanxi Province), the State of Yan (now the northern part of Hebei Province and the west part of Liaoning Province), the State of Wei (now the northern part of Henan Province and the southern part of Shanxi Province), the State of Haan (now the northwest part of Henan Province and the southern part of Shanxi Province) and the State of Qin (now Shaanxi Province, Sichuan Province and the east part of Gansu Province).

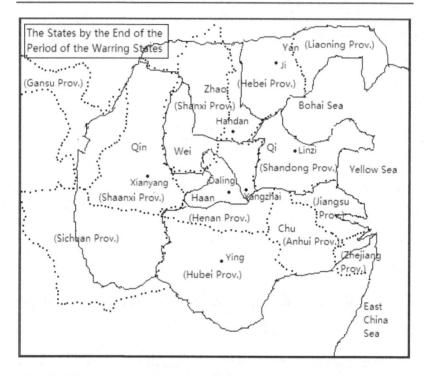

The States by the End of the Period of the Warring States

The States by the End of the Period of the Warring States

The seven states waged wars against one another. Of the seven states, the State of Qin was the strongest and had a topographical advantage. It was protected by the Yellow River and great mountains. The capital of the State of Qin was Xianyang (now Xianyang, Shaanxi Province).

Ying Zheng succeeded his father Ying Yi Ren to the throne of the State of Qin in May 247 BC. In 230 BC the King of the State of Qin sent troops to attack the State of Haan. The Qin army conquered the State of Haan and captured Haan An, the king. The King of the State of Qin turned the State of Haan into the Prefecture of Yingchuan.

In 229 BC the King of the State of Qin sent troops to attack the State of Zhao. They took Handan (now Handan, in the southern part of Hebei Province), the capital of the State of Zhao, and captured Zhao Qian, the King of the State of Zhao. The State of Zhao was conquered.

In 227 BC the King of the State of Qin sent troops to attack the State of Yan. The next year the Qin took Ji (now Beijing), the capital of the State of Yan. The King of the State of Yan escaped to Liaodong (now Liaoyang, Liaoning Province).

In 225 BC the King of the State of Qin sent troops to attack the State of Wei. They dug a channel to divert water from the Yellow River to flood the city of Daliang (now Kaifeng, Henan Province), the capital of the State of Wei. Wei Jia, the King of the State of Wei, surrendered. The State of Wei was conquered.

In 224 BC the King of the State of Qin sent a great army of 600,000 men to attack the State of Chu. In 223 BC they captured Fu Chu, the King of the State of Chu. The State of Chu was conquered. In the next year the King of the State of Qin sent troops to attack Liaodong, where they captured Ji Xi, the King of the State of Yan who had escaped from Ji (now Beijing). The State of Yan was finally conquered.

In 221 BC the King of the State of Qin sent a great army to attack the State of Qi. The Qin army captured Tian Jian, the King of the State of Qi, and the State of Qi was conquered. From then on the whole China was unified as one.

Thus Ying Zheng, the King of the State of Qin, conquered the other six states and unified China as one. He changed the name of the State of Qin into the Qin Dynasty and he named himself the First Emperor. He hoped that his dynasty would last forever.

The First Emperor was a cruel ruler. In order to prevent the people from rebelling, he ordered that all the weapons from the original six states be collected and he had such weapons melted into twelve enormous figures, each of which weighed 170 tons. He did not allow the people to have any weapons: five households were allowed to share one metal knife for kitchen use.

He sent General Meng Tian to drive the Huns out of the area of the Great Bend of the Yellow River (in Ningxia Hui and Inner Mongolia, two Autonomous Regions of China). In order to prevent the Huns from entering the areas of the Qin Dynasty, he ordered a great wall to be built. Thousands and thousands of people were sent to build this great wall, and many of them died performing this extraordinary task. And many people were sent to build the Epang Palaces and the mausoleum of the First Emperor of the Qin Dynasty. The people lived in great suffering.

帝 皇 始 秦

3. Portrait of the First Emperor of the Qin Dynasty

In July 210 BC the First Emperor of the Qin Dynasty died while he was making a tour to the east part of China. Before he died, he asked Zhao Gao, a eunuch (a castrated manservant), to write a letter to his eldest son Prince Ying Fu Su, asking the Prince to go back to Xianyang to preside over his funeral. At that time Prince Ying Fu Su was the supervisor of a great army of 300,000 men under the command of General Meng Tian stationed in the north border around the Great Wall. Zhao Gao and Li Si, the premier, made a scheme to get rid of Prince Ying Fu Su and put Prince Ying Hu Hai, the younger son of the First Emperor of the Qin Dynasty, on the throne. They wrote another letter in the name of the First Emperor of the Qin Dynasty. It was ordered in the letter that Prince Ying Fu Su and General Meng Tian should kill themselves. When Prince Ying Fu Su got the letter, he killed himself. General Meng Tian refused to kill himself. He was arrested and put in jail. Not long later he was killed.

Prince Ying Hu Hai was put on the throne and became the Second Emperor of the Qin Dynasty. He was strictly under the control of Zhao Gao and Li Si. Power was in the hands of Zhao Gao and Li Si.

2. Liu Bang Rises Up in Rebellion

Liu Bang was born in Zhongyangli of Fengyi (now Peixian, Jiangsu Province) within the State of Chu in 256 BC in a peasant family. His father was Liu Zi Jia. He had two elder brothers. When he grew up, he became a tall, handsome man with a straight and high nose and a beautiful beard. He became the chief of the sub-township in Pei County, the lowest ranking official at that time, at the age of 36. In the prime of his life he married a girl named Lü Zhi. Not long later she gave birth to a baby girl. The girl was named Liu Yuan. Several years later Lü Zhi gave birth to a baby boy. The boy was named Liu Ying.

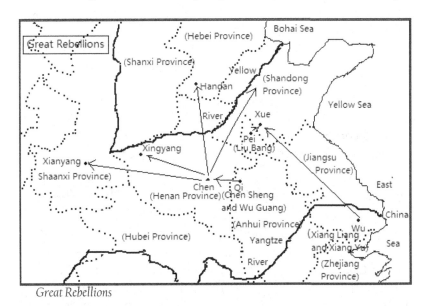

Great Rebellions

In 209 BC the Second Emperor of the Qin Dynasty issued an order to all the counties to send people to Lishan Mountain to complete the construction of the First Emperor's mausoleum. The county government of Pei rounded up about a hundred criminals from the jails. Liu Bang was assigned the task of escorting the convoy to Lishan Mountain near Xianyang. On the way more than thirty criminals escaped. According to the laws of the Qin Dynasty, he would be put to death even if he managed to get the rest of the conscripts to the destination. When they got to the bank of a big marsh which was a hundred miles from Pei, Liu Bang made up his mind. He set all the criminals free and let them go where they wanted. About ten criminals would not leave him and they said that they would go wherever Liu Bang would go. Then Liu Bang led these ten persons to past the big marsh and into Mang-Dang Mountains.

When the governor of Pei County found out that Liu Bang had freed all the criminals and he himself had also run away, the governor ordered Liu Bang's home to be searched, but no one could find him. The governor ordered the arrest of Liu Bang's wife Lü Zhi and had her thrown into jail. She had no money to bribe the jail keepers, so she was treated badly and was often insulted crudely. With the help of Xiao He, an official in the government of Pei County, and Ren Ao, a jail keeper, Lü Zhi was released from jail. As soon as she got out, she went looking for her husband, taking her two children with her. They went past the great marsh and into the remote area of Mang-Dang Mountains. About fifteen days later, Lü Zhi and her children arrived at the cave where Liu Bang and his followers were hiding. Liu Bang asked Lü Zhi how she had managed to find him. She told Liu Bang that wherever he went there was a cloud of five colors in the sky over his head, and she just followed that cloud of five colors and found him. From then on, many people of Pei County came and joined him. Very soon Liu Bang had an army of about a hundred men.

3. Chen Sheng and Wu Guang Rebel, and the Five States are Reinstated

Chen Sheng was a poor peasant in Yangcheng area (now Dengfeng County, Henan Province); Wu Guang was a peasant in Xiayang (now Taikang County, Henan Province). In July 209 BC, nine hundred poor people were conscripted to serve as frontier guards in Yuyang (a place in Miyun near Beijing); the 900 people were gathered together and stationed in Daze Village (now in Suxian area of Anhui Province), ready to march to Yuyang.

Chen Sheng and Wu Guang were among them; they were appointed leaders. They had to get the people to Yuyang at an appointed time. But torrential rains came down and prevented them from leaving. They were badly delayed. No matter how fast the men marched, there was no way for them to make it to their destination on time. According to the law of the Qin Dynasty, anyone who missed the deadline would be put to death. Chen Sheng and Wu Guang decided to revolt. One day the two of them killed the military officers. Then they gathered together the 900 people being sent to garrison the frontiers and called on them to rise up against the rulers of the Qin Dynasty. All the 900 people decided to follow Chen Sheng and Wu Guang. Chen Sheng named himself General, and Wu Guang was made Captain. They attacked Daze Village and took it. Then Chen Sheng led his army to storm Qi, the county town, and captured it. Very soon his army grew to more than 10,000 men with cavalry and chariots. Chen Sheng marched his army to Chen (now Huaiyang, Henan Province). After a battle Chen Sheng's army captured the city. Several days later Chen Sheng proclaimed himself King of the State of Zhang Chu (meaning the Greater State of Chu) and he made the city of Chen the capital of the State of Zhang Chu.

Zhang Er and Chen Yu were both from Daliang (now Kaifeng, Henan Province). They went to join Chen Sheng. They offered their assistance to take the former State of Zhao. Chen Sheng accepted their offer. He appointed Wu Chen general and appointed Zhang Er and Chen Yu captains. He put 3,000 men under Wu Chen's command, and ordered them to occupy the areas of the former States of Zhao and Yan. He sent Zhou Shi to take the areas of the former States of Qi and Wei.

Chen Sheng appointed Wu Guang Acting King to supervise all the generals in the westward march to take Xingyang (now Xingyang, Henan Province), a strategic point of military importance.

Chen Sheng sent Zhou Wen, a local man of virtue, to lead an army to march into Qin. Zhou Wen marched his army westward, gathering soldiers and horses on the way. When he reached Hanguguan Pass (now in the northeast of Lingbao, Henan Province), his forces had grown into an army of 300,000 men. They stormed the pass and took it. Zhou Wen's army marched quickly into Qin and very soon they reached Xi (to the east of Lintong, Shaanxi Province), threatening Xianyang, the capital of the Qin Dynasty.

The army under the command of Wu Chen crossed the Yellow River at the point of Baima (now in the northeast of Huaxian, Henan

Province); then they marched into the former State of Zhao. With the help of Zhang Er and Chen Yu, Wu Chen's army expanded from 3,000 men into an army of 50,000 men. In a short time Wu Chen took more than thirty cities and marched smoothly into Handan (now Handan, Hebei Province), the capital of the former State of Zhao. Wu Chen declared himself King of the State of Zhao. He made Chen Yu the chief general and Zhang Er the premier of the State of Zhao.

Wu Chen sent General Han Guang to occupy the former State of Yan. Han Guang and his troops fought bravely and they occupied Ji (now Beijing), the capital of the former State of Yan. Han Guang followed Wu Chen's example and declared himself King of the State of Yan.

Tian Dan, a descendant of the former King of the State of Qi, with his cousins Tian Rong and Tian Heng, killed the governor of Di (now Gaoqing, Shandong Province) appointed by the government of the Qin Dynasty and proclaimed himself King of the State of Qi. He led his army to fight against the army under Zhou Shi, the general sent by Chen Sheng to occupy the former State of Qi. Tian Dan's army defeated Zhou Shi's army.

Zhou Shi regrouped his army and turned to the former State of Wei. After some fighting, Zhou Shi put down all the resistance in the former State of Wei. He installed Wei Jiu, a descendant of the former King of the State of Wei, on the throne of the State of Wei, and Wei Jiu appointed Zhou Shi premier of the State of Wei.

By September 209 BC, the State of Chu (under King Chen Sheng), the State of Zhao (under King Wu Chen), the State of Wei (under King Wei Jiu), the State of Yan (under King Han Guang), and the State of Qi (under King Tian Dan) had been reinstated, they had broken off the rule of the Qin Dynasty.

4. LIU BANG REVOLTS IN PEI COUNTY

People of many counties killed their governors in solidarity with Chen Sheng's uprising. The governor of Pei County was afraid that he would meet the same fate. In September 209 BC, he decided to take the initiative and lead the whole county in rebellion against the Qin Dynasty. Xiao He and Cao Shen, two officials in the government of Pei County, said to the governor, "You are a high ranking official appointed by the court of the Qin Dynasty. Now you are going to betray the government that has appointed you. What if the people of Pei do not follow you? You'd better call back those who are now in exile and you might gather together several hundred of them. With their help, you might force the people of the county to follow you in the rebellion." The governor agreed with them and said, "Then send someone to look for them and bring them here to assist me."

Xiao He and Cao Shen hurried out of the governor's office to the market place to find Fan Kuai, a butcher and the brother-in-law of Liu Bang. (Fan Kuai was the husband of Lü Xu, younger sister of Liu Bang's wife Lü Zhi.) Xiao He said to him, "The governor wants to revolt against the Qin Dynasty; that means betraying his master, and he is afraid that the people of Pei may not follow him. He needs reinforcements to help get the people of Pei to follow him. Since you know the whereabouts of Liu Bang, you should go to find him and ask him to bring all the people under him to hurry back to Pei." Fan Kuai set out for Mang-Dang Mountain immediately. Very soon he found Liu Bang and conveyed to him what Xiao He had said. Then Liu Bang gathered together the people under him, several hundred in all, and marched to Pei.

Before Liu Bang reached Pei, the governor changed his mind because he suspected that Xiao He and Cao Shen's plan was a trick. He gave the order to arrest Xiao He and Cao Shen and kill them. Xiao He and Cao Shen escaped by getting out over the city wall in a basket held with ropes, and they joined Liu Bang. Liu Bang wrote letters to call on the people in the city to kill the governor and join in to rebellion against the rule of the Qin Dynasty. The letters were wrapped around arrows and shot into the city. People read the letters and decided to take action. They killed the governor and then opened the city gates to let in Liu Bang and his followers. The people of Pei made Liu Bang the Duke of Pei.

Xiao He, Cao Shen, Fan Kuai, Xiahou Ying and Ren Ao joined Liu Bang. Lu Wan, a friend of Liu Bang from childhood, became the captain of his bodyguards. Zhou Bo, a local from Pei, also joined Liu Bang. Yong Chi, a man from a rich and powerful family in Pei, also joined Liu Bang.

Xiao He and Cao Shen recruited 3,000 men in Pei. Liu Bang put Xiao He in charge of the general affairs of the army. Xiahou Ying became the driver of Liu Bang's carriage and was appointed commander of the troops of chariots. Liu Bang divided the 3,000 men into several groups and put them under the command of Cao Shen, Fan Kuai, Zhou Bo and Yong Chi. With this army, Liu Bang attacked Huling and Fangyu (both now in the southwest part of Shandong Province), but could not take them. Then he withdrew to Feng (now Feng County of Jiangsu Province).

5. Xiang Liang and Xiang Yu Rebel in the Area East of the Yangtze River

Xiang Liang, a son of the famous General Xiang Yan of the former State of Chu, and his brother's son Xiang Yu lived in Wu (in the southern part of Jiangsu Province). Xiang Yu was eight feet tall and strongly built. He was very powerful. He could lift up a big brass tripod with one had. When he was young, he did not like to learn how to read and write. His uncle Xiang Liang taught him how to use the sword. But very soon he ran out of patience with that, too. His Liang was angry. Xiang Yu said, "I can write my name, so it is no use learning reading and writing any more. Using a sword, I can only fight against one or two persons. I want to learn something with which I can fight against 10,000 enemies." Xiang Liang was glad to hear that. So he taught his nephew the art of war.

In September, 209 BC, when the news that Chen Sheng and Wu Guang had held an uprising against the Qin Dynasty reached Wu, the Governor of Guiji (now Suzhou City, Jiangsu Province) wanted to respond to the rebellion. He told Xiang Liang that he would raise an army and put him in command of it — with Huan Chu. At that time Huan Chu was in hiding, in the marsh area. Only one person knew where he was. Xiang Liang told the governor that Xiang Yu was the only one who could find Huan Chu and offered to call him in to see the governor. Then he went out of the office and told Xiang Yu what to do. When Xiang Yu was summoned before the governor, he drew out his sword and cut off the governor's head; then he picked up the official seal of the governor and fastened it to his belt.

With the head of the governor in his hand, Xiang Liang ordered the other officials to surrender. Some officials and guards resisted; Xiang Yu fought and killed nearly a hundred of them. The rest prostrated themselves on the ground in submission.

Xiang Liang gathered together the gentry of Guiji and told them that he had decided to rebel against the Qin Dynasty. They all expressed their support for him. Then an army of 8,000 men was organized. Xiang Liang and Xiang Yu led this army to occupy the rest of Wu Prefecture.

6. Great Changes in the State of Zhao

Wu Chen, King of the State of Zhao, sent Li Liang with 5,000 soldiers to take Changshan (now in in Hebei Province). Li Liang soon accomplished this and returned to Handan to report his victory to the King of the State of Zhao. In November of 209 BC, the King sent him to take Taiyuan (now in Shanxi Province). But when the army made it to Jingxing (now in southwestern Hebei Province), it could not go any further because the Qin army blocked the way. Li Liang turned back to Handan to ask for more troops. When he was near the capital, he saw a great procession with a hundred horsemen and many banners. Li Liang thought it was the procession of the King of the State of Zhao, so he prostrated himself by the roadside and touched his head to the ground until the procession passed. In fact it was not the king but the king's elder sister in the main carriage. Li Liang felt greatly humiliated. He sent one of his officers with a party of soldiers to kill the king's sister.

Li Liang then quickly went on with his main force to start a surprise attack on Handan. The defending army was not vigilant, and Li Liang took the city easily, then rushed into the palace and killed Wu Chen. A friend of Zhang Er got news of Li Liang's rebellion, and he sped to inform Zhang Er and Chen Yu of the news. They immediately escaped the city in fear for their lives. Then they gathered 5,000 scattered soldiers.

A local person suggested to Zhang Er and Chen Yu that they should find a descendant of the former king of the State of Zhao and put him on the throne so as to get the support of the people of the State of Zhao. Zhang Er and Chen Yu agreed, and they sent out officers to look for Zhao Xie. He was made King of the State of Zhao. However, since Handan was still in the hands of Li Liang, Zhang Er and Chen Yu escorted the new King to Xindu (now Xingtai, Hebei Province).

7. Liu Bang's Military Operations

After Liu Bang withdrew back to Feng, after attempting to take Huling, Ping, the supervisor of the Qin army in Sishui Prefecture, led his army and laid siege to Feng. This was in September 208 BC. Liu Bang gave the order to shut all the gates and not to meet the Qin army in battle. Two days later, Liu Bang led his army out of the city. In the ensuing battle the Qin army was defeated and Ping fled back to Huling. Liu Bang ordered Xiao He and Xiahou Ying to give chase. Xiao He urged Ping to surrender; he was persuaded, and surrendered and handed over the city of Huling to Liu Bang.

Liu Bang ordered Yong Chi to defend the city of Feng with some troops, while he himself led the main force to Xue (now Weishan, Shandong Province) to attack Zhuang, the governor of Sishui Prefecture appointed by the court of the Qin Dynasty. Zhuang was defeated and ran away to Qi, but he was caught and killed by one of Liu Bang's officers. Then Liu Bang and his army moved to Kangfu (south of Jining, Shandong Province) and stationed themselves in Fangyu (south of Jining, Shandong Province).

At that time, Zhou Shi came with an army to attack Feng under orders from the King of the State of Wei. Zhou Shi sent an envoy to talk to the city leaders. The envoy said to Yong Chi, "The city of Feng formerly belonged to the State of Wei. Now the State of Wei has been reinstated and it has recovered most of the cities of the former State of Wei. You'd better surrender Feng to us, and you'd better come over to our side as well. If you surrender, we will make you governor of Feng and the Lord of Feng. If not, we will attack the city. If the city falls into our hands, we will kill everyone in the city."

Yong Chi did not like Liu Bang; they had had some conflicts in their youth and he still held a grudge. Now he thought for some time and decided to turn over and hold the city of Feng for the State of Wei. Very soon, the news was reported to Liu Bang. Liu Bang was shocked, and he led the main force back to Feng. Yong Chi was at the top of the city wall. Liu Bang shouted from below: "I have been very kind to you and have entrusted the city of Feng to you. Why have you betrayed me?" Yong Chi said, "What do you think you are? You are not a nobleman. You are not qualified to be the Duke of Pei. You were a humble junior official from a peasant's family. I feel ashamed to be your subordinate. Now I have been appointed Governor of Feng and made Lord of Feng by the King of the State of Wei. I am defending this city for the King of the State of Wei, not for you."

Liu Bang could not tolerate such insults. He was in a great rage and ordered his army to attack. But Yong Chi had mobilized the townsfolk. Many people went up to the top of the city wall to help Yong Chi's army defend the city. When Liu Bang's soldiers got close, volleys of arrows and stones rained down. They could not get to the foot of the city wall. Liu Bang had to give up the attack and withdraw to Pei. Liu Bang hated Yong Chi and the people of Feng for their betrayal. But for now he had to suppress his anger and wait for another chance.

8. The Death of Chen Sheng, King of Zhang Chu

Chen Sheng had sent Zhou Wen to take an army and march into Qin. The Second Emperor of the Qin Dynasty was shocked when a great army of 300,000 men reached Xi, not far from Xianyang, the capital of the Qin Dynasty. He held court and asked the courtiers what to do. Zhang Han, the Tax minister, spoke up. He said, "Now the enemy is very close to the capital. It is impossible to mobilize the armies in other counties to come to the rescue. But there are many convicts working in Lishan Mountain. If we set them free and arm them, we can organize an army in a very short time to meet Zhou Wen's army."

The Emperor accepted his suggestion and immediately issued an order to pardon all the criminals in the realm. In a short time, an army of several hundred thousand men was mustered. The Second Emperor put this army under Zhang Han's command.

In November 209 BC, Zhang Han led the army to meet Zhou Wen at Xi. After a fierce battle, Zhou Wen was defeated. He withdrew through Hanguguan Pass to Caoyang, with Zhang Han in hot pursuit. Another battle was fought, and Zhou Wen was defeated again. He fled to Mianci (now in Henan Province). Ten days later Zhang Han caught up with him. Zhou Wen saw that there was no hope to escape. He drew his sword and killed himself.

Zhang Han now directed his victorious army to relieve the siege of Xingyang. Wu Guang was killed by one of his subordinates. A battle was fought outside the city, and the army Chen Sheng had sent was totally destroyed.

Zhang Han sent an envoy to report his victories to the Second Emperor of the Qin Dynasty. The Emperor was overjoyed and sent Generals Sima Xin and Dong Yi with 10,000 men to support Zhang Han. Thus reinforced, the Qin army under Zhang Han swept east, destroying many armies who were in rebellion against the Qin. In December 208 BC, the Qin army reached the City of Chen, the capital of Zhang Chu. At that time, only General Zhang He and his army were there. King Chen Sheng ordered the General to lead his army out of the city to fend off the Qin army. The King himself supervised the army from the top of the city wall. In the fierce battle, the army under Zhang He was defeated and he himself was killed. King Chen Sheng had no more army to defend him and he had to escape to Ruyin (now Fuyang, Anhui Province), then to Chengfu (now Guoyang, Anhui Province). On the way to Chengfu, Chen Sheng's driver Zhuang Jia killed him. Zhuang Jia then surrendered to Zhang Han, with Chen Sheng's head in hand. Lü Zhen, one of the defeated King's generals, led an army to storm the City of Chen and took it. The driver, Zhuang Jia, was caught and executed for the crime of murdering the King of Zhang Chu. Lü Zhen collected King Chen Sheng's remains and buried them in the Mang-Dang Mountains.

9. Qin Jia Makes Jing Ju King of the State of Chu

Qin Jia was originally a general under Chen Sheng. When Chen Sheng was defeated and left the city of Chen, no one was aware of his whereabouts. So Qin Jia made Jing Ju, a descendant of the royal family of the former State of Chu, the acting king. Qin Jia and Jing Ju stationed their army in Liu (25 kilometers south of Pei Xian, Jiangsu Province).

When Liu Bang got the news that Qin Jia and Jing Ju were stationed in Liu, he decided to go there to ask them to help take back the city of Feng. When his army of 3,000 men was marching towards Liu, the vanguard came to Liu Bang and reported, "There is a contingent of armed men marching towards us." Liu Bang galloped forward and saw a group of armed men headed by a tall, slim man. Liu Bang and the man greeted each other. After the formalities, they introduced themselves. The man said, "My surname name is Zhang, given name Liang. I am going to Liu to see Qin Jia and Jing Ju." Liu Bang said, "My surname is Liu, given name Bang. I am from Pei. I am also going to see Qin Jia and Jing Ju. Since we are going to the same place, let's go together." On the way they talked freely and heartily as if they had known each other for a long time.

Who was this Zhang Liang? He was a descendant of an eminent family of the former State of Haan. His grandfather Kai Di served as premier for three generations of the kings of the State of Haan, and his father Ping served as premier for two generations of the kings of the same state. Twenty years after Zhang Liang's father died, the State of Qin conquered the State of Haan. At that time Zhang Liang had not become an official of the State of Haan. Three hundred members of his clan, including his younger brother, were killed by the Qin soldiers. He was determined to avenge the State of Haan. In 218 BC, the First Emperor of the Qin Dynasty made a tour to the east. Zhang Liang learned that the First Emperor would be going past Bolangsha (now Yuanyang County, Henan Province). Zhang Liang and a brave, particularly strong man, lay in ambush by the roadside, looking to kill the Emperor. When they caught sight of the procession, they were surprised to see that there were more than ten carriages and all of them looked exactly the same. They could not make out which one the First Emperor was sitting in. So they made their best guess and the man threw his huge hammer with all his might at one of them. The carriage was totally destroyed. Then they ran as fast as they could into the forest and disappeared.

Unfortunately, the hammer had hit a decoy carriage. The First Emperor was in a great rage and gave the orders to search for the assassins all over the realm. Zhang Liang's original surname was Ji. In order to avoid being caught, he changed his surname to Zhang and went into hiding in Xiapi (now Suining, Jiangsu Province).

An old man saw that Zhang Liang was a young fellow with a lot of promise. He gave Zhang Liang a book and said, "Read this and you will become the military adviser to an emperor. Ten years from now, there will be great turmoil all over the realm. You may use what you learn from this book to assist the true emperor." The book was "On the Art of War by Jiang Tai Gong". Jiang Tai Gong was regarded as the greatest military theorist in Chinese history. He helped King Wu of Zhou to establish the Zhou Dynast,y which lasted for eight hundred years (1122 BC–256 BC). Zhang Liang was immensely impressed by the book. He read it every day and learned it by heart.

And when Chen Sheng rose up in Daze in rebellion against the Qin Dynasty, Zhang Liang organized an army of more than a hundred young men in Xiapi. When Chen Sheng died and Qin Jia made Jing Ju King of the State of Chu, Zhang Liang had in mind joining Qin Jia and Jing Ju. So he led this group of young men to Liu. On the way he met Liu Bang. He talked with him and found that he was a broadminded man and would become a real leader. So Zhang Liang changed his mind, and instead of joining Qin Jia and Jing Ju, he put himself and his men under the command of Liu Bang. And Liu Bang appointed Zhang Liang as military adviser.

Liu Bang reached Liu and was received by Qin Jia and Jing Ju. Liu Bang asked Qin Jia and Jing Ju to lend him some troops to get back the city of Feng. Qin Jia said that he would most like to assist Liu Bang to recover the city of Feng, but the Qin army was coming and they must deal with the Qin army first.

At that time Zhang Han was leading his army in pursuit of Chen Sheng's other generals. He sent General Yi to pacify the State of Chu. General Yi's army swept from the south, destroyed the city of Xiang (now north to Suixi County of Anhui Province) and killed all the people in that city. Then they reached the east of Dang (now northeast to Yongcheng, Henan Province). Qin Jia and Jing Ju led their army to meet the Qin army in battle. The army of Qin Jia and Jing Ju could not overcome the enemy. They had to retreat back to Liu.

In February 208 BC Liu Bang led his army of 3,000 men to attack Dang. He laid siege to the city. Three days later Liu Bang gave the order to attack. Cao Shen, Fan Kuai and Zhou Bo led the soldiers under their command to storm the city and took it. Six thousand Qin soldiers surrendered. Liu Bang incorporated them into his own forces, so that he now had an army of 9,000 men. Carrying on the momentum of victory, Liu Bang marched to Xiayi (now Dangshan, Anhui Province). Zhou Bo led his soldiers to storm the city and took it. After the victory at Xiayi, Liu Bang led his army back to Feng.

10. Xiang Liang and Xiang Yu Lead Their Army West of the Yangtze River and Liu Bang Joins Them

In January 208 BC, Zhao Ping, a general sent by Chen Sheng to take Guangling (now Yangzhou, Jiangsu Province), heard that Chen Sheng had been defeated and the Qin army was coming, so he sailed across the Yangtze River to see Xiang Liang. He asked Xiang Liang to lead his army west to attack the Qin. So Xiang Liang and Xiang Yu and the 8,000 men crossed the Yangtze River.

And they marched westward. Chen Ying, an official of Dongyang (now northwest to Taichang, Anhui Province), led 20,000 followers to join them.

Xiang Liang's army continued its march to the west. When Xiang Liang's army was crossing the Huai River (in the mid-west part of Jiangsu Province), Ying Bu, the head of a band of 1,000 bandits, joined up with them. At the same time General Pu also brought over his army to join Xiang Liang by the Huai River.

Xiang Liang's army grew into an army of 60,000 men. The army was stationed in Xiapi (now Suining, Jiangsu Province). At that time Qin Jia had made Jing Ju Acting King of the State of Chu. Qin Jia and Jing Ju stationed their army in Pengcheng (now Xuzhou, Jiangsu Province) to resist Xiang Liang's army. Xiang Liang had his army attack Qin Jia and Jing Ju's army. After several battles, Qin Jia and Jing Ju were killed.

When Liu Bang learned that Xiang Liang and Xiang Yu had reached Xue (now Weishan, Shandong Province) with a great army, he decided to go to see them. In April 208 BC, with a hundred horsemen, Liu Bang rode to Xue. When he arrived, Xiang Liang warmly welcomed him. Liu Bang said that he would most willingly join forces with Xiang Liang, but he first requested Xiang Liang to assign some troops to take back the city of Feng. Xiang Liang assigned 5,000 soldiers with ten high ranking military officers to help him get back the city of Feng. In May, with these reinforcements, Liu Bang stormed Feng. The army under Yong Chi could not withstand the attack, and very soon the city fell. Yong Chi fled to the State of Wei. Liu Bang left some troops to defend the city, and he himself led the main force to join Xiang Liang. By that time Xiang Yu had been away to Xiangcheng (now Xiangcheng, in the middle part of Henan Province) for a month. He led his army to attack Xiangcheng, but the defenders of the city fought bravely and repulsed them. The following day, Xiang Yu launched another attack, and the city fell. Xiang Yu gave the order to kill everyone in the city. Then he led his army back to Xue, and Liu Bang and Xiang Yu met for the first time.

Fan Zeng, an old man, over seventy, was resourceful and astute. He suggested to Xiang Liang that he should reinstate the State of Chu and put a descendant of King Huai on the throne, because King Huai of the State of Chu had been kidnapped into the State of Qin and never returned; this left the people of Chu nostalgic for their king and resentful of the Qin Dynasty. By reversing this, Xiang Liang might gain the support of the people. Xiang Liang accepted Fan Zeng's suggestion and sent out people to look for a descendant of King Huai of the State of Chu. At last they found Xiong Xin, the grandson. In June, the state of Chu was reinstated, with its capital in Xuyi (now in Jiangsu Province), and Xiong Xin was made King Huai of Chu, and he lasted for a couple of years..

When Zhang Liang saw that Xiang Liang had made Xiong Xin the new King of the State of Chu, he went to see Xiang Liang. He pointed out that of the former six states, five had been reinstated: the States of Chu, Qi, Zhao, Yan and Wei. Only the State of Haan had not been reinstated. He asked Xiang Liang to help to reinstate the State of Haan by putting Haan Cheng, a descendant of the former King of the State Haan, on the throne. Xiang Liang agreed. Then Zhang Liang went out to seek Haan Cheng.

Very soon Zhang Liang found Haan Cheng and brought him back to see Xiang Liang. Xiang Liang made Haan Cheng King of the State of Haan, and made Zhang Liang premier of the State of Haan. Xiang Liang gave Haan Cheng an army of 1,000 men to recover the State of Haan. Before Zhang Liang left for his mission, he said to Liu Bang that he would come back to Liu Bang when he had completed his mission.

Since Zhang Han had defeated Chen Sheng, he directed his army to attack Linji (now to the southwest of Changyuan of Henan Province, to the north of the Yellow River) where the King of the State of Wei was. Wei Jiu, King of the State of Wei, sent Zhou Shi to the State of Qi to ask for help. Tian Dan, King of the State of Qi, with Tian Rong, immediately led a great army to rescue the King of the State of Wei. One night, Zhang Han's army moved very quickly and silently to the camps of the army of the State of Qi and hit them with a surprise attack. Tian Dan, the King of the State of Qi, was killed and his army scattered. Then Zhang Han laid siege to Linji. Wei Jiu, the King of the State of Wei, sent an envoy to take a letter to Zhang Han. Wei Jiu wrote to offer that he would kill himself, and he begged Zhang Han not to harm the people in Linji after he died. Zhang Han gave his word. When Wei Jiu got Zhang Han's promise, he went up to the top of the city wall. Then he set fire to himself and was burned to death. Linji fell into the hands of Zhang Han. Wei Jiu's younger brother Wei Bao fled to the State of Chu. King Huai of the State of Chu gave Wei Bao several thousand men to recover the former State of Wei.

When this news reached the people of the State of Qi, they put Tian Jia on the throne of the State of Qi. Tian Jia was the younger brother of the last king of the State of Qi before the State of Qin conquered the State of Qi. Tian Jiao was made premier and Tian Jian was made chief general.

Tian Rong gathered together the scattered soldiers of the State of Qi who had come to rescue the King of the State of Wei, and retreated to Dong'e (now in Shandong Province). But Zhang Han pursued Tian Rong to Dong'e and laid siege to the city.

At that time Xiang Liang was leading the armies under the command of Liu Bang and Xiang Yu in an attack on the city of Kangfu (now to the south of Jining, Shandong Province). When Xiang Liang heard that Tian Rong was surrounded by the Qin army under Zhang Han and that Tian Rong was in great danger, he gave up the attack of Kangfu and led his army to rescue Tian Rong. They moved fast and very soon reached Dong'e. Xiang Liang arranged his army into battle formation. Xiang Yu was in charge of the middle formation. Liu Bang was in charge of the left and Ying Bu was in charge of the right.

Zhang Han immediately responded. He left some troops to maintain the siege, and arranged the rest of his troops in battle formation facing the Chu army. Xiang Liang gave the order to attack, and the Chu soldiers fell upon the Qin army. Xiang Yu galloped smartly to the Qin battle formation and found Zhang Han. They fought fiercely. At the same time the soldiers under Cao Shen, Zhou Bo and Fan Kuai fell upon the Qin army and destroyed their battle formation. After several exchanges, Zhang Han found that he was not a match for Xiang Yu, and he turned round and waved to the Qin soldiers laying siege to the city of Dong'e to retreat. The Qin army collapsed.

At this time, the army of the State of Qi under the command of Tian Rong came out of the city and joined in attacking the defeated

Qin army. He led his soldiers back to the State of Qi. Before Tian Rong with his army reached the State of Qi, Tian Jia, the King of the State of Qi, knew that he was no match for Tian Rong, so he fled to the State of Chu. Tian Jiao, the premier, ran away to the State of Zhao. Tian Jian, the chief general, was already in the State of Zhao asking for help, so he stayed there.

Tian Rong put Tian Shi, son of his cousin Tian Dan, on the throne of the State of Qi. Tian Rong became the premier, and Tian Heng became the chief commander of the army of the State of Qi.

Having defeated Zhang Han in Dong'e, Xiang Liang directed his army in hot pursuit of the defeated Qin army. He sent an envoy to the State of Qi to urge Tian Rong to send an army to join in the fight Zhang Han and his army. Tian Rong sent an envoy to the State of Chu to ask King Huai to kill Tian Jia, King of Qi. But King Huai of the State of Chu refused to do so. So Tian Rong refused to send any army to assist Xiang Liang. Since the King of the State of Qi would not assist him, Xiang Liang had to rely on his own forces to pursue Zhang Han and his army. He sent Xiang Yu and Liu Bang to attack Chengyang (now a place to the north of Heze, Shandong Province).

They attacked the city and took it. In the battle in Dong'e and the battle in Chengyang, Xiang Yu and Liu Bang fought side by side, and they became very good friends. After the battle of Chengyang, Xiang Yu said to Liu Bang, "I see that you are a kind and trustworthy person. We have fought side by side like two brothers. Shall we become sworn brothers?" Liu Bang said, "That's a good idea." They held a ceremony and pledged their mutual loyalty. Liu Bang was older than Xiang Yu, so that in terms of fraternal hierarchy Liu Bang was the elder brother and Xiang Yu the younger brother.

Then Liu Bang and Xiang Yu moved their army from Chengyang to Puyang (now Puyang City of Henan Province). East of Puyang, they fought against Zhang Han's army. Again Zhang Han was defeated. Then he regrouped the scattered soldiers and the Qin army became strong again. Zhang Han and the Qin army withdrew into the city of Puyang and defended the city resolutely. The Chu army had to give up taking the city. Xiang Yu and Liu Bang maneuvered the Chu army southward to attack Dingtao (now in the west part of Shandong Province), but the Chu army could not take it.

Then Xiang Yu and Liu Bang moved their troops to Yongqiu (now Qixian of Henan Province). The defender of Yongqiu was Li Yong, the son of Premier Li Si of the Qin Dynasty. A battle was fought. Li Yong was killed by Xiang Yu and the Qin soldiers ran for their lives in all directions. Then, under the order of Xiang Liang, Liu Bang and Xiang Yu led their army to Waihuang (now north of Minquan, Henan Province) and laid siege to the city.

Xiang Liang marched from Dong'e to Dingtao. The general of the Qin army in Dingtao led his troops to cope with the Chu army. In the battle, the Chu army defeated the Qin. The Qin army retreated into the city. Xiang Liang laid siege, but the Qin army shut all the gates of Dingtao and would not come out for a decisive battle. At that time Zhang Han and his troops were sitting tight in the city of Puyang and would not come out to fight, either.

Now, since Liu Bang and Xiang Yu had won a great victory in Yongqiu and killed Li Yong, and Xiang Liang himself won a victory outside Dingtao, Xiang Liang became very conceited and arrogant. He thought that Zhang Han had been defeated and did not have the strength to fight with him. The Chu army's vigilance against the Qin army was relaxed. Xiang Liang held banquets frequently to celebrate his victories.

Song Yi, a general under Xiang Liang, was very worried because he found out that Qin army reinforcements had arrived secretly and thus the Qin army might launch a surprise attack any time. But Xiang Liang ignored this fact and still believed that Zhang Han did not have the strength to attack him. Song Yi went to see Xiang Liang. He said, "After a victory, the general who underestimates the force of his enemy and the soldiers who become relaxed will surely be defeated. Now as I see it, the soldiers have become relaxed after these victories. More and more Qin soldiers have been sent to reinforce Zhang Han's army. This is very dangerous." But Xiang Liang would not listen. He sent Song Yi as an envoy to persuade the King of State of Qi to send troops to cooperate in the action against the Qin army under Zhang Han. On his way to the State of Qi, Song Yi met with Xian, the envoy sent by the King of the State of Qi to see Xiang Liang. He predicted to Xian that the Qin army's surprise attack would take place within the next few days and Xiang Liang would be defeated.

In Puyang, Zhang Han was secretly preparing a surprise attack on the Chu army. The Second Emperor of the Qin Dynasty had sent reinforcements to him and Zhang Han's army was strong enough to fight with the main force of the Chu army. One day in September 208 BC, Zhang Han led his army out of Puyang. Each of his soldiers kept a stick clamped in his mouth so that no sound would be made during the march. After one day and one night's march, the Qin army reached the camps of the Chu army under Xiang Liang outside the city of Dingtao at dawn. Their action had not been discovered because the Chu army had let down their guard and no scouts had been sent out by Xiang Liang to watch the activities of the Qin army. The Qin soldiers burst into the Chu army's camps and set fire to the tents. They fell upon the sleeping Chu soldiers with uproarious war cries, killing everyone they saw. Many Chu soldiers were killed while sleeping. Some woke up but were killed before they could put up a fight. Many Chu soldiers woke up and ran out of their tents without armor and weapons. They ran in all directions. Xiang Liang woke up and stepped out of his tent with a sword in his hand to see what had happened. Zhang Han rode at him and killed him with his spear. Very few Chu soldiers escaped. It was a tremendous disaster for the State of Chu.

Xiang Yu and Liu Bang were on their way to Chenliu (now in Henan Province) after several unsuccessful attacks on Waihuang (near Minquan, Henan Province) when some soldiers who had escaped from Dingtao caught up with them and reported to them the disaster in the Chu army camps outside Dingtao. When Xiang Yu learned that Zhang Han had killed his uncle, he was so sad that he cried bitterly. He swore that he would kill Zhang Han and avenge his uncle with Zhang Han's head. Liu Bang was very sad too. He tried his best to comfort Xiang Yu. Then he suggested that they should move their army east to join forces with General Lü Chen who was nearby, and retreat together. Xiang Yu agreed with him. Then they joined forces with General Lü Chen. General Lü Chen's army was stationed in the east of Pengcheng. Xiang Yu's army was stationed in the west of Pengcheng. Liu Bang's army was stationed in Dang (now northeast to Yongcheng, Henan Province).

King Huai of the State of Chu didn't think Xuyi was a safe place to stay since Zhang Han might attack it at any time. He decided to move to Pengcheng, with all his ministers. He merged the army under General Lü Chen and the army under Xiang Yu into one and put this army directly under his own command. He appointed Liu Bang governor of Dang Prefecture, in command of all the armies in Dang.

11. The Promise Made by King Huai of the State of Chu

After Xiang Liang's army was defeated, Zhang Han thought that the rest of the State of Chu's armies were no threat to him anymore, so he directed his army across the Yellow River and marched north to attack the State of Zhao.

At that time, Xian, the envoy from the State of Qi, was in the State of Chu. He said to King Huai, "On my way to Dingtao to see Xiang

Liang, I met Song Yi. He predicted that Xiang Liang would be defeated, and several days later Xiang Liang was indeed defeated. Song Yi must have great military talent if he could see the signs of defeat before the battle took place." When Song Yi came back to the State of Chu from the State of Qi, King Huai received him and talked with him about military affairs. Song Yi answered the King's questions fluently and made many sound suggestions. He made a good impression.

King Huai of the State of Chu decided to send an army to Guanzhong (the Qin area within the mountain passes of Hanguguan, Wuguan, Xiaoguan and Sanguan) to overthrow the Qin Dynasty. He called together his court to discuss the selection of a suitable general. When all the military officers and civil officials had come, King Huai of the State of Chu said, "We must send an army to march into Guanzhong and root out the Qin Dynasty. We need a capable general to lead this army. Now I solemnly make the following promise: the general who is the first to march into Guanzhong and put down that area will be made king of Guanzhong. Will any one of you take up this task?" Liu Bang responded, "I will." Xiang Yu said, "I will go, too." The other generals were silent. They did not want to go into Guanzhong because the Qin army was very strong.

King Huai of the State of Chu intended to send Liu Bang only. He tried to persuade Xiang Yu to stay behind. But Xiang Yu insisted in going with Liu Bang.

It happened that at this time an envoy sent by Zhao Xie, King of the State of Zhao, arrived with a letter, begging to see King Huai of the State of Chu. King Huai granted him a reception and the envoy presented the letter. It read, "Zhang Han has led a great army to attack our state. Our army suffered a great set back. We have retreated into the city of Julu. The Qin army has laid siege to the city, which may fall at any time. Please send an army to rescue us as soon as possible."

The envoy explained to King Huai of the State of Chu how the situation in the State of Zhao had unfolded: having defeated the Chu army under the command of Xiang Liang outside Dingtao, Zhang Han with his victorious army crossed the Yellow River and marched into the State of Zhao; the Qin army defeated the army of the State of Zhao and took Handan, the capital of the State of Zhao; Zhang Han forced all the people in Handan to move to Henei (now Wuzi, Henan Province) and then he ordered the Qin army to destroy the city of Handan; when the Qin army left for the north, the city was totally in ruins; the King of the State of Zhao, and Zhang Er, the premier of the State of Zhao, retreated to Julu (now in Hebei Province); the

Qin army under Zhang Han surrounded the city of Julu; Chen Yu, the chief general of the State of Zhao, gathered all the scattered Zhao soldiers, and he got 30,000 men; he stationed his army to the north of the city of Julu; Zhang Han stationed his army in Jiyuan to the south of Julu; a road with walls on both sides had been built to ensure the transportation of food to the Qin army laying siege to Julu; the King of the State of Zhao had sent several envoys to King Huai of the State of Chu, to the King of the State of Qi and the King of the State Yan for help.

King Huai of the State of Chu immediately summoned all the generals and ministers to discuss the matter. He showed the letter of the King of the State of Zhao to them. Xiang Yu stood up and said, "I swear I will kill Zhang Han to revenge my uncle. I am willing to lead an army to rescue the King of the State of Zhao." Then King Huai of the State of Chu declared his decision: he appointed Song Yi commander-in-chief, Xiang Yu second commander-in-chief and Fan Zeng the third commander; all the generals of the State of Chu should be under the command of Song Yi; and meanwhile, Liu Bang should lead the army under him to march into Guanzhong in accordance with the original plan.

In the second September of 208 BC (that year was a leap year and thus it had two Septembers), Liu Bang left Pengcheng and rode back to Dang where his army was stationed. Then he started his march to Guanzhong with his army. This was the first time that Liu Bang alone led an army to penetrate deep into the hostile land of Qin. He knew that it would be a very difficult task but he was confident that he could accomplish it.

On the way he gathered the scattered soldiers under Chen Sheng and those under Xiang Liang. The next month, Liu Bang's army reached Chengwu (now Chengwu, Shandong Province). The commanding general of the Qin army stationed in Chengwu was Wang Li. When Liu Bang led his army to the city of Chengwu, General Wang Li led his army out of the city and arranged his men in battle array to the south of the city to block Liu Bang's advance. Liu Bang's officers and men fought bravely and defeated the Qin army. General Wang Li led his defeated army northward in retreat and joined Zhang Han, who was leading his army to destroy the State of Zhao.

In December 208 BC, Liu Bang's army marched north to Chengyang (north of today's Heze, Shandong Province). An army of the Qin Dynasty was stationed in Gangli, a county near Chengyang. Liu Bang's army attacked them in their camps and defeated them.

The envoy sent by the King of the State of Zhao reached the State of Qi to ask the King to send an army to his rescue in Julu. Tian Rong, the premier of the State of Qi, refused, because the King of the State of Zhao had refused to kill Tian Jiao and Tian Jian. Tian Du, a general of the State of Qi, resented the attitude of Tian Rong. He had his troops march out of the State of Qi to rescue the King of the State of Zhao, against the will of Tian Rong.

The King of the State of Zhao's envoy reached Ji, the capital of the State of Yan, and was received by Han Guang, the King of the State of Yan. The King of the State of Yan sent General Zang Tu with an army to rescue the King of the State of Zhao.

12. The Battle of Julu

Other events were unfolding simultaneously. In the second September of 208 BC, Song Yi with his army started from Pengcheng and marched north to rescue the King of the State of Zhao in Julu. They marched northward to Baima (now within, Henan Province), where the whole army crossed the Yellow River. Then the army continued its march to Anyang (now in Hebei Province). Once there, Song Yi gave the order to stop marching and pitch camps. Song Yi's army stayed in Anyang without moving a step forward. One day in October 208 BC, Xiang Yu went to see Song Yi and said to him, "The Qin army has besieged the King of the State of Zhao in the city of Julu. The city may fall at any moment. We should march north quickly and cross the Zhang River. If the Chu army attacks the Qin army from outside and the Zhao army from inside of the city, the Qin army will surely be defeated."

But Song Yi said, "That is not correct. Now the Qin army is fiercely attacking the State of Zhao. If the Qin army wins, the Qin soldiers will be very tired. Then we have a better chance to attack the Qin army. On the other hand, if the Zhao army defeats the Qin army, then I will lead my army westward in marching formation accompanied by drums. The Qin Dynasty will surely fall. So it is better to let the Qin army and the Zhao army fight each other first. I am not as good as you in actual combat face to face with the enemy. But when it comes to devising strategies and making plans, you are not as good as I am." Then Song Yi issued a warning to the whole army. It read, "Anyone who is as fierce as a tiger, as cruel as a wolf and greedy as a bear but does not obey orders shall be put to death."

Song Yi sent his son Song Xiang to the State of Qi to take the position of a high ranking official. Song Yi saw his son off in Wuyan (now Dongping, Shandong Province) where a grand banquet was given. This was during the winter and there was rain. The soldiers of the State of Chu were suffering cold and hunger.

One morning in November 208 BC, when the Chu army had already been staying in Anyang for 46 days, Xiang Yu went into Song Yi's tent, killed Song Yi and then went out of the tent with Song Yi's head in one hand and his sword in the other. He gathered the officers and men together and said, "Song Yi conspired with the State of Qi to betray the State of Chu. King Huai of the State of Chu gave me a secret order to kill him." At the same time, all the officers and men were awed by what he had done and nobody said anything against him. They said that it was the Xiangs that had re-established the State of Chu and that what he had done was just, suppressing a traitorous act, so they made him acting commander-in-chief.

Then Xiang Yu sent a party of soldiers to catch Song Yi's son. They caught up with him within the territory of the State of Qi and killed him. Xiang Yu sent Huan Chu to Pengcheng to tell King Huai of the State of Chu what had happened. Then King Huai of the State of Chu officially appointed Xiang Yu commander-in-chief of the army and sent him to rescue the State of Zhao.

The Qin army under Zhang Han was attacking the city of Julu fiercely. Zhang Han ordered Wang Li to lead the Qin army of 100,000 men under him to lay siege to Julu. Zhang Han stationed the Qin army of 200,000 men in Jiyuan, south of Julu. Zhang Han had built a walled road leading to Julu to protect the supply route to General Wang Li, who was the commanding general in charge of attacking the city of Julu. The Qin army had sufficient food, so their attack became more and more fierce. There were just a few troops from the State of Zhao inside the city of Julu and they did not have enough food. Zhang Er sent several messengers to Chen Yu asking him to fight hard to rescue them. But Chen Yu considered that he had too few troops and he would not be able to defeat such a strong army. So he did not dare to fight his way through. Now, as sworn friends, Zhang Er and Chen Yu had pledged to share life and death. Zhang Er sent Zhang Yan and Chen Ze to reprimand Chen Yu and force him to attack the Qin army. Chen Yu replied, "I think, even if we fight our way forward, we cannot rescue the King. But there is a risk that the whole army will be destroyed. The reason why I do not want to die together with the King and Zhang Er is that I may take revenge for them on the Qin army. It is no use dying together. If I attack the strong Qin army with this small number of troops, it would be like putting meat into the mouth of a hungry tiger."

Zhang Yan and Chen Ze insisted that Chen Yu should engage the Qin army in spite of the fact that that there would be no hope for Chen Yu to come back alive. Zhang Yan said, "The situation is critical. Julu may fall at any time. You must fulfill your promise with Zhang Er by fighting to the death. You should not consider what would happen after you die." Chen Yu said, "It is no use dying in such a way. If you want to have a try, you go ahead." Chen Yu gave them 5,000 men to give it a try. But as soon as they met the Qin army in battle, all of them were killed in action.

At that time, the army of the State of Qi under General Tian Du and the army of the State of Yan under General Zang Tu arrived to help the State of Zhao. But the Qin army was so strong that they did not dare to go into battle. So they just pitched camp beside Chen Yu's army. Zhang Ao, Zhang Er's son, also came from the State of Dai with an army of 10,000 men to rescue the King of the State of Zhao and his father. He too pitched camp beside Chen Yu's army.

Since Xiang Yu killed Song Yi, he had become the most powerful man all over the State of Chu. In December 208 BC, he sent Ying Bu and General Pu with 20,000 men as vanguards. They cross the Zhang River and then marched quickly to relieve the city of Julu. They went into battle as soon as they arrived. When Wang Li saw that the Chu army was marching towards Julu, he sent a detachment to check their advance. The two armies confronted each other. Ying Bu gave the order to engage the enemy. Then he urged his horse to gallop forward and took the lead in the assault. His soldiers followed him and charged the enemy. The Qin army was defeated and retreated back to join the main force. Then Ying Bu and General Pu commanded their army to attack the walled road on which Zhang Han transported food to the Qin army under Wang Li's command. The Qin soldiers could not resist the attack, and they ran away.

The Chu soldiers destroyed the walled road and no more food could be transported to the Qin army under General Wang Li, and several days later, the Qin soldiers began to starve. The Chu army had achieved a victory. But they were greatly outnumbered by the Qin army. Zhang Han ordered his men to stage a counterattack; they drove the Chu army back and were able to rebuild the walled road. The supply route was back in business and the Qin army under Wang Li prospered. So Ying Bu and General Pu had to pitch camp and wait for the main force to come.

Chen Yu sent a messenger to Xiang Yu asking for more troops. In January 207 BC, Xiang Yu with his army crossed the Zhang River. After they all reached the northern bank of the river, Xiang Yu ordered that the ships be sunk to the bottom of the river and all the cooking utensils be destroyed. He also ordered that every soldier should carry enough solid food for three days. After these orders were carried out, before the army started to march, Xiang Yu said to all his officers and men, "The ships have all been sunk and the cooking utensils have all been destroyed. We will have to fight to the death. We will not return without victory!" Then the whole army was set on a forced march with the determination that they would fight to win; otherwise they would die in battle. They went past the ruins of Handan and continued their march to Julu, covering a distance of eighty kilometers in one day and one night. It was about midnight when they reached Julu. Ying Bu and General Pu joined Xiang Yu and reported to him about their action. After a short discussion, Xiang Yu decided to surround the Qin army under the command of Wang Li.

Morning came. The sun rose. The Chu army was drawn up in calm and confident array with Xiang Yu in command of the middle formation, Ying Bu in command of the right and General Pu in command of the left. Wang Li immediately made his arrangement. He sent a strong army out of the camp in battle array face to face with the Chu army. Xiang Yu issued the order to assault. The two armies joined and the battle began. The battle went on fiercely. The spirit of the Chu soldiers was keen. They fell upon the Qin soldiers with uproarious war cries that shook the sky. They were irresistible. They made their way forward fiercely, killing every Qin soldier on their way. Although the Chu army was inferior in number, each Chu soldier could take on nine or ten Qin soldiers. The soldiers of the armies of the other states were so shocked at the sight of the fierce fighting that they all stayed inside the walls of their camps and just looked on. They did not dare to go out to join in the battle. The fighting went on from morning till sunset, when the two sides withdrew for the night. The Chu soldiers were very tired. They did not bother to pitch camp. They just spent the night in the open. The next morning, they got up and were ready for battle again.

Zhang Han had commanded his army from Jiyuan to reinforce the Qin army under Wang Li. Xiang Yu personally led an army to stop the advance of the Qin army commanded by Zhang Han. A fierce battle was fought. Zhang Han had to withdraw back to Jiyuan. The walled road was totally destroyed. There was no hope for the Qin army under

Wang Li to get any support from Zhang Han and there was no hope for them to get any food supplies. Nine battles were fought. General Su Jiao of the Qin army was killed. Wang Li saw that his last moment had come. Leaving General She Xian to guard the camp, he rode out for a decisive battle. He met Xiang Yu in the battle field. After several bouts, he was hit by Xiang Yu and fell from his horse. The Chu soldiers rushed up and captured him. When the Qin soldiers saw that their chief commander was captured, they threw down their weapons and surrendered. General She Xian saw that the Qin army had lost the battle but he would not surrender. He set fire to the tents inside the camp and to himself. The fire rose high and burned up everything in the camp, and burned General She Xian to death.

After the battle, the Chu soldiers puled together all the wagons and carts to form walls for a campsite. Two wagons were erected in the middle of the wall with their shafts up to form the gate.

The generals of the armies of the other states who had looked on within the walls of their camps saw that the battle was over and that Xiang Yu had won a glorious victory, without their assistance. They were ashamed. They all rode out to the campsite of the Chu army. When they reached the gate made of the shafts of two wagons, they got down off their horses and crawled on all fours into the campsite, prostrating themselves at Xiang Yu's feet with great shame. They all expressed their respect for this great general and said that they would put themselves and their armies under Xiang Yu's command. Xiang Yu became the commander-in-chief of the united army of the States of Chu, Qi, Yan, Zhao and Dai.

The siege of Julu was raised. The King of the State of Zhao and Zhang Er came out of the city to the Chu campsite and Xiang Yu received them. They expressed their hearty thanks to Xiang Yu and the generals of the other states for their effort to save them from destruction.

When Zhang Er met Chen Yu, they had a fierce quarrel. Zhang Er blamed Chen Yu for not fighting hard enough to rescue them. Chen Yu was very angry. He took out the general seal and pushed in front of Zhang Er. Zhang Er was so surprise that he did not know what to say. Then Chen Yu stood up and went to use the toilet. One of Zhang Er's subordinates said that he should take the seal. Then Zhang Er took the seal and took all the troops under his command. When Chen Yu came back, he found that Zhang Er had pocketed his seal and would not give it back to him.

Zhang Er escorted the King of the State of Zhao to Xindu (now Xingtai, Hebei Province). Then he returned with all the army under him to Julu to join Xiang Yu in the confrontation with the Qin army under Zhang Han. Chen Yu left with several hundred followers to a place near the Yellow River, fishing and hunting for a living. From then on, the two men who had sworn to be friends unto death drifted apart and became mortal enemies.

13. Liu Bang's March to Guanzhong

While Xiang Yu was fighting his battles in Julu, Liu Bang was on his way marching to Guanzhong. In February 207 BC, Liu Bang reached Changyi (now western Jinxiang in Shandong Province). With the help of Peng Yu, the head of a group of 1,000 local people from around Changyi, Liu Bang led his army to attack the city. But the Qin army defended the city of Changyi resolutely. Liu Bang's army could not take it. Liu Bang had to give up the attack and withdraw. Liu Bang asked Peng Yu to go west with him. But Peng Yu would stay in Changyi. So Liu Bang continued his march to the west with his army. Peng Yue led his army to the marshes of Juye (now Juye, Shandong Province).

Liu Bang maneuvered his army west. When they passed Gaoyang (now near Chenliu of Henan Province), a Confucian scholar named Li Yi Ji came to join Liu Bang. He suggested that Liu Bang should take Chenliu because Chenliu was a strategic point and a lot of food was stored there; and he was acquainted with the governor of Chenliu. If Liu Bang would officially appoint him as his envoy, he would try to persuade the governor to surrender; if the governor would not surrender, he would help attack the city from within. Liu Bang took his advice and appointed him as an envoy to go first, and Liu Bang's army followed.

Liu Bang unleashed a surprise attack and successfully took the city of Chenliu (now Chenliu, Henan Province) with the help of Li Yi Ji. In appreciation he granted Li Yi Ji the title of the Lord of Guangye and entrusted to him the responsibility of diplomatic envoy to handle the relations among different states. Li Yi Ji's younger brother Li Shang had gathered together several thousand young men in Chenliu. When Liu Bang conquered Chenliu, Li Shang led his army of 4,000 men to join Liu Bang. Liu Bang appointed him general to command this army.

Liu Bang moved his army southwest to attack the city of Kaifeng (now in Henan Province). Liu Bang's army defeated the Qin army under Zhao Ben, the commander of the Qin army defending Kaifeng, outside the city. Zhao Ben ordered all the remaining Qin troops to retreat into the city and seal all the gates. Liu Bang laid siege to the city.

A scout came hurriedly to report to Liu Bang that General Yang Xiong of the Qin army was marching his army from Baima to relieve the city of Kaifeng. Liu Bang immediately raised the siege of Kaifeng and moved his army eastward to intercept Yang Xion's army. A battle was fought in the area west of Baima. But Yang Xiong forced his way to the east of Quyu (northeast of what is now Zhongmou, Henan Province) where he arranged his army into battle formation. Liu Bang led his army in pursuit of the Qin army. When he saw that Yang Xiong was ready in battle array, he ordered his army to fan out and a fierce battle began. In the heat of the fray, an army of 1,000 men arrived and joined in the attack of the Qin army. The Qin army broke formation and the soldiers fled in disorder. Many Qin soldiers were captured. Yang Xiong escaped to Xingyang. Liu Bang won a great victory.

When the battle was over, the leader of the army which had recently arrived rode up to Liu Bang. To his great surprise, Liu Bang found it was Zhang Liang. The two friends talked freely and happily. Zhang Liang told Liu Bang that after he left Xue with the King of the State of Haan and 1,000 soldiers, they went back to the former State of Haan; they had taken several cities but very soon they were retaken by the Qin army; so they had to move to Yingchuan area and carry out guerrilla warfare; when he got the news that Liu Bang had arrived to that area, Zhang Liang decided to come to join Liu Bang.

In April 207 BC, with the help of Zhang Liang, Liu Bang moved his army south to occupy Yingchuan (now the area from the south of Xinzheng to the Ying River, Henan Province) and several cities. When Liu Bang was ready to continue his march west, news came that General Sima Wang of the State of Zhao had taken Henei (now Wuzhi, Henan Province) and was moving west, planning to cross the Yellow River. He intended to march into Guanzhong. Liu Bang conferred on this matter with Zhang Liang. Zhang Liang said, "I think that Sima Wang will most probably cross the Yellow River in Pingyin, because Pingyin is where the Yellow River is comparatively narrow. We should occupy that place to prevent Sima Wang from crossing the river and marching into Guanzhong. But we have to pass Luoyang before we can get to Pingyin. Luoyang is a big city and heavily defended by the Qin army. There are many Qin troops stationed south of Luoyang. We must try our best to avoid fighting on our way. We'd better go through Huangyuan Mountain where there are no Qin troops; Huangyuan was such a dangerous and difficult mountain that the Qin generals consider it a natural barrier and they do not station any troops to defend it." Liu Bang accepted his suggestion and led his army in the march to Pingyin (on the south bank of the Yellow River near Mengjin, Henan Province). On the way they passed Huangyuan Mountain (between Dengfeng and Goushi, Henan Province). The winding road was narrow with ninety-two twists and turns with precipices on one side. Liu Bang's army crossed this mountain with great difficulty. When they came out on the other side, Liu Bang's army marched quickly north. Then they marched to Pingyin and occupied that place. When Sima Wang saw that the ferry crossing port had been occupied by Liu Bang and there was no hope for him to cross the Yellow River, he turned back to Henei with his army.

In June 207 BC, Liu Bang and his army returned from Pingyin to Yingchuan (now the area near Yuzhou, Henan Province) through the same route. Then Liu Bang asked King of the State of Haan's permission to let Zhang Liang to go with him to Guanzhong. The King of the State of Haan agreed.

Having taken his leave of the King of the State of Haan, Liu Bang, accompanied by Zhang Liang, went on his way south with his army. When they reached Nanyang (around Nanyang City, Henan Province), Yi, the commander of the Qin army in this area and the governor of Nanyang Prefecture, led an army to intercept the advancing army in Chou (now near Yexian, Henan Province). They fought to the east of the city of Chou. The Qin army was crushed and Yi led his defeated army to Wuyang (now Fangcheng, Henan Province). Liu Bang's army pursued the Qin army to Wuyang. Another battle was fought to the east of that city. The Qin army was defeated again. Yi retreated to the city of Wan (now Nanyang City, Henan Province).

Liu Bang reached the city of Wan. The city walls were very strong and the Qin soldiers were standing in combat readiness along the top. Liu Bang pondered his options. If he tried to storm the city, his army would suffer many casualties; if he laid siege, he would be delayed in his march to Guanzhong. So he simply ordered his army to go around the city of Wan and leave it unconquered and continue their march west.

After Liu Bang's army had marched fifteen kilometers, Zhang Liang rode up to Liu Bang and said to him, "I know that you are eager to reach Guanzhong. But the Qin troops are still many and they have occupied strategic points. If we leave the city of Wan untaken, then the Qin army of Wan will attack us from behind; and there are strong

Qin troops ahead of us. We will be in a very dangerous situation." Liu Bang recognized the danger and when night fell, he led his army back to Wan by another path. They arrived outside the city of Wan before dawn and surrounded the city in three rings. Yi saw that he could not resist the attack. He drew out his sword, put it to his own throat and was ready to kill himself. Chen Hui, an official under the governor, rushed forward and took away the sword from Yi's hand. Chen Hui offered to go out of the city to negotiate with Liu Bang. After negotiation, Liu Bang accepted Yi's surrender and made Yi Marquis of Yin and let him still be the governor of Nanyang Prefecture. Liu Bang put the troops of Wan in the van of his army and marched west. All the cities ahead were taken without a fight.

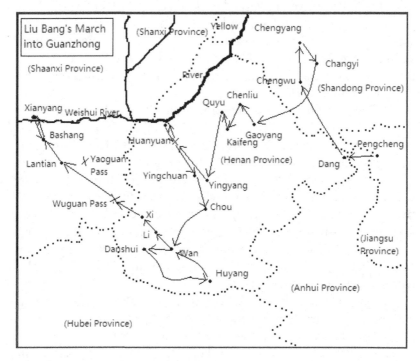

Liu Bang's March into Guanzhong

When Liu Bang's army was marching along the road to Danshui (now Danshui in the southwest part of Henan Province), he met with Wang Ling, who was from Pei — like Liu Bang. He and Liu Bang were good friends. He had organized an army in Nanyang and carried out military operations there. Liu Bang invited him to join him to march to Guangzhong. But Wang Ling preferred to go on with his fighting in the area of Nanyang. Then Liu Bang went on his way and Wang Ling stayed behind. Liu Bang's army swung southeastward to Huyang (now in Henan Province). Then his army passed the city of Wan again and took Li (northwest of Nanyang). Then Liu Bang's army marched westward and took Xi (now Xixia, Henan Province). By the end of July 207 BC, Liu Bang was marching towards Wuguan Pass. He was sure to be the first general to enter the areas of Guanzhong.

14. Zhang Han Surrenders to Xiang Yu

After the battle of Julu, the army of the State of Chu under Xiang Yu wiped out the army of the Qin Dynasty under General Wang Li. In February 207 BC, Zhang Han and his army retreated from Jiyuan (south of Julu) to Yinxu (now Xiaotun Village of Anyang, Henan Province). In April 207 BC, Zhang Han sent Sima Xin, one of his generals, back to Xianyang, the capital, to ask the Second Emperor of the Qin Dynasty for reinforcements. But at that time, all the power was in the hands of Zhao Gao, the premier. Zhao Gao refused to receive Sima Xin. Sima Xin ran back and said to Zhang Han that he was in a very difficult situation.

While Zhang Han was trying to find a solution, he received a letter from Chen Yu, the former commander-in-chief of the army of the State of Zhao. In the letter, Chen Yu wrote that the Qin Dynasty was doomed to fall; he pointed out that the only solution for Zhang Han was to turn over to the side of the people and unite with the forces of the other states to overthrow the rule of the Qin Dynasty.

In June, Zhang Han sent an envoy to Xiang Yu to negotiate a truce. But Xiang Yu turned down his offer, for he still hated Zhang Han. In July 207 BC Xiang Yu's army defeated Zhang Han south of the Zhang River. Zhang Han sent Sima Xin, who had once saved Xiang Liang from trouble, to negotiate with Xiang Yu. Sima Xin succeeded in persuading Xiang Yu to accept Zhang Han's offer of a truce.

Xiang Yu and Zhang Han met in Yinxu, where they signed the treaty. Xiang Yu made Zhang Han King of Yong (the western part of Guanzhong). Xiang Yu kept Zhang Han in the army of the State of Chu. He appointed Sima Xin commander-in-chief of the Qin army of 200,000 originally under the command of Zhang Han. Xiang Yu already had an army of 400,000 men from the States of Chu, Zhao, Yan, Qi and Dai. Now with the 200,000 Qin soldiers, his army grew to 600,000 men. He led this great army on the march towards Guanzhong.

At that time Wei Bao had taken more than twenty cities of the former State of Wei. Xiang Yu named him King of the State of Wei. He was grateful for this honor, and repaid Xiang Yu by sending his elite troops to join him in his march on Guanzhong.

15. Zhao Gao Kills the Second Emperor and Puts Ying Zi Ying on the Throne

Once Zhang Han surrendered to Xiang Yu, things looked very bad for the Qin Dynasty. By the end of July 207 BC, Liu Bang's army was very close to Wuguan Pass, and Xiang Yu was leading a great army towards Guanzhong. Zhao Gao was afraid that the Second Emperor of the Qin Dynasty would hold him responsible for the failure and punish him. He made up his mind to depose the Second Emperor. But how?

In August, Zhao Gao hatched a plot with his son-in-law Yan Yue, the commander of the Xianyang garrison, and his younger brother Zhao Cheng, the commander of the Wangyi Palace garrison. Yan Yue led 1,000 soldiers into the palace on the pretext that thieves had snuck into the grounds and buildings. And then Yan Yue and Zhao Cheng forced the Second Emperor of the Qin Dynasty to kill himself.

Zhao Gao decided to give the throne to Ying Zi Ying, the son of the elder brother of the Second Emperor, on the throne. On the day when Ying Zi Ying was to go to the Ancestral Temple to receive the seal of the King, Zhao Gao went to the palace to make sure the new candidate was going to show up. Ying Zi Ying was waiting for him: he drove a dagger into Zhao Gao's heart and killed him. Only after avenging his uncle did Ying Zi Ying ascend the throne of the State of Qin.

16. Liu Bang Takes Qin, and Ying Zi Ying Surrenders

In August 207 BC, Liu Bang took Wuguan Pass by storm and succeeded in entering the territories of Guanzhong. Liu Bang ordered his army not to loot the Qin people. His army marched with great discipline; the people of Qin liked Liu Bang and welcomed his army.

Ying Zi Ying, the new King of the State of Qin, sent generals with a great army to Yaoguan Pass (northwest of Shangzhou, Shaanxi Province) to fend off Liu Bang's advance. Liu Bang wanted to send 20,000 men to attack them but Zhang Liang suggested buying off their commanding officer, stationed in Yaoguan Pass — he was the son of a butcher and known to be greedy. Good idea. Liu Bang sent

Li Yi Ji as his envoy to present a load of gold to the Qin general. The officer readily offered to join forces with Liu Bang and march together to take Xianyang. Li Yi Ji conveyed this offer to Liu Bang, who was very glad. He was about to give his consent. But Zhang Liang pointed out that as far as anyone knew, only the commanding general wanted to come over; what about the officers and men? Zhang Liang suggested starting a surprise attack while the commanding general of the Qin army had his guard down. And that is what they did. In a surprise attack, the Qin army was defeated. They fled to Lantian (now in Shaanxi Province). Another battle was fought in Lantian, where the Qin were totally defeated. From then on, the State of Qin had no real army to resist the advance of Liu Bang.

In October 207 BC, Liu Bang reached Bashang (now Baqiao, a district in Xi'an; it is named for the bridge over the Ba River. In ancient times, when people saw off friends who were leaving the capital, they would say farewell at this scenic spot). He sent an envoy to see Ying Zi Ying, the King of the State of Qin, with a letter demanding that he surrender. Seeing that he could do nothing to save his State, Ying Zi Ying decided to submit. He went to Zhidao Pavilion, which was just a stone's throw from Bashang, and surrendered. Liu Ban accepted his surrender and handed him over to the charge of the officers of justice.

Liu Bang marched his army from Bashang to Xianyang. He ordered his army to pitch camps while he went into the city with his generals and some troops. Liu Bang entered the palace with some friends, where he was charmed by the splendid halls and chambers. He wanted to stay in the palace. Fan Kuai tried to persuade him to leave, but Liu Bang would not listen to him. Fan Kuai asked Zhang Liang to talk to him. Zhang Liang pointed out that the reason the Qin Dynasty had been destroyed was that the Emperor had oppressed the people cruelly and he himself led a luxurious life. He advised Liu Bang to lead a simple life and show his sympathy for the poor people. Liu Bang accepted his advice and turned back to Bashang with his army.

In November 207 BC, Liu Bang declared that all the laws enacted by the Qin Dynasty would become null and void. He would enact three chapters of Law. Anyone who killed a person would be killed; anyone who wounded another person would be given punishment equal to the harm he had done; anyone who stole from another would be given punishment equal to what he had stolen. The people of Qin were very happy. Their only worry was that Liu Bang could not become king of the areas of Guanzhong.

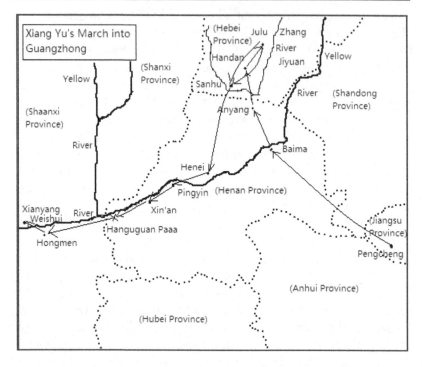

Xiang Yu's March into Guanzhong

17. Xiang Yu's March to Guanzhong

Since Xiang Yu had put down any resistance north of the Yellow River, he now led the army of all the states in the march to Guanzhong. However, on the way, the Qin soldiers planned to rebel. One night in September 207 BC, the Chu army hit the sleeping Qin soldiers with a surprise attack at midnight, disarmed them, and then killed all of them, 200,000 in total, by burying them alive in a place south of the city of Xin'an (now Xin'an, Henan Province). Then Xiang Yu and his great army marched towards Hanguguan Pass.

As Xiang Yu's 400,000 men were approaching Hanguguan Pass, someone suggested to Liu Bang to send an army to guard Hanguguan Pass to keep them out, suggesting that when Xiang Yu came, he would not make Liu Bang king of Guanzhong. Liu Bang took his advice and sent an army to guard Hanguguan Pass.

When Xiang Yu reached the Pass, he asked the general defending it to open the gate and let his army in. When the general refused, Xiang Yu ordered Ying Bu and his army to storm the pass. Ying Bu and his soldiers soon took it. Then Xiang Yu and the united army of the states went through the pass into Guanzhong.

In December, Xiang Yu reached Xi (east of Xianyang). He ordered his army to camp in a place named Hongmen (in Xinfeng Town, Shaanxi Province), which had been a campsite of the garrison army of the Qin Dynasty. That night a man came to the gate of the camp of Hongmen, claiming that he had important information to tell Xiang Yu. He was brought to Xiang Yu's tent. The man announced, "I am an envoy sent by General Cao Wu Shang of Liu Bang's army. He has sent me to tell you: Liu Bang wants to be the king of Guanzhong. He has appointed Ying Zi Ying, the former King of the State of Qin, as the premier, and he has taken all the treasures in the palaces for his own." When Xiang Yu heard that, he was furious. Then he ordered, "Tomorrow morning, provide food for the soldiers. We will crush Liu Bang's army tomorrow!" Hongmen and Bashang, where Liu Bang's army was stationed, were just thirty kilometers away.

When Xiang Bo, Xiang Yu's uncle, got the order, he immediately thought of Zhang Liang, who was now in Liu Bang's army. Ten years ago, Xiang Bo had killed a local bully and he ran away from home. He had found refuge in Zhang Liang's home in Xiapi. It was Zhang Liang who had saved his life. Now Zhang Liang was in great danger. It was his turn to save him from destruction. So he rode quickly to Liu Bang's camp in Bashang. He found Zhang Liang and told him of the upcoming attack, and urged him to leave immediately. Zhang Liang went to Liu Bang's tent and informed him of the danger. Zhang Liang suggested Liu Bang to ask Xiang Bo to tell Xiang Yu that Liu Bang did not intend to prevent Xiang Yu from entering the Qin area, and that he sent an army to guard the pass to keep out the bandits; Xiang Bo was Xiang Yu's uncle; perhaps he could persuade Xiang Yu to give up the attack. Then Zhang Liang brought Xiang Bo into Liu Bang's tent. Liu Bang said to Xiang Bo, "When I entered the areas of Guanzhong, I did not touch anything. I have pacified all the officials and people of the Qin area. I have sealed all the treasure houses for General Xiang Yu. I sent troops to guard Hanguguan Pass only to prevent bandits from going through the pass. I have been longing for General Xiang Yu to come. I do not dare to betray him. Please tell General Xiang Yu that I will not forget his kindness to me." Xiang Bo promised to do so and said, "You must go to see General Xiang Yu first thing tomorrow morning and apologize to him personally." Liu Bang said that he would go early the next morning.

Xiang Bo rode back to his army and reported to Xiang Yu what Liu Bang had said. Then Xiang Bo said, "If the Duke of Pei had not taken the pass first, could you have entered the region so early? The Duke of Pei has made great contributions, but you are going to attack him. That is not a righteous thing to do. I think we'd better treat him kindly instead." Xiang Yu agreed

18. The Banquet in Hongmen

Early the next morning, Liu Bang set out in a carriage drawn by two horses. Xiahou Ying was his driver. Zhang Liang, Fan Kuai, Jin Jiang and Ji Xin with a hundred men on horses followed. When they reached the gate of Xiang Yu's camp, Liu Bang got out of the carriage and his followers dismounted from their horses. Zhang Liang asked the guard of the camp to inform Xiang Yu that Liu Bang had come to visit him. Liu Bang and Zhang Liang were shown to Xiang Yu's tent and the others stayed inside the camp by the gate.

When Liu Bang met Xiang Yu, he apologized to Xiang Yu by saying, "You and I have been fighting side by side against the Qin army. You fought in the area north of the Yellow River, and I fought in the area south of the Yellow River. I do not expect that I could reach the areas of Guanzhong first and overthrow the rule of the Qin Dynasty. I am very happy to meet you here again. But some ill-intended person has passed false information to cause misunderstanding between you and me." Xiang Yu said, "It is Cao Wu Shang of your army who gave the information. Otherwise I would not have prepared the action against you."

Then Xiang Yu invited Liu Bang into a big tent where a banquet was spread. Xiang Yu and Xiang Bo sat on the west side of the tent. Fan Zeng sat on the north side. Liu Bang sat on the south side and Zhang Liang sat on the east side. In front of each one, there was a table on which wonderful food and wine were laid out. There was an open space in the middle of the tent. During the banquet, Fan Zeng eyed Xiang Yu several times to urge him to kill Liu Bang, but Xiang Yu ignored his signals. Fan Zeng went out of the tent and called Xiang Zhuang. He asked him to present a sword dance at the banquet and seize the opportunity to kill Liu Bang.

Xiang Zhuang went into the tent and proposed a toast to Liu Bang, and then he said he would present a sword dance to entertain him. He drew out his sword and began to dance. He was moving closer and closer to Liu Bang. Then Xiang Bo also drew his sword and joined in the sword dance. He protected Liu Bang with his own body. Zhang

Liang went out of the tent and told Fan Kuai that Liu Bang was in danger; so Fan Kuai went to the tent with a shield in his left hand and a sword in his right hand. The guards would not let him in. He shoved the guards with his shield and several fell down. Then he went through the curtain at the opening into the tent facing westward. When Xiang Zhuang saw Fan Kuai, he immediately stopped his sword dance and exited. With Fan Kuai in the tent, no one could do any harm to Liu Bang.

A moment later, Liu Bang got up and said that he wanted to go to the toilet. On his way out of the tent he called Fan Kuai and Zhang Liang to go with him. When they were outside, Liu Bang said to Zhang Liang that he would head back to Bashang by way of a small path along Lishan Mountain, and he could get back to his army very soon. He asked Zhang Liang to stay behind and say good-bye to Xiang Yu when he estimated that Liu Bang would have reached his army. Then Liu Bang set out on the path and slipped back to Bashang. As soon as he reached his army's camp, Liu Bang ordered that Cao Wu Shang be arrested and put to death.

When Zhang Liang reckoned that Liu Bang had reached his camp, he went into the tent to tell Xiang Yu that Liu Bang had left and gone back to his army. Fan Zeng said to Xiang Yu with a long sigh, "How foolish you are to have let Liu Bang go. It is Liu Bang who will take away all your power. We will all be his prisoners someday!"

19. The Making of Kings

Several days later, Xiang Yu marched his army westward to Xianyang. He had Ying Zi Ying, the former King of the State of Qin, executed. He ordered his army to burn all the palaces of the State of Qin. The fire lasted for three months. He let his soldiers loot the people of Qin, and they suffered terribly. He went back eastward with all the treasures and beautiful women taken from the Qin palaces.

Now Xiang Yu held the great power in his own hands. He had no intention of letting Liu Bang be the king of Guanzhong as King Huai of the State of Chu had promised. After discussion with Fan Zeng, he decided to make him King of Ba and Shu (now Sichuan Province), which were blocked by great mountains. He would make Zhang Han, Sima Xin and Dong Yi kings of the Qin area to block Liu Bang from coming out of the areas of Ba and Shu. When Liu Bang got this information, he was very angry and wanted to attack Xiang Yu. But Xiao He persuaded him to give up the idea. Liu Bang wanted Hanzhong (now the southwest part of Shaanxi Province) because that area was a small part of Guanzhong. Zhang Liang went to see Xiang Bo and asked him to persuade Xiang Yu to give Liu Bang the area of Hanzhong. After persuasion by Xiang Bo, Xiang Yu at last agreed to give Hanzhong to Liu Bang and grant him the title of King of the State of Han.

In January 206 BC, Xiang Yu made King Huai of the State of Chu (that is Xiong Xin, who had been given back his grandfather's throne), Acting Emperor. He moved the Acting Emperor to the area south of the Yangtze River. The capital was Chen (now Chenzhou, Hunan Province). In February, he named himself the Conqueror, Great King of Western Chu. He ruled over nine prefectures in the Chu and Liang areas. The capital was Pengcheng. He made Liu Bang King of the State of Han, ruling over Ba and Shu areas and Hanzhong Prefecture, with the capital in Nanzheng (now Nanzheng, Shaanxi Province). In order to block the way from which Liu Bang would come out of Hanzhong, Xiang Yu decided to divide Guanzhong into three states. He made Zhang Han, the Qin general who had surrendered to him, King of the State of Yong, ruling over an area west of Xianyang with the capital in Feiqiu (now a place near Xingping, Shaanxi Province). He made Sima Xin, another Qin general who had surrendered, King of the State of Sai, ruling over an area from Xianyang east to the Yellow River with the capital in Yueyang (now a place near Xingping, Shaanxi Province). He named Dong Yi (another Qin General who had surrendered) King of the State of Zhai, to rule over Shang Prefecture (northern part of Shaanxi Province) with the capital in Gaonu (now a place near Yan'an, Shaanxi Province).

Xiang Yu changed Wei Bao, the King of the State of Wei, into King of the State of Western Wei, ruling over Hedong (now Shanxi Province) with the capital in Pingyang (now a place near Linfen City, Shanxi Province). He made Shen Yang, a general under Zhang Er, King of the State of Henei with the capital in Luoyang (now Luoyang, Henan Province). Haan Cheng, King of the State of Haan, remained King of the State of Haan with the capital in Yangzhai (now Yuzhou, Henan Province). He made Sima Wang King of the State of Yin, ruling Henei Prefecture with the capital in Zhaoge (now Qixian, Henan Province). He moved Zhao Xie, King of the State of Zhao, to Dai Prefecture as King of the State of Dai. He made Zhang Er, the former premier of the State of Zhao, King of the State of Changshan, ruling over the former State of Zhao with the capital in Xiangguo (now Xingtai, Hebei Province). He made Ying Bu King of the State of Jiujiang with the capital in Liucheng (now Liu'an, Anhui Province).

He made Wu Rui, a king in the southern part of China, King of the State of Hengshan with the capital in Zhu (now Huanggang, Hubei Province). He made Gong Ao, the premier to King Huai of the State of Chu, King of the State of Linjiang with the capital in Jiangling (now Jiangling, Hubei Province). Haan Guang, King of the State of Yan, was moved to Liaodong as King of Liaodong with the capital in Wuzhong (now Jixian, Tianjin Municipality). Xiang Yu made Zang Tu, a general of the former State of Yan, King of the State of Yan with the capital in Ji (now a place in the southwest part of Beijing). Tian Shi, King of the State of Qi, was moved to Jiaodong as King of the State of Jiaodong with the capital in Jimo (now a place in Pingdu, Shandong Province). Xiang Yu made Tian Du, a former general of the State of Qi, King of the State of Qi with the capital in Linzi (now Linzi, Shandong Province). Xiang Yu made Tian An, a former general of the State of Qi, King of the State of Jibei with the capital in Boyang (now a place near Tai'an, Shandong Province).

Tian Rong was not granted any title because he had refused to cooperate with Xiang Liang and refused to lead his army to join with Xiang Yu in fighting against the Qin. Xiang Yu made Chen Yu Marquis of Nanpi (now Nanpi, Hebei Province).

20. LIU BANG'S MARCH INTO HANZHONG

In April 206 BC, all the generals began to leave for the states where they had been made kings. When Xiang Yu led his army out of Hanguguan Pass, he sent some envoys ahead to Pengcheng to force the Acting Emperor (King Huai of the State of Chu) to leave Pengcheng for a remote area in the south.

Xiang Yu allowed Liu Bang to take 30,000 soldiers to go to Hanzhong with him; this was a way to make sure that Liu Bang would not turn back on his way to Hanzhong. Over 10,000 men from the armies of the State of Chu and other states voluntarily followed Liu Bang to Hanzhong.

Liu Bang and his army marched southward and went into the great mountain of Qin Ling from the south of Chang'an (now Chang'an County, Shaanxi Province). They passed Ningshan, Shiquan and Yangxian. They covered a distance of 450 kilometers and reached the Hanshui River Basin where Nanzheng was situated. They did not go to Nanzheng directly but turned westward along the north bank of Hanshui River. Then they reached Baogukou (the entrance of Baogu Valley, now Baocheng, Shaanxi Province) where the south end of the plank road built along the face of the cliff was situated. The north end of the plank road was in Xiegukou (the entrance of Xiegu Valley, now southwest to Meixian of Baoji, Shaanxi Province). At 210 kilometers long, it was the shortest of the three roads leading to Guanzhong. Zhang Liang suggested to Liu Bang to burn up the plank road to show to Xiang Yu and all the kings that Liu Bang had no intention of going back to Guanzhong. Liu Bang agreed. Then Zhang Liang said that he had to go back to assist the King of the State of Haan. Liu Bang and Zhang Liang said good bye to each other. Liu Bang and his army turned south to Nanzheng. When Zhang Liang and his party of soldiers got to the plank road, they burned it up, section by section. When they reached Xiegukou, the north end, the whole plank road of 210 kilometers had been burned away. When Zhang Han, the King of the State of Yong, heard about this, he was relieved because he understood this meant he did not need to worry about Liu Bang anymore.

When Liu Bang and his men reached Nanzheng, they settled down there. He appointed Xiao He premier. Cao Shen, Fan Kuai, Xiahou Ying, Zhou Bo, Lu Wan and Guan Ying were promoted to the rank of general.

21. The Rebellions of the State of Qi and the State of Zhao against Xiang Yu

When Tian Rong found out that Xiang Yu had decided to move Tian Shi, King of the State of Qi, to Jiaodong (the eastern part of Shandong Province) as King of that State, and had made Tian Du King of the State of Qi, he was very angry. He refused to let Tian Shi move to Jiaodong and decided to rebel against Xiang Yu. He sent an army to prevent Tian Du from getting to Linzi to take the throne of the State of Qi. Tian Du had to go to the State of Chu for refuge. Tian Rong asked Tian Shi to stay in Linzi as King of the State of Qi instead of going to Jimo as King of Jiaodong. But Tian Shi was afraid of Xiang Yu, so he secretly left Linzi and went to Jimo as King of the State of Jiaodong. Tian Rong was so angry that he chased Tian Shi to Jimo and killed him. Then he directed his army northward and attacked Tian An, the King of the State of Jibei, and killed him, too. Tian Rong unified the three states in the Qi area as the State of Qi and declared himself King of the State of Qi.

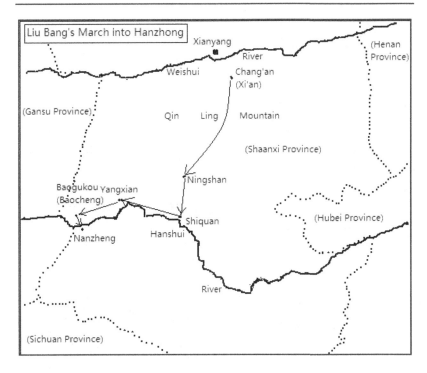

Liu Bang's March into Hanzhong

Zhang Er went to Xiangguo (now Xingtai, Hebei Province) to take the throne of the State of Changshan. Chen Yu sent an envoy to ask Tian Rong to lend him some troops to defeat Zhang Er and put Zhao Xie back on the throne of the State of Zhao. Tian Rong obliged and sent Chen Yu some troops. Chen Yu also raised an army from the three counties under his jurisdiction. With these men he defeated Zhang Er. Chen Yu escorted Zhao Xie from the State of Dai to Handan to resume the throne of the State of Zhao. In order to repay Chen Yu's kindness, the King of the State of Zhao made Chen Yu King of the State of Dai.

When Zhang Er was defeated and fled, he could not decide whether he should go to Xiang Yu or Liu Bang. He consulted with an astrologer. The astrologer predicted that Liu Bang would finally unify China. So Zhang Er decided to go to Liu Bang.

Xiang Yu did not allow King of the State of Haan to go back to his realm because Zhang Liang went with Liu Bang to Guanzhong. He took the King of the State of Haan to Pengcheng and then disposed of him. Sometime later, Haan Cheng was killed.

Zang Tu, made King of the State of Yan by Xiang Yu, led an army to Ji, the capital, and forced Han Guang, the former King of the State of Yan, to go to Liaodong. Han Guang refused to go. Then Zang Tu attacked and took the city of Ji. Han Guang ran, but he was killed.

22. Han Xin Is Appointed Commander-in-Chief of the Army of Han

Han Xin was from a poor family in Huaiyin (now in Anhui Province). He was a capable man. He first joined Xiang Liang's army. After Xiang Liang was killed, Han Xin was a low ranking officer in Xiang Yu's army. When Liu Bang went into Hanzhong, Han Xin left Xiang Yu and joined Liu Bang's army. Liu Bang appointed him to take charge of the food supply. When Liu Bang and his army reached Nanzheng, Han Xin got the impression that Liu Bang would not put him in a more important position, so he ran away. Xiao He, the premier, knew that Han Xin was a very clever man, so he jumped on a horse and went after him. He was in such a hurry that he did not report to the King of Han. Two days later Xiao He came back. He recommended Han Xin to Liu Bang. Then Liu Bang appointed Han Xin commander-in-chief of the whole army.

A grand ceremony was held. Liu Bang declared the appointment before all the generals, ministers and soldiers of his army. When Liu Bang declared that he would appoint Han Xin commander-in-chief of the whole army, everybody was stunned.

After the ceremony, Han Xin presented a detailed analysis to show that Xiang Yu would be finally defeated by Liu Bang.

23. Liu Bang's Actions to Pacify Guanzhong

One day in August 206 BC, the King of Han and Han Xin with an army of 100,000 men secretly embarked on their northern expedition. They passed Mian Xian and then went up the great mountains of Qin Ling. The mountains were covered with forests. The army went forward with great difficulty. Then they moved westward and reached Gudao (now Fengxian, Shaanxi Province). Han Xin ordered Cao Shen to lead the troops under him to take Gudao. Cao Shen led his troops to attack the town and took it.

From the north end of Gudao, there was a secluded ancient road leading to Chencang (now Baoji, Shaanxi Province). The Han army marched very quickly along this secluded ancient road and they reached Sanguan Pass which was the only access from the southwest into Guanzhong.

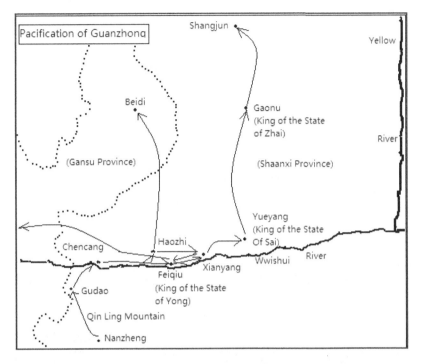

The Pacification of Guanzhong

Han Xin ordered General Cao Shen to select fifty strong and brave soldiers. The fifty soldiers disguised themselves as woodcutters. When sundown was approaching, every one of the fifty soldiers carried a heavy load of firewood on his back. They went to the gate of the pass. The soldiers of the State of Yong guarding the pass examined every one of them. The guards did not find anything suspicious and let them go into the pass. When midnight came the fifty soldiers took out their swords that were hidden in the loads of firewood. They started a surprise attack on the gate guards and took the pass. They opened the gate and the Han army rushed through, then marched quickly towards Chencang.

The Han army hit the city of Chencang with a surprise attack as soon as they arrived. The general of the State of Yong defending the city of Chencang could not hold them off. The general and his soldiers abandoned the city and ran away. The Han army easily took the city.

The general who had been defending Chencang rode quickly to Feiqiu (now Xingping, Shaanxi Province), the capital of the State of Yong, to report to Zhang Han, the King of the State of Yong, that the Han army had arrived suddenly and conquered the city. Zhang Han led his army to prevent the advance of the Han army because he understood very well that the task assigned to him by Xiang Yu was to stop Liu Bang from ever coming back to Guanzhong. When Zhang Han reached Chencang, the Han army was already arranged in battle formation. Zhang Han's army was defeated. Zhang Han led the main part of his army to retreat to Feiqiu. Han Xin ordered Fan Kuai to lead his army to lay siege to Feiqiu and sent Cao Shen and Zhou Bo to attack Xianyang. Cao Shen and Zhou Bo captured Xianyang, the former capital of the State of Qin.

Han Xin sent General Guan Ying to attack Yueyang, the capital of the State of Sai. When Guan Ying with his army arrived, Sima Xin, the King of the State of Sai, opened the city gate and surrendered Yueyang to the Han army. Liu Bang moved his headquarters to Yueyang. Liu Bang sent a great army to march north to Gaonu, the capital of the State of Zhai. Dong Yi, King of the State of Zhai, knew that he could do nothing to save his state from destruction. When the Han army arrived, he opened the city gate and surrendered. Now, apart from the city of Feiqiu which was still in the hands of Zhang Han and under siege by the Han army, the whole area of Guanzhong had been brought into line.

24. XIANG YU'S DECISION TO ATTACK THE STATE OF QI

When Xiang Yu got word that Liu Bang had burst out of Hanzhong and was taking over Guanzhong, he was furious. At this time an envoy sent by Zhang Liang arrived and presented Xiang Yu with a letter. In the letter Zhang Liang explained that Liu Bang only wanted to get back Guangzhong and he had no intention of going further east. After reading the letter, Xiang Yu felt a bit easier.

Soon after, another envoy from Zhang Liang arrived in Pengcheng to report further news. Zhang Liang wrote that Tian Rong, the King of the State of Qi, had made arrangements to threaten the State of Western Chu; he had lent an army to Chen Yu to drive out Zhang Er, King of Changshan, and put Zhao Xie back to the throne of the State of Zhao; the State of Zhao controlled by Chen Yu constituted a threat to the State of Western Chu. So Xiang Yu made up his mind to attack the State of Qi.

And Zhang Liang made up his mind to go to Guanzhong and offer to serve Liu Bang wholeheartedly. When he arrived in Yueyang, Liu Bang welcomed him warmly and granted him the title of Marquis of Chengxin.

Xiang Yu urged the Acting Emperor to leave Pengcheng for Chen, south of the Yangtze River. Then in October 206 BC, Xiang Yu sent undercover agents to take secret orders to Ying Bu, King of Jiujiang, and Wu Rui, King of Hengshan, and Gong Ao, King of Linjiang: and they killed the Acting Emperor in the Yangtze River.

In December 206 BC, Xiang Yu led his army in the march northward to Chengyang (now to the north of Heze, Shandong Province). Tian Rong met Xiang Yu's army there and a battle was fought in January 205 BC. Tian Rong was defeated; he retreated to Pingyuan (now in Shandong Province). The people there killed him.

In January 205 BC, Xiang Yu reinstated Tian Jia as King of the State of Qi. Xiang Yu then led his victorious army in a vicious campaign, fighting all the way north to the sea, destroying cities, killing Qi soldiers who had surrendered, capturing old people and women. So the people of the State of Qi rose against him.

Tian Heng, Tian Rong's younger brother, gathered the scattered Qi soldiers. He got about 50,000 men. In March 205 BC, Tian Heng put Tian Guang, Tian Rong's son, on the throne of the State of Qi. So Xiang Yu was stuck in the State of Qi.

25. Liu Bang's Action to Conquer the Areas around the Yellow River

After Guanzhong had been largely pacified, Liu Bang decided to go into action to put an end to the fighting in the east. He appointed Xiao He to stay in Yueyang to administer of Guanzhong. Han Xin was also to stay in Guanzhong to continue the siege of Feiqiu. Liu Bang personally to lead a strong army to march out of Guanzhong.

In September 206 BC, Liu Bang exited Hanguguan Pass with a great army of 100,000 men. They reached Shan (now Shanxian, Henan Province), where he established his headquarters. From there, he sent out an army to attack the State of Henan. In October 206 BC, when the Han army reached Luoyang, the capital of the State of Henan, Shen Yang, King of the State of Henan, surrendered to Liu Bang.

Liu Bang sent Haan Xin, the grandson of the former King of the State of Haan (before the State of Haan was conquered by the State of Qin), to put down the unrest in the State of Haan. He promised to make Haan Xin the King if he could pacify the State of Haan. In

November 206 BC, the army under Haan Xin and the army under Zheng Chang, King of the State of Haan made by Xiang Yu, met in Yangcheng (now a place between Dengfeng and Yuzhou, Henan Province). Zheng Chang was defeated and he surrendered. The whole State of Haan put down arms. Liu Bang made Haan Xin King of the State of Haan as he had promised.

After the State of Henan and the State of Haan, which were located south of the Yellow River, were pacified, Liu Bang returned to Yueyang. In November 206 BC, Liu Bang made Yueyang the capital of the State of Han.

While Liu Bang was in Yueyang, Zhang Er, the King of Changshan, who had been defeated by Chen Yu, went to Yueyang to ask Liu Bang for help. Liu Bang promised to help him and asked him to stay in the State of Han for the time being.

Not long later, Liu Bang set out to the areas to the north of the Yellow River. In March 205 BC, Liu Bang crossed the River from Linji (now to the east of Dali, Shaanxi Province). The Han army marched to Pingyang (now Linfen, Shanxi Province), the capital of the State of Western Wei. Wei Bao, the King, opened the city gate to welcome Liu Bang, and he put himself under the command of Liu Bang. Then Liu Bang marched his army to Henei (now Wuzhi, Henan Province) which belonged to the State of Yin. Sima Wang (King of the State of Yin) led an army from Zhaoge (now Qixian, Henan Province), the capital of the State of Yin, to prevent the advance of the Han army. After a battle, Sima Wang was captured and he surrendered. The State of Yin was brought under control.

Chen Ping, a high-ranking officer in Xiang Yu's army, crossed the Yellow River and joined Liu Bang's army in Xiuwu (now Huojia, Henan Province). Liu Bang appointed him to a responsible position as a supervisor of the generals.

Liu Bang crossed the Yellow River again and was riding his horse, heading south to Luoyang (Henan Province), when an old man stopped him and informed Liu Bang that Xiang Yu had moved King Huai of the State of Chu to the south side of the River and had him killed there. He suggested Liu Bang to openly declare what a crime Xiang Yu had committed and to order all his officers and men to wear white clothes to mourn for King Huai of the State of Chu; then, he advised, Liu Bang should openly call the kings of different states all over China to launch an expedition against Xiang Yu. Liu Bang took this advice and held a mourning ceremony for the Acting King (King

Huai of the State of Chu). Then he sent envoys to all the kings to call upon them to embark on an expedition against Xiang Yu.

When Liu Bang's envoy reached the State of Zhao with the message, Chen Yu said, "If the King of Han kills Zhang Er, then I will do what he has instructed." Liu Bang found a person who resembled Zhang Er in appearance and had him killed. Then he sent an envoy with the head of this person to Chen Yu. Then Chen Yu sent his army to the King of Han.

26. THE BATTLE OF PENGCHENG

After Tian Rong died, his brother Tian Heng collected the soldiers who had fled in disarray; he pulled together more than 30,000 of them and stationed his army in Chengyang. In April 205 BC, Tian Heng made Tian Rong's son Tian Guang King of the State of Qi, with orders to resist Xiang Yu's attack. Xiang Yu charged Chengyang several times but could not take it. Although he learned that Liu Bang was advancing eastward, he could not withdraw from Chengyang to stop the advance of the King of Han. So Liu Bang commanded the united army of the kings of other states, 560,000 in all, in an expedition against Xiang Yu.

In April 205 BC, the Han army and the armies of other kings marched towards Pengcheng in three routes: the north route, the middle route and the south route. (A "route" was a typical military formation consisting of at least a couple of corps or maybe several divisions.) The north route mainly comprised of the Han army under Generals Cao Shen, Fan Kuai, Zhou Bo and Guan Ying. They started from Henei. They marched to Xiuwu (now Huojia, Henan Province) and then to the Port of Baima (now Huaxian, Henan Province). From the Port of Baima, the Han army crossed the Yellow River and marched south to Dingtao (Shandong Province). There they fought with the Western Chu army and defeated them. Then the Han army marched to Dang (in the southwest of Henan Province) and Xiao (Xiaoxian, Jiangsu Province); then they were ready to enter Pengcheng.

The army of the south route comprised the Han army commanded by Generals Wang Ling, Xue Ou and Wang Xi, which had already marched to Yangxia (now Taikang, Henan Province) and was stopped by the army of the Western Chu. The Han started an attack and took Yangxia. This route of the army marched towards Pengcheng.

Liu Bang led the middle route. Zhang Liang, Chen Ping, Xiahou Ying, Jin She, Lu Wan, Haan Xin (King of the State of Haan), Wei Bao (King of the State of Western Wei), Zhang Er (original King of the

State of Changshan), Shen Yang (original King of the State of Henan), Sima Xin (original King of the State Sai), Dong Yi (original King of the State of Zhai), Sima Wang (original King of the State of Yin) were in this route. They started from Luoyang and took Quyu (now Zhongmao, Henan Province), then marched to Waihuang (a place near Zhongmao, Henan Province). Peng Yue joined Liu Bang with 30,000 men under his command. There Liu Bang made Wei Bao (King of the State of Western Wei) King of the State of Wei and appointed Peng Yue premier of the State of Wei.

Liu Bang's army marched to Pengcheng and took the city. Liu Bang confiscated all the treasures and beautiful women in Xiang Yu's palaces. Then Liu Bang held banquets day and night to celebrate the victory.

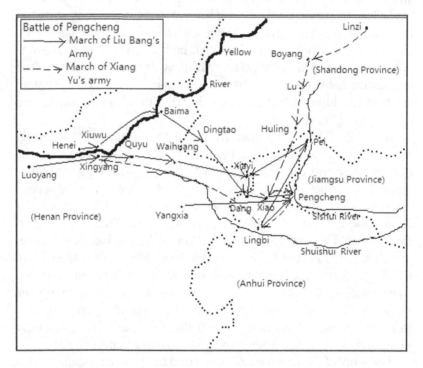

The Battle of Pengcheng

Xiang Yu got word that Liu Bang had entered Pengcheng. He ordered other generals to continue the fighting with the Qi army while he himself with an army of 30,000 select troops all on horseback moved quickly and secretly south through Lu (now Qufu, Shandong Province) to Huling (in the southwest of Shandong Province), then to Xiao (now Xiaoxian, Anhui Province) which was to the west of Pengcheng. Liu Bang did not notice his opponent's movement at all, because he thought that Xiang Yu was still busy fighting with the State of Qi. He went on holding celebrations every day without taking the least precautions.

One day in April 205 BC, in the early morning, Xiang Yu commanded the Western Chu army to launch a surprise attack on the Han army, sweeping from west to east to Pengcheng. The Han army was caught entirely off guard, and it collapsed. At noon the Western Chu army inflicted a crushing blow upon the Han army. More than 200,000 Han soldiers were killed.

Xiang Yu spotted Liu Bang in the confusion and ordered his soldiers to surround him. The Western Chu army surrounded the King of Han in three rings. But suddenly, a fierce wind blew up from the northwest. The wind was so strong that big trees broke and houses were lifted from the ground. Sand and stone were blown up into the air. The sky went dark. The wind blew directly against the Western Chu army and the men were in great confusion and then scattered. Liu Bang and about ten followers on horseback seized the chance to make their escape.

They soon encountered many Han soldiers who were looking for him. On their way, Liu Bang wanted to go past Pei and take his family with him, but at that time Xiang Yu sent an army after them. Liu Bang's family got wind that Xiang Yu had sent an army after them and they ran away, so that when Liu Bang got there, he could not find them. On their way, Liu Bang found his son Liu Ying and daughter Liu Yuan.

At that time Liu Bang's wife's brother Lü Ze was a general under Liu Bang and stationed his army in Xiayi (now Dangshan, Henan Province). Liu Bang went into Lü Ze's camps and put Lü Ze's army under his own command. But Liu Bang's wife, his father, and Shen Yi Ji were unlucky. They tried to run away along the side road to look for King of Han. They did not meet the King of Han. Instead, they fell into the hands of Xiang Yu. And Xiang Yu kept them in his custody as hostages.

After Liu Bang was defeated by Xiang Yu, many kings who were originally on Liu Bang's side betrayed him and turned to Xiang Yu's side. Sima Xin, King of Sai, and Dong Yi, King of Zhai, went over to join Xiang Yu. Sima Wang, the former King of Yin, was missing in action.

In May 205 BC, Liu Bang retreated from Xiayi to Xingyang (now Xingyang, Henan Province). All the troops which had been defeated and scattered in the battle of Pengcheng congregated in Xingyang.

Xiang Yu recovered Pengcheng. Then he led his army in the march west to Xingyang to fight against the King of Han. Liu Bang's cavalry fought a battle against the cavalry of Western Chu to the east of Xingyang. The Han cavalry won a great victory over the Chu cavalry. From then on, the march of the Western Chu army to the west was stopped.

In June 205 BC, Liu Bang returned to Yueyang, the capital of the State of Han in Guanzhong. Liu Bang appointed his son Liu Ying Crown Prince of the State of Han. Liu Bang decided to conquer Feiqiu which had been in siege for a long time. As Commander-in-Chief, Han Xin ordered the soldiers to dig a channel from the side of Weishui River to the foot of the city wall. The water flooded through the channel to the foot of the city wall. Several days later, the city wall fell. Then the Han army entered the city. Zhang Han drew out his sword and killed himself.

In August Liu Bang went back to Xingyang. Before he left, he ordered Xiao He to stay in Guangzhong to help the Crown Prince.

27. Wei Bao's Betrayal of Liu Bang

Wei Bao, King of the State of Wei, had a concubine named Bo Ji. One day Bo Ji's mother Lady Wei invited Xu Fu, a famous fortune-teller, to the palace of Wei in Pingyang (now Linfen of Shanxi Province), the capital of the State of Wei, to tell Bo Ji's fortune. After reading Bo Ji's face carefully, Xu Fu said to Lady Wei, "Your daughter will give birth to an emperor!" Lady Wei was very glad and sent Xu Fu to Xingyang to tell King of the State of Wei about this.

Xu Fu traveled all the way from Pingyang to Xiangyang where Wei Bao, King of the State of Wei, was staying. Wei Bao was allied with Liu Bang. Wei Bao had led his army to help Liu Bang attack Pengcheng. But later they were defeated by Xiang Yu and ran back to Xingyang. When Xu Fu arrived, Wei Bao invited her to a private room. Xu Fu said, "I have read your concubine Bo Ji's face. I can predict that she will give birth to an emperor!" Wei Bao said excitedly, "My concubine will give birth to an emperor! That is to say, I shall be the father of an emperor!" So he decided to leave Liu Bang.

Wei Bao went to see Liu Bang and asked for leave because his mother was missing him. Liu Bang gave his permission.

In May 205 BC, as soon as he crossed the Yellow River and stepped on the territory of the State of Wei, Wei Bao ordered the army of Wei to block all the ports by the Yellow River to prevent Liu Bang's army from crossing the River and attacking them. When he arrived at Pingyang, he openly declared that the State of Wei was no more an ally of the State of Han. Later he even declared that he would be on the side of Xiang Yu.

28. THE BATTLE TO DEFEAT THE KING OF THE STATE OF WEI

When Liu Bang heard that Wei Bao had openly declared his betrayal and gone over to the side of Xiang Yu, he sent Li Yi Ji to go to the State of Wei to talk him out of it. When Li Yi Ji went to the State of Wei and conveyed Liu Bang's intention to Wei Bao, Wei Bao refused resolutely.

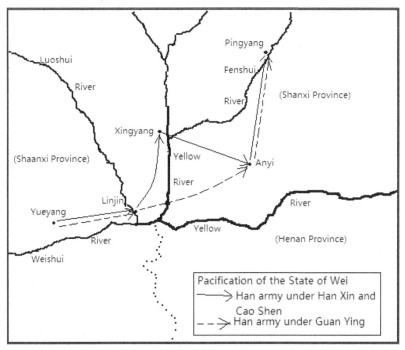

The Pacification of the State of Wei

When Li Yi Ji went back to Xingyang and reported the attitude of Wei Bao, Liu Bang decided to attack the State of Wei and to bring Wei Bao to his knees. In August 205 BC, Liu Bang sent Han Xin, together with Guan Ying and Cao Shen, to attack.

Han Xin commanded his army to advance to Linjin (now to the east of Dali, Shaanxi Province). Wei Bao deployed his army in Puban (now Puzhou, west to Yongji, Shanxi Province) to prevent Han Xin's army from crossing the Yellow River from Linjin. When the Han army reached Linjin, Han Xin ordered his army to show to the Wei army that the Han army would cross the Yellow River from Linjin.

One night, Han Xin ordered Guan Ying to stay in Linjin and attract the attention of the Wei army. He led Cao Shen and 20,000 men to go up north secretly to Xiayang (now Xiayang Village, Heyang County, Shaanxi Province) where the bank of the Yellow River was low and there were no Wei soldiers guarding the opposite bank. There the Han army crossed the Yellow River with rafts made of jars and poles. When the troops reached the opposite bank, they marched quickly towards Anyi (now Xiaxian, Shanxi Province). A battle was fought outside the city of Anyi, and the Han army was victorious.

When the news of the fall of Anyi reached Pingyang, Wei Bao immediately ordered the Wei army in Puban to come back to defend the capital. When General Guan Ying saw that the Wei army in Puban had retreated, he immediately ordered all his cavalry to get on board the boats and cross the Yellow River. General Guan Ying and his cavalry joined forces with Han Xin and Cao Shen. They marched to Pingyang. Wei Bao personally led his army out of the city of Pingyang to fight against the Han army. But Wei Bao was captured; and the guards of Pingyang opened the city gate and the Han army took Pingyang.

When Wei Bao was brought before Liu Bang, he begged him to spare his life. Then Liu Bang set him free. But he ordered that all of Wei Bao's concubines, including Bo Ji, be sent to work as slaves in a weaving room to weave cloth.

29. The Pacification of the State of Dai, the State of Zhao and the State of Yan

When the Han army was defeated in Pengcheng by the Western Chu army, Chen Yu, the premier of the State of Zhao, found that Zhang Er was still alive. So the State of Zhao controlled by Chen Yu turned against Liu Bang.

Since Commander-in-Chief Han Xin had squelched any resistance in the State of Wei, he sent an envoy to Liu Bang to ask permission to attack the State of Zhao, the State of Yan, and the State of Dai in the north, and the State of Qi in the east with 30,000 troops. Liu Bang gave him permission.

In September 205 BC, Han Xin, Zhang Er, the former King of the State of Changshan, and General Cao Shen marched their army to the State of Dai. The king of the State of Dai was Chen Yu. He was made King of the State of Dai by Zhao Xie, King of the State of Zhao. But Chen Yu had not gone to the State of Dai to take the throne of the state. He continued to stay in the State of Zhao to assist Zhao Xie. He just entrusted the state affairs to Xia Yue, the premier of the State of Dai. When the Han army arrived at the east of Wuxian (now Jiexiu, Shanxi Province), Premier Xia Yue led an army to block their advance. After a battle, General Cao Shen killed him. Han Xin decided to continue his march to Jingxing with Zhang Er. He ordered Cao Shen to lay siege to Wuxian. Not long later Cao Shen took Wuxian and pacified the State of Dai.

In October 205 BC, Han Xin and Zhang Er maneuvered an army of 30,000 men eastward to the State of Zhao. When Zhao Xie and Chen Yu got word that the Han army was advancing to the State of Zhao, they concentrated their army of 200,000 men in the entrance of Jingxing Pass.

When the Han army was fifteen kilometers away, Han Xin ordered the army to stop marching and pitch camps for the night. At midnight he sent 2,000 men from the cavalry to go through side roads to get to a place overlooking the camps of the Zhao army secretly. Each of them carried a red flag.

Then Han Xin sent 10,000 troops into the pass and the troops were deployed in a battle formation with the Jinman River at their backs. When the Zhao officers and soldiers saw that the Han troops were deployed in battle formation with a river behind them, they all laughed out loud. For it was a general rule, written in the military books, that an army should be deployed facing a river; if the army is deployed with a river behind them, they cannot retreat. Only foolish generals would deploy their armies this way.

In the morning, Han Xin and his officers and men marched into the pass. The Zhao soldier came out of their camps to fight. The battle went on for some time, and then Han Xin and Zhang Er pretended they were defeated. When the Zhao soldiers remaining in their camps saw that the Han army was defeated, they all came out of their camps to run after Han Xin and Zhang Er. Han Xin and Zhang Er and their army ran to the battle formation by the river. Since there was a river behind them, the soldiers had nowhere to escape. So the Han soldiers fought fiercely for their lives. They held their ground. When the 2,000 cavalrymen hiding in the hills near the camps saw that all the Zhao solders had left their camps, they rode as quickly as they could into the empty camps and pulled up all the flags of Zhao and put up the red flags of Han. When the Zhao soldiers saw that their camps had been taken by the enemy, they were in great disorder and they scattered and began to run for their own lives. The Han army attacked the Zhao army from two sides. They won a great victory. They killed Chen Yu in the battle and took prisoner Zhao Xie, King of the State of Zhao. The State of Zhao dropped all resistance.

Han Xin sent an envoy to the King of the State of Yan. The envoy showed all the advantages and strength of Han Xin to the King of the State of Yan. Then the King of the State of Yan agreed to submit to the King of Han.

30. The Fall of Xingyang

In May 204 BC, the situation became worse and worse. Food rations for the Han army became very short. The Western Chu army attacked the city of Xingyang fiercely. The city could fall at any moment. One night, General Ji Xin who bore a strong resemblance to Liu Bang, disguised himself as Liu Bang, was driven out of the city though the east gate. In the carriage, he shouted to the western Chu soldiers, "I am King of Han. My army has run out of food. I have decided to surrender." When the soldiers of the Western Chu army got the news that the King of Han had surrendered, they all rushed to the east gate to watch the great scene of the surrender of the King of Han.

Meanwhile Liu Bang and about thirty followers rode on horseback out of the city of Xingyang from the west gate.

After the King of Han left Xingyang, he went to Chenggao. When Xiang Yu heard that Liu Bang had escaped to Chenggao, he sent his army in pursuit. Liu Bang had to leave Chenggao. He went into Guanzhong through Hanguguan Pass. He raised an army there. Then he maneuvered his army through Wuguan Pass in the south to the area between Wan (now the area around Nanyang, Henan Province) and Ye (now Yexian, Henan Province). Ying Bu was also there with the King of Han. When Xiang Yu heard that the King of Han was in the area between Wan and Ye, he led his army to the south to meet the army of the King of Han.

When the King of Han was defeated in Pengcheng and retreated to the east, Peng Yue also lost all the cities he had occupied in Wei. Then he led his army to the area along the Yellow River to carry out guerrilla attacks. He launched raids on the food transportation units of the Western Chu army. This greatly disrupted the food supply of the Western Chu army. In May 204 BC, Peng Yue crossed the Suishui River and fought the Western Chu army in Xiapi (now northwest of Suining, Jiangsu Province). Peng Yue defeated the Western Chu army. At the same time, General Han Xin and Zhang Er led a great army to march south; they marched down to the north bank of the Yellow River, forming a threat to the army of Western Chu.

Xiang Yu decided to deal with Peng Yue and Han Xin first, so he sent an army across the Yellow River to fight with Han Xin and Zhang Er's army. Xiang Yu ordered General Zhong Gong to take some troops to defend Chenggao and he himself commanded his army to march east to deal with Peng Yue.

The King of Han seized the chance to move his army north to Chenggao; they defeated the Western Chu army at Chenggao under General Zhong Gong, and they took the city of Chenggao. In June, Xiang Yu defeated Peng Yue and drove Peng Yue out of the area of Xiapi. In June 204 BC, Xiang Yu got the news that Liu Bang had taken Chenggao, he moved swiftly west and made a severe strike at Xingyang and broke into the city.

Before Xingyang fell, Wei Bao, the former King of the State of Wei, intended to surrender to Xing Yu. His intension was found out by Zhou Ke. Then Zhou Ke killed Wei Bao with his sword.

When Xingyang fell, Zhou Ke, Zong Gong and Haan Xin (King of the State of Haan) were captured. Xiang Yu demanded them to surrender. Zhou Ke and Zong Gong would not surrender and were killed. Haan Xin surrendered and was spared. Later he found a chance and ran away. He went to Chenggao to Liu Bang. Liu Bang forgave him and made him King of the State of Haan again.

Then Xiang Yu directed his army north to lay siege to Chenggao. The King of Han and Xiahou Ying drove away from the north gate of Chenggao in a carriage. They crossed the Yellow River to the north bank. They stayed in Xiuwu (now Huojia, Henan Province) for the night. Early next morning, they reached the camp of the Han army under the command of Han Xin and Zhang Er. Liu Bang pretended that he was the envoy sent by the King of Han, and the guards of the camp let them into the camp. At that time Han Xin and Zhang Er were sleeping fast. The King of Han went into Han Xin's tent and Zheng Er's tent and seized their seals for the command of their army. With the seals in his possession, the King of Han had the army under his own command. Then Liu Bang ordered Han Xin to lead an army to take the State of Qi. After taking the State of Qin, Han Xin should lead his army to threaten the Western Chu from the north.

Peng Yue started his military operations in Wei and took seventeen cities including Suiyang (now south of Shangqiu, Henan Province) and Waihuang (now northwest of Minquan, Henan Province).

In September Xiang Yu ordered Cao Jiu to defend Changgao and he himself led his army to march east. They attacked the city of Chenliu (now of Kaifeng, Henan Province) and took it. But when Xiang Yu attacked the city of Waihuang, he met with strong resistance. Peng Yue's army and the people of Waihuang put up a brave defense. Still, Xiang Yu took the city after several days of hard fighting with severe casualties. Then he marched his army to east again. When Xiang Yu reached Suiyang, the people of Suiyang surrendered.

31. Han Xin Defeats the State of Qi

Han Xin marched his army from Xiuwu to Pingyuan (now Pingyuan, Shandong Province) and crossed the Yellow River. In October 204 BC, Han Xin suddenly attacked the Qi army in Lixia and defeated them. Then the Han army pursued the defeated army to Linzi, the capital city of the State of Qi (now Linzi, Shandong Province).

The King of the State of Qi appointed Tian Guaang as the acting premier to defend Linzi, and he maneuvered his army to cross the Wei River to Gaomi (now Gaomi, Shandong Province). He sent an envoy to Xiang Yu to ask for help. Tian Heng, the premier of the State of Qi, retreated to Boyang with an army. When the Han army attacked Linzi, Acting Premier Tian Guaang fled to Chengyang. General Tian Ji stationed his army in Liaodong (now Jimo, Shandong Province).

32. The Battles of Chenggao

Liu Bang decided to go on and take Chenggao. The Han army marched along the north bank of the Yellow River to the Port of Pingyin, where they crossed the Yellow River to the south bank. Then they marched east to attack Chenggao. Cao Jiu, the general of the Western Chu army defending Chenggao, came out of the city to fight with the Han army. After a battle, the Western Chu army was defeated and Cao Jiu killed himself. Liu Bang took Chenggao again. He stationed his army on a hill west of Guangwu Mountain (now in Henan Province) and established food supply lines from Aochang.

Guangwu Mountain was situated to the north of Xingyang and east of Chenggao. It rose abruptly on the south bank of the Yellow

River and extended to the south. There was a great ravine, the Guangwu Ravine, 200 meters deep and 100 meters wide, that cut Guangwu Mountain in two — the Western Guangwu Hill and the Eastern Guangwu Hill. At the bottom of the ravine there was a canal dug by the people of the State of Wei during the period of Warring States for the purpose of irrigation. Liu Bang stationed his army on the Western Guangwu Hill and ordered his soldiers to build a wall of 1,200 meters long and 10 meters high around the hill to defend the camps.

33. Bo Ji Becomes Liu Bang's Concubine and Liu Heng Is Born

When Liu Bang went back to Chenggao, he went to the weaving room where the concubines of Wei Bao, the former King of the State of Wei, were working. He saw a particularly pretty young lady sorrowfully working at the looms. He asked one of the keepers, "Who is that young lady?" The keeper said, "She is Bo Ji, one of Wei Bao's concubines." Liu Bang had pity on her and said, "I have decided to select her as one of my concubines. Send her to my harem."

One night, Liu Bang called Bo Ji to his bed. When she was undressed and lying in the bed of the King of Han, she said shyly, "Last night, I dreamed that a dragon coiled upon my belly." King of Han said, "I will make your dream come true." They spent the night together. Not long later, Bo Ji found that she was pregnant, and in nine months, she gave birth to a baby boy. He was named Liu Heng.

34. The Confrontation between Liu Bang and Xiang Yu at Guangwu Mountain

Xiang Yu went east to fight with Peng Yue and won back more than ten cities. When he heard that Cao Jiu had been defeated and Chenggao had been taken by Liu Bang, he immediately went back with his army. At that point, the Han army had just laid siege to the city of Xingyang which was defended by the Western Chu army under General Zhong Li Mei. When the Han army found out that Xiang Yu was coming, they all retreated to a tenable defensive position on the Western Guangwu Hill. Xiang Yu stationed his army on Eastern Guangwu Hill opposite them. He also ordered his soldiers to build a wall 1,000 meters long, 15 meter high and 26 meters wide. The two hostile armies were in a stalemate for several months.

As Peng Yue began to attack the supply lines of the Western Chu army, so their food supplies began to run short. Xiang Yu was worried.

One day, he had his soldiers build a platform at the foot of Eastern Guangwu Hill beside the canal. Then a big block for cutting meat was put on the platform, and a big pot was set there over a big fire. Then Liu Bang's father was dragged to the platform by an executioner with a big axe in his hand. Xiang Yu shouted to Liu Bang on the other side of the canal, "Liu Bang, if you don't surrender immediately, I will chop your father to pieces and cook him into soup!" From the other side of the canal, Liu Bang could see his father's mournful and helpless eyes. He felt pain in his heart. His struggle with Xiang Yu had dragged his father into disaster. His heart was breaking and tears were about to run down his face. But with a great effort, he held back his tears, and he shouted back, "When we both served King Huai of the State of Chu and were fighting side by side against the rule of the Qin Dynasty, we swore to be brothers. Since we were brothers, my father is also your father. If you are so cruel as to cook your father into soup, when it is ready, please give me a bowl of the soup." Xiang Yu was so angry that he ordered the executioner to chop Liu Bang's father to pieces. But Xiang Bo intervened. He stopped the executioner and said to Xiang Yu, "Now, we cannot tell who will win the final victory. Liu Bang is an ambitious man and will reach his goal regardless his family. He will not care even if you kill his father. It will bring you more trouble." Xiang Yu backed down, and ordered Liu Bang's father to be taken back into custody.

The confrontation between Liu Bang and Xiang Yu continued.

35. HAN XIN PACIFIES THE STATE OF QI

After Commander-in-Chief Han Xin took Linzi, he commanded his army in the pursuit of the King of the State of Qi in the east. Xiang Yu sent Long Ju with an army of 200,000 men to relieve the State of Qi. Long Ju joined the King of the State of Qi in Gaomi.

In November 204 BC, the armies of Qi and Western Chu were stationed on the east bank of the Wei River. The Han army commanded by Han Xin was stationed on the west bank of the same river. Han Xin sent some of his soldiers upstream at night to divert the course of the river with sand bags. When morning came, there was little water flowing downstream, allowing Han Xin and his army to cross the river and attack the Western Chu army under Long Ju.

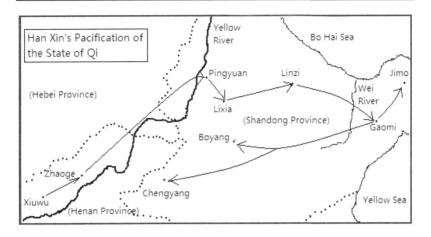

Han Xin's Pacification of the State of Qi

When Long Ju started a counterattack, Han Xin's army pretended to be overwhelmed and fled back to the west bank. Long Ju sent his army across the river to pursue them. At this, Han Xin gave the signal to the troops upstream to remove the sandbags. Water rushed down and the river was full again. Only Long Ju, General Zhou Lan and a small number of Western Chu soldiers reached the west bank. The army under Han Xin turned back and fought with the Western Chu troops who had crossed the river. Long Ju was killed and Zhou Lan was captured. Since the Western Chu army on the west bank had lost their commander, they scattered and ran away. Tian Guang, the King of the State of Qi, escaped. Han Xin went after him and captured him at Chengyang (north of Heze, Shandong Province). General Guan Ying pursued Tian Guaang, the premier of the State of Qi, and captured him too. Then he moved his army to Boyang (now a place near Tai'an, Shandong Province).

When Tian Heng got the news that the King of the State of Qi had been killed, he made himself King of the State of Qi and led his army into battle against the army of Han under Guan Ying. A battle was fought in Ying (a place near Laiwu, Shandong Province) and Tian Heng was defeated. He escaped and joined Peng Yue who was operating in Wei. Then Guan Ying marched his army to Qiancheng (now northeast of Gaoqing, Shandong Province) to fight with Tian Xi, commander-in-chief of the army of the State of Qi. Tian Xi was killed in battle. Cao Shen attacked Tian Ji in Shandong Peninsula and killed him. And in the State of Qi, the fighting stopped.

In November 204 BC, Liu Bang made Zheng Er King of the State of Zhao. In February 203 BC, Liu Bang made Han Xin King of the State of Qi. And then Liu Bang ordered Han Xin to attack the State of Western Chu. In July 203 BC, Liu Bang made Ying Bu King of the State of Huainan and sent him to Jiujiang. Ying Bu's task was to block Xiang Yu's return route to the south.

36. The Decisive Battle in Gaixia

In August 203 BC, Xiang Yu realized that he could not get help from anywhere; and he had run out of food for the army. Han Xin's army was advancing from the State of Qi to attack the State of Western Chu. At that time Liu Bang sent Hou Gong as his envoy to Xiang Yu to convey his intention to make peace with him. Liu Bang set out two conditions. The first condition was to draw a demarcation line to divide the whole realm into two parts. Xiang Yu would take the eastern part and Liu Bang would take the western part. Each would stay in his own territory and would not invade the territory of the other. The second condition was that Xiang Yu should release Liu Bang's father and wife. Xiang Yu thought that the conditions were reasonable. Then he summoned Xiang Bo into his tent and appointed him the representative to negotiate the detailed terms for peace.

Hou Gang on behalf of the King of Han and Xiang Bo on behalf of the King of Western Chu held negotiations for several days. They reached an agreement on the terms for peace. They decided that the demarcation should be along the Hongguo. Honggou was the name of an ancient canal taking water of the Yellow River from the north of Xingyang through the north of Taikang to the Yingshui River in the southeast of Huaiyang of Henan Province. It ran between Western Guangwu Hill, where the camp of Liu Bang's army was situated, and the Eastern Guangwu Hill, where the camp of Xiang Yu's army was situated. The areas to the east of Honggou belonged to Xiang Yu, King of the Western Chu. The areas to the west of Honggou belonged to Liu Bang, King of Han.

Then Hou Gong and Xiang Yu's envoy went to Liu Bang's camp. Liu Bang read the agreement and approved the terms. After that, Hou Gong and Xiang Yu's envoy went back with the agreement approved by Liu Bang to Xiang Yu. Then Xiang Yu released Liu Bang's father and wife, and Shen Yi Ji who had been captured together with them.

In September, since the peace agreement had been made, Xiang Yu left Xingyang on his way back to the east with the army. He was eager to return to Pengcheng, his capital. His soldiers longed to go back home. So his army marched very quickly east.

The King of Han wanted to go back to the west. He ordered his army to get ready to return to Guangzhong. But Zhang Liang and Chen Ping suggested to the King of Han to take the chance to destroy Xiang Yu. The King of Han took their advice. He led his army of 100,000 men to cross Honggou, the demarcation, to pursue the army of Western Chu.

In October 203 BC, the King of Han pursued Xiang Yu to Yangxia (now Taikang, Henan Province). Then Liu Bang stopped advancing. He sent out envoys to Han Xin, King of the State of Qi, and Peng Yue, Premier of the State of Wei, ordering them to lead their armies to join with him in Guling to destroy Xiang Yu's army.

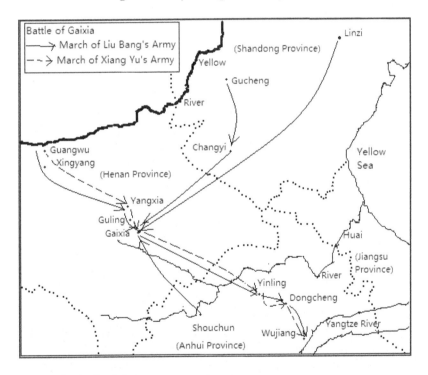

The Battle of Gaixia

When the envoy reached the State of Qi and conveyed Liu Bang's order, Han Xin led an army of 300,000 men to join King of Han. Peng Yue led all the army under him to march to Guaixia (near Suiyang, Henan Province) from the area of Wei. General Liu Jia led an army to march to Gaixia from Shouchun (now Shouxian, Anhui Province).

In December Liu Bang's great army of over 500,000 men had gathered in Gaixia and was ready to attack Xiang Yu's army. There were about 100,000 men in Xiang Yu's army. Now over 600,000 men gathered in Gaixia to fight a decisive battle.

Xiang Yu's army pitched camp on high ground. Liu Bang's great army marched to Xiang Yu's camp to challenge them to battle. Xiang Yu led his army out of camp and arranged the men in battle formation. Then a great battle began. The battle went on for a long time. Nearly half of the men of Xiang Yu's army fell. Xiang Yu was defeated. He retreated with his remaining army into his camp.

At midnight Zhang Liang arranged the Han soldiers surrounding the Chu army to sing a sad song in the tune of the area of Chu repeatedly urging the Chu soldiers to leave Xiang Yu and go back home. When the soldiers of the Western Chu army heard this tune from their homeland, they shed tears. Then the soldiers stood up, snuck out of the camp and left. Even Xiang Bo, Xiang Yu's uncle, slipped out and turned over to the side of the King of Han. Only eight hundred soldiers remained.

Xiang Yu and his eight hundred followers jumped on the backs of their horses and broke through the encirclement. They galloped quickly southward. When they reached Yinling (now northwest of Dingyuan, Anhui Province), the Han cavalrymen caught up with them. Xiang Yu killed the commander of the Han cavalrymen in battle. Then Xiang Yu and his followers reached Wujiang (now in Anhui Province), on the west bank of the Yangtze River. Xiang Yu was too ashamed to go back to the east bank of the Yangtze River. So he put his sword to his neck and killed himself.

37. Liu Bang Becomes Emperor of the Han Dynasty

In February 202 BC, Han Xin (King of the State of Chu) together with Peng Yue (King of the State of Liang), Ying Bu (King of the State of Huainan), Haan Xin (King of the State of Haan), Wu Rui (King of the State of Hengshan), Zhang Er (King of the State of Zhao), and Zang Tu (King of the State of Yan), jointly presented a memorandum to Liu Bang, King of the State of Han, proposing that he ascend the throne as an emperor. Premier Xiao He and the civil officials and the generals also presented a memorandum to Liu Bang proposing that he ascend the throne of emperor.

4. Portrait of Liu Bang, Emperor Gaozu of the Han Dynasty

One day in late February 202 BC, a grand ceremony was held in a place to the south of Jishui River, south of Dingtao. Liu Bang stepped up onto a stage and sat on the throne in the middle of the stage. All the kings, officials and general went up to the stage to express their congratulations to Liu Bang upon the occasion of his ascension to the throne of the Emperor of the Han Dynasty. It was declared that Lü Zhi, the Queen of the State of Han, had become the Empress of the Han Dynasty, Liu Ying, the Crown Prince of the State of Han, became the successor to the throne of the Han Dynasty. The Emperor declared he was making Luoyang (Henan Province) the capital of the Han Dynasty. But later Liu Bang accepted Lou Jing's suggestion and decided to move his capital from Luoyang to Chang'an (now Xi'an, Shaanxi Province). Emperor Liu Bang put Xiao He in charge of building new palaces in Chang'an.

38. Under the Rule of Emperor Liu Bang

In July 202 BC, Zang Tu, King of the State of the State of Yan, rebelled against the Han Dynasty. He sent an army to attack the area of Dai (now an area around Weixian in the north part of Hebei Province) and took it.

Emperor Liu Bang sent a great army to suppress the rebellion. The army of the Han Dynasty took Ji (now Beijing), the capital of the State of Yan. After the battle, Zang Tu was captured and executed. Emperor Liu Bang made Lu Wan, a good friend of Liu Bang from childhood, King of the State of Yan.

Zhong Li Mei, one of Xiang Yu's fiercest generals, was a good friend of Han Xin. After Xiang Yu died, Zhong Li Mei escaped to Han Xin for protection. Liu Bang hated Zhong Li Mei very much. When Liu Bang found out that Zhong Li Mei was in the State of Chu under the protection of Han Xin, he sent an order to the State of Chu to arrest Zhong Li Mai.

In October 202 BC, the Emperor received a secret written statement informing him the Han Xin was plotting a rebellion. Emperor Liu Bang sent out envoys to all the states to call the kings to meet him in Chen (eastern Hebei Province and western Anhui Province). In December 202 BC, the Emperor and the kings met. Han Xin brought Zhong Li Mei's head and went to see the Emperor.

As soon as he arrived, the Emperor ordered two strong warriors to arrest Han Xin. The Emperor brought him back to Luoyang, and then pardoned him and made him Marquis of Huaiyin (now Huaiyin, Jiangsu Province). However, Han Xin was deposed as the King of the State of Chu. The Emperor divided the State of Chu in two: the State of Jing, which had fifty-three counties, and the State of Chu, which had thirty-six counties. He made Liu Jia, his cousin, King of the State of Jing, and made his younger brother Liu Jiao King of the State of Chu. The Emperor created Zhang Liang Marquis of Liu (now southeast of Peixian, Jiangsu Province), Chen Ping Marquis of Huyou (now Chenliu, Henan Province), and Cao Shen Marquis of Pingyang (now Linfen, Shanxi Province). The Emperor created twenty-nine marquises in the period from December 202 BC to January 201 BC. From March to August 201 BC, and in the later years, Liu Bang created 124 marquises.

39. THE RISE OF THE HUNS

The Huns lived in the grasslands of Mongolia. They were nomadic people. They raised livestock such as horses, cattle and sheep. All the people of the Huns, even children, were able horsemen. So the Huns were called "people on horseback." They could draw strong bows and shoot arrows. The Hun armies could move rapidly because they were all on horseback.

During the period of Warring States, they moved into the Great Bend of the Yellow River (Ningxia Hui and Inner Mongolia Autonomous Regions). After the First Emperor of the Qin Dynasty unified China, he ordered General Meng Tian to drive the Huns out of the Great Bend in 215 BC with an army of 300,000 men. The Huns returned to the grasslands of Mongolia. Then the First Emperor of the Qin Dynasty sent more than 100,000 men to garrison along the frontier to prevent the Huns from coming back.

At that time, the name of the king of the Huns was Tumen Luandi. He could not resist the army commanded by General Meng Tian of the Qin Dynasty. He led the Huns to retreat to the north. Ten years later, General Meng Tian died and China was in great chaos. All the people who were garrisoned at the frontier left. So Tumen Luandi led the Huns back to the Great Bend of the Yellow River.

Tumen's son Modu was the crown prince. Modu's mother had died early. Tumen took another wife, and she became queen. Not long later the queen gave birth to a son. Tumen liked the younger son better than the elder son, and he wanted to deprive Modu the title of crown prince and make his younger son the crown prince. But in 209 BC Modu killed his father Tumen during a hunting trip and then killed his stepmother and his younger brother. Thus Modu became the king of the Huns.

Modu led his army to defeat the State of Dong Hu (the Eastern Minority Nationality in the Northeast China) and the State of Yuezi (in Gansu Province). He invaded the areas of the State of Yan and the State of Dai. At that time Liu Bang was hard at war with Xiang

Yu. China was in great chaos. So Modu took this opportunity to take back all the areas in the Great Bend of the Yellow River.

40. HAAN XIN, THE KING OF THE STATE OF HAAN, BETRAYS THE HAN DYNASTY AND DEFECTS TO THE HUNS

In the autumn of 201 BC, Modu led an army of the Huns to lay siege to Mayi (now Shuozhou, in the northwest part of Shanxi Province), the capital of the State of Haan. The King of the State of Haan sent several envoys to the Huns suing for peace. Meanwhile the Emperor sent an army to relieve the King of the State of Haan. When the Emperor found out that the King of the State of Haan had sent several envoys to the Huns, he suspected that he was looking to form an alliance with the Huns. So he sent an envoy to reproach the King of the State of Haan. The King of the State of Haan was afraid of being punished by the Emperor. So in September 201 BC he surrendered to the Huns and handed Mayi to them. Then Modu led his army through Yanmenguan Pass (now in the north of Daixian, Shanxi Province) to attack Jinyang in the Taiyuan area (now in Shanxi Province).

In October 201 BC, the Emperor personally led an army on an expedition against Haan Xin. The Han army marched to Tongti (now Qixian, Shanxi Province). The army of the State of Haan tried to resist the army of the Han Dynasty and a battle was fought. The State of Haan was defeated. Then the Han army moved northward to Taiyuan, and then to Jinyang. Haan Xin's army and the Hun cavalrymen were there. A battle was fought outside the city. The army of the Han Dynasty won, and the King of the State of Haan fled to the Huns.

The Emperor was in Jinyang. He got word that Modu was in Daigu (now northeast to Datong City, Shanxi Province) and he wanted to attack him there. He sent several teams of scouts to Daigu to spy on the Huns. Modu hid his strongest warriors and strongest horses, so the scouts only saw the old and weak soldiers and weak horses. More than ten teams of scouts came back and reported to the Emperor what they had seen and said that the Huns could be easily defeated.

Then the Emperor sent Liu Jing to spy on the Huns. Before Liu Jing came back, the Emperor sent all his army of 320,000 men north to pursue Modu, and the army had passed Gouzhu Mountain (also called Yanmen Mountain, in the north of Daixian, Shanxi Province). The Emperor had advanced to Guangwu (now southwest of Daixiaan, Shanxi Province). Liu Jing came back and said to the Emperor that Modu was playing a trick and had laid an ambush to trap the Han army. But the Emperor would not listen to his advice.

The Emperor reached Pingcheng (now northeast to Datong City, Shanxi Province) ahead of his main force. Modu sent 400,000 elite soldiers to surround the Emperor in Baideng, which was situated five kilometers southeast of Pengcheng. The Emperor was surrounded for a whole week. The Emperor could not get any reinforcements and the food was running out. This is when the Emperor adopted Chen Ping's stratagem: he sent a secret envoy to present precious gifts to Modu's wife. Then Modu's wife said to Modu, "We should not press the Emperor of the Han Dynasty too hard. If you occupy the lands of the Han Dynasty, you will not inhabit these lands. May Heaven protect the Emperor of the Han Dynasty. You'd better think it over carefully." Then Modu lifted one corner of the encirclement. Incidentally there was a heavy fog that day. The Emperor made his breakthrough from the corner of the encirclement. When the Emperor reached Pingcheng, the main force also arrived. So the Huns withdrew and left. The Han army also withdrew.

41. Liu Jing's Advice to Improve Relations with the Huns

Modu led his army to invade the territory in the north of the Han Dynasty many times. The Emperor was worried, and he asked Liu Jing for advice. Liu Jing suggested the Emperor carry out a long term plan to make the future generations of the Huns the subjects of the Emperor. The Emperor asked, "What plan is that?" Li Jing said, "If Your Majesty is willing to send Your Majesty's eldest daughter to Modu as his wife, Modu will be very happy and make her queen. When she gives birth to a son, he will surely be made crown prince. Every year, Your Majesty can offer Modu gifts of articles that are abundant in China but are scarce in the State of the Huns. Then Modu will be grateful to Your Majesty. At the same time, Your Majesty may send some eloquent persons to the Huns to persuade the Huns to adopt a sense of propriety and righteousness. While Modu is alive, he will be the son-in-law of Your Majesty. After Modu dies, his son, that is, the grandson of Your Majesty, will ascend the throne of the Huns. I have never heard of a grandson who was hostile to his grandfather. In this way, the Huns will be brought to submission by and by. However," he warned, "if Your Majesty cannot bring himself to send his own daughter, but just sends any girl of your clan or any girl pretending to be the daughter of Your Majesty, it will be of no use, because when Modu finds out that she is not the daughter of Your Majesty, he will not make her queen." The Emperor said, "Your point is well made."

The Emperor decided to send his first-born daughter Princess Liu Yuan to Modu. But Empress Lü Zhi cried every day, begging the Emperor not to send their only daughter. The Empress said to the Emperor, "We have just this one daughter. Why should we abandon her to the wild area of the Huns?" And Princess Liu Yuan had been married to Zhang Ao, the former King of the State of Zhao. In the end, the Emperor gave up the idea of sending Princess Liu Yuan to Modu. At last he selected a girl by the family name of Liu and sent her to Modu to be his wife.

42. The Emperor's Intention to Replace the Crown Prince

Liu Bang loved his concubine Qi Ji very much. She gave birth to a son for him. This son was name Liu Ru Yi. Unfortunately, the Emperor thought that Crown Prince Liu Ying was soft and incompetent and would not become a ruler as powerful as he was. He loved the younger son better than the older son. Although Liu Ru Yi had been made King of the State of Zhao, he did not go to the State of Zhao but stayed in Chang'an.

The Emperor wanted to depose Crown Prince Liu Ying and replace him with Liu Ru Yi. All the ministers tried their best to persuade the Emperor not to do it. Zhou Chang, the vice premier, was resolutely against the Emperor's intention to replace the Crown Prince. The Emperor asked him why. Zhou Chang had a stutter, and he was very angry, so he stammered, "I can't say it well. But I think, think, think that won't, won't, won't do. Your Majesty wants to depose the Crown Prince. I think, think, think I won't, won't, won't take your order." The Emperor laughed heartily. The Empress was standing in the side room, listening. After court was over, the Empress met Zhou Chang. She knelt before him and expressed her hearty thanks to him. She said, "Without you, the Crown Prince would have been replaced."

43. Chen Xi's Rebellion and the End of Han Xin

Originally, the Emperor appointed Chen Xi, the Marquis of Yangxia, the premier of the State of Zhao. Chen Xi was also commander of the army stationed at the frontier in the area of Dai (now north Shanxi Province). Before he went to the State of Zhao to take the position, he visited Han Xin. Han Xin and Chen Xi plotted to launch a rebellion.

In September 197 BC, Chen Xi started his rebellion. Chen Xi made himself King of Dai. He occupied the areas of Zhao and Dai. The Emperor personally led an army in an expedition against Chen

Xi. When he arrived in Handan, he was very glad and said, "Chen Xi does not occupy Handan and defend it with the Zhang River as its natural barrier. This means that Chen Xi will certainly lose." When the Emperor found out that many of the generals under Chen Xi were originally merchants, he spent a lot of money to buy them over. And many of Chen Xi's generals surrendered. After several battles, Chen Xi's army was totally defeated.

Han Xin did not go with the Emperor to put down Chen Xi's rebellion, on the excuse that he was ill. Han Xin conspired with his followers to release all the criminals in Chang'an on a false order from the Emperor to pardon them in order to make a surprise attack on the Empress and the Crown Prince. When he was ready to act, he waited for Chen Xi's reply. But at that critical moment, one of his followers committed some offence against Han Xin. Han Xin put that man into prison and was going to kill him. In January 196 BC, that man's brother reported to the Empress that Han Xin was preparing to attack the Empress and the Crown Prince. Then the Empress consulted with Xiao He to make a plan. They sent a man out of the capital, and the man came back pretending that he had been sent by the Emperor. He reported to the Empress that Chen Xi had been killed. Xiao He personally went to Han Xin's residence and said to Han Xin, "Although you are ill, you must go to the palace to express your congratulations on the great victory." Han Xin had to go. As soon as he arrived, the Empress ordered the warriors to seize him and tie him up. Then he was dragged to a room in the palace and executed.

44. THE END OF HAAN XIN, THE FORMER KING OF THE STATE OF HAAN

In the spring of 196 BC, Haan Xin, the former King of the State of Haan, was staying in Sanhe (now Dingxiang, Shanxi Province) with the Huns, opposing the Han Dynasty. The Emperor sent General Cai Wu with a great army to attack Haan Xin and the Huns in Sanhe. General Cai Wu commanded his army to attack the city of Sanhe. The Han army broke into the city. General Cai Wu and Haan Xin met in the battlefield. After several bouts, General Cai Wu killed Haan Xin.

After the area of Dai had settled down, the Emperor made his son Liu Heng King of the State of Dai. The capital of the State of Dai was Jinyang (now Taiyuan, Shanxi Province).

45. THE DEATH OF PENG YUE, THE KING OF THE STATE OF LIANG

When the Emperor started his expedition against Chen Xi, he ordered Peng Yue to command his army to join in the expedition. But Ying Bu did not go personally; he said he was ill. He sent some generals commanding his army to Handan. The Emperor was very angry and sent an envoy to reprimand him. The King of the State of Liang was full of fear and wanted to go personally to apologize to the Emperor.

The premier of the State of Liang committed some offence against the King of Liang and Peng Yue was going to punish him. He ran away to see the Emperor and reported to the Emperor that the King of the State of Liang was conspiring to rebel. The Emperor sent some envoys to the State of Liang and arrested Peng Yue by surprise. In March 196 BC Peng Yue was executed.

The Emperor made his fifth son Liu Hui King of the State of Liang. Not long later the Emperor made his sixth son Liu You King of the State of Huaiyang.

46. THE REBELLION OF YING BU, THE KING OF THE STATE OF HUAINAN

When Ying Bu, the King of the State of Huainan, heard that Han Xin, Marquis of Huaiyin, had been executed, he was full of fear. When Peng Yue was killed, the Emperor had Peng Yue's flesh made into chopped salted meat and had it put into pots to present to the other kings. When the pot of meat was presented to Ying Bu, the King of the State of Huainan, he secretly ordered his generals to mobilize his army and sent agents to other prefectures to watch how things evolved.

Ying Bu suspected that his most loved concubine had committed adultery with Ben He, the minister in charge of the military affairs of the State of Huainan, and he wanted to arrest Ben He. Ben He escaped and went to Chang'an. Ben He reported to the Emperor that Ying Bu was plotting a rebellion.

When Ying Bu found that Ben He had escaped to Chang'an and reported to the Emperor that he was going to rebel, he knew that the Emperor must be suspicious of him. In July 196 BC, when the envoy was sent to investigate him, Ying Bu did rise in rebellion.

The Emperor personally led an army to fight against Ying Bu. The Emperor sent an envoy to the State of Qi to order the King of the State of Qi to lead an army to join him in the expedition against Ying Bu. When the King of the State of Qi got the order, he led an army of 120,000 men commanded by Cao Shen, the premier of the State of Qi, to march out of the State of Qi to join force with the Emperor.

Ying Bu first attacked the State of Jing (now south part of Jiangsu Province). Liu Jia, the King of the State of Jing, was defeated and was killed in Fuling (now Xuyi, Jiangsu Province). Then Ying Bu crossed the Huai River to attack the State of Chu. A battle was fought in the area between Xu and Tong (now Suining, Jiangsu Province). The army of the State of Chu was defeated. Ying Bu marched his army to the west. In October 196 BC, the army of the State of Qi commanded by Liu Fei and Cao Shen joined force with the army of the Han Dynasty under the command of the Emperor in Dan (now Dancheng, Henan Province). The Emperor's army met Ying Bu's army in the west of Dan. A fierce battle was fought. Ying Bu's army was defeated. They crossed the Huai River and stopped to fight some more. Several battles were fought. Ying Bu lost all the battles and escaped to the south of the Yangtze River. Ying Bu was at last killed by the local people of Boyang (in Hunan Province).

47. Lu Wan's Rebellion

When Chen Xi rose up in rebellion, Lu Wan, the King of the State of Yan, sent an army to attack the Army of Chen Xi from northeast. At that time Chen Xi sent Wang Huang into the Huns to ask for help, but Lu Wan sent Zhang Sheng, one of the ministers in the court of the State of Yan, to tell the Huns that Chen Xi's army had been defeated. When Zhang Sheng arrived, he spoke with Zang Yan, the son of Zang Tu, the former King of the State of Yan, who had been exiled to the Huns. Zang Yan told Zhang Sheng that if Chen Xi and the others were all destroyed, soon it would be the King of the State of Yan's turn. He asked Zhang Sheng to persuade the King of the State of Yan to delay the attack against Chen Xi and made peace with the Huns. When Zhang Shang came back to the State of Yan, he succeeded in persuading Lu Wan to delay the attack against Chen Xi. Lu Wan sent Zhang Sheng to the Huns as his envoy.

The Emperor found out that Lu Wan had conspired with Chen Xi and had united with the Huns. In February 195 BC he appointed Fan Kuai premier and sent him with an army to attack Lu Wan. And the Emperor made his son Liu Jia King of the State of Yan. Now except for the King of Changsha and the King of Nanyue, all the kings of the states in China bore the family name of Liu.

General Fan Kuai's wife Lü Xu was Empress Lü Zhi's younger sister, so General Fan Kuai was considered to belong to the clique of Empress Lü Zhi. When Fan Kuai was leading an army to pacify the rebellion of Lu Wan, some persons spread rumors that Fan Kuai would kill Qi Ji and Liu Ru Yi, the King of the State of Zhao. The Emperor ordered Chen Ping and General Zhou Bo to catch up with the army commanded by Fan Kuai; General Zhou Bo should replace Fan Kuai to command the army to continue the expedition to pacify the rebellion of Lu Wan; Chen Ping should arrest Fan Kuai and execute him on the spot.

On the way Chen Ping and Zhou Bo decided not to kill Fan Kuai but send him back to Chang'an and let the Emperor decide whether he should be executed. When they were getting close, they stopped and ordered the soldiers to build a platform. They sent an envoy to the army to summon Fan Kuai with the tally given by the Emperor. As soon as Fan Kuai arrived, he was arrested and put on a prisoner carriage. Zhou Bo took over the power to command the army and continued on to the State of Yan. At that time, Lu Wan had run away to the foot of the Great Wall with the queen, all his concubines and maids and several thousand cavalrymen. He stayed there in the hope that the Emperor would pardon him.

When the army under the command of General Zhou Bo reached Ji (now Beijing), the capital of the State of Yan, Zhou Bo launched an assault on the city. After a battle was fought, all the generals defending the city were captured. Then Zhou Bo marched his army northwest. He defeated the Yan army in Shanglan (in the northwest part of Hebei Province), then defeated the Yan army in Juyang (in the northwest part of Hebei Province). All the areas of the State of Yan were brought under control.

48. The Death of Liu Bang, the Emperor of the Han Dynasty

During the expedition against Ying Bu, Liu Bang was wounded by an arrow. The Emperor became seriously ill. The Empress sent for the best doctor, but the Emperor said that his life was decided by Heaven's will, and no doctor could cure him. He decided not to have his disease treated. He paid the doctor handsomely and sent him away. In April 195 BC, Liu Bang died in Changle Palace at the age of sixty-one.

In May the Emperor was buried in Changling (now in the northeast of Xianyang City, Shaanxi Province). He was given the posthumous title of Emperor Gao. He temple title was Gaozu. In the same month, Liu Ying, the Crown Prince, ascended the throne of the Han Dynasty at the age of sixteen. Lü Zhi, the Empress and mother of Liu Ying, was made Empress Dowager.

CHAPTER TWO: EMPEROR LIU YING AND EMPRESS DOWAGER LÜ ZHI

49. TROUBLES IN THE PALACE AFTER LIU BANG'S DEATH

Liu Bang had tried several times to replace the Crown Prince, Liu Ying, with Liu Ru Yi, and for this the Empress hated Liu Ru Yi and his mother Qi Ji very much. She couldn't do much about them while Liu Bang was alive. But as soon as Liu Bang died, and Liu Ying ascended the throne, Lü Zhi, now the Empress Dowager, took action. She ordered that Qi Ji be put in jail. She summoned Liu Ru Yi, King of the State of Zhao, to Chang'an. Emperor Liu Ying understood perfectly well how his mother felt about Liu Ru Yi, so Liu Ying personally met him in Bashang and put him in his own palace. But one day in December, Emperor Liu Ying had to get up early to practice archery. The King of the State of Zhao was too young to get up so early, so he stayed in bed. After Emperor Liu Ying left, the Empress Dowager sent a person to the Emperor's palace and forced the young King to drink poison. When Emperor Liu Ying came back, he found that the King of the State of Zhao was already dead.

The Empress Dowager then had Qi Ji's hands and legs cut off, her eyes gouged out, and made her deaf and dumb with a poisonous potion. The Empress Dowager put Qi Ji in a toilet and invited Emperor Liu Ying to see this "human pig." When the young Emperor saw the "human pig," he did not realize who she was. When he found out that it was Qi Ji, he burst into tears. He fell terribly ill and could not attend to state affairs. He sent someone to tell the Empress Dowager, "This is an inhuman atrocity you have committed. And although I am your son, I do not have the ruling power." From then on, he indulged in sensual pleasure and did not hold court any more.

50. Empress Dowager Lü Zhi Takes Over

In order to better control Emperor Liu Ying, Empress Dowager married her daughter's daughter to him. She was the daughter of Zhang Ao and Princess Liu Yuan. The Empress Dowager made her Empress, and she was called Empress Zhang. For several years she did not have any children. When one of the many concubines of Emperor Liu Ying got pregnant, under the instruction of the Empress Dowager, Empress Zhang pretended to be pregnant, too. When that concubine gave birth to a boy, Empress Zhang took away the child as her own and the Empress Dowager had that concubine killed. Liu Ying was on the throne for seven years and he died in August 188 BC at the age of twenty-three. Empress Dowager put that baby on the throne of the Han Dynasty.

After Liu Ying died, all the power was in the hands of Empress Dowager Lü Zhi. She wanted very much to make her brothers and her brothers' sons kings. But Liu Bang had made a rule with all the ministers and generals that no one with a family name other than the family name of Liu should be made king. So she summoned all the ministers and generals to court. She asked them their opinion. Premier Wang Ling was against her idea resolutely. But Chen Ping, the second premier, and Zhou Bo, the minister in charge of the national military affairs, agreed with her idea. Then Empress Dowager Lü Zhi made her elder brother Lü Ze, who had already died, King of Dao Wu. In April 187 BC, Lü Zhi made Lü Ze's eldest son Lü Tai King of the State of Lü. Empress Dowager Lü Zhi ordered Liu Shang, the King of the State of Qi, to cede the territory of Jinan Prefecture (now in Shandong Province) and made it the territory of the State of Lü. In November 187 BC, Lü Tai, the King of Lü died, and his son Lü Jia succeeded the throne of the State of Lü.

When the baby emperor was a little older, he heard that he was not Empress Dowager Zhang's son. He heard that his mother had been killed. He said angrily, "It is unjust that Empress Dowager Zhang killed my mother and took me as her own son. I will avenge my mother when I grow up." Lü Zhi kept the little emperor in a cold, derelict house. In February 184 BC, Lü Zhi had the baby emperor killed and made Liu Yi, another son of Liu Ying, emperor. In October 183 BC Empress Dowager Lü Zhi deposed Lü Jia as the King of the State of Lü because Lü Jia had carried out many unlawful activities. In

November 183 BC, she made Lü Chan, the younger brother of Lü Tai, King of the State of Lü.

In April 182 BC, Empress Dowager Lü Zhi made Liu Xing Ju Marquis of Dongmao (now Maoping, Shandong Province). Liu Xing Ju was a strong and brave man. He was appointed a commander of the guards of the palace.

In December 182 BC Empress Dowager Lü Zhi kept Liu You, King of the State of Zhao, locked in a house and withheld all food from him because he did not love her nephew, the daughter of her younger brother. Liu You was starved to death. In February 181 BC, Empress Dowager Lü Zhi moved Liu Hui, King of the State of Liang, to be the King of the State of Zhao. At the same time she moved Lü Chan, the King of Lü, to be the King of the State of Liang. Lü Chan did not go to the State of Liang to take the throne of the State of Liang, though. Empress Dowager Lü Zhi asked him to stay in Chang'an to serve as tutor to the young emperor. Empress Dowager Lü Zhi forced Liu Hui, King of the State of Zhao, to marry Lü Chan's daughter and made her queen of the State of Zhao. Liu Hui did not like the queen. He loved one of his concubines. The queen sent someone to kill that concubine by forcing her to drink poison. Liu Hui, the King of the State of Zhao, could not stand that anymore and committed suicide. Then Empress Dowager Lü Zhi made her brother's son Lü Lu King of the State of Zhao. In September, Liu Jian, King of the State of Yan, died. He had only one son, born by one of his concubines. Empress Dowager Lü Zhi sent an agent to kill that child. Then since there was no one to succeed to the throne of the State of Yan, Empress Dowager Lü Zhi made Lü Tong, a son of her brother, King of the State of Yan.

51. THE DEATH OF EMPRESS DOWAGER LÜ ZHI

In March 180 BC, Empress Dowager Lü Zhi held a ceremony in the outskirts of Chang'an to offer sacrifices to the gods, praying to ward off disasters and ask for blessings. Not much use: on her way back to Chang'an city, when her carriage was passing Zhidao, some kind of beast which resembled a huge dog rushed up to her carriage and thrust its head at her, biting her near the armpit. Then, just as suddenly, the animal disappeared. The Empress was terribly frightened. Her wound soon began to ulcerate and she became ill.

By July 180 BC, Empress Dowager Lü Zhi was ailing. She had to make arrangements to strengthen the power of the Lü family before she died. She appointed Lü Lu (King of the State of Zhao) commander-in-chief of the army and ordered him to take command of the army north of the capital and ordered Lü Chan (King of the State of Liang) to take command the army south of the capital. She ordered Emperor Liu Hong to marry one of Lü Lu's daughters and appointed that girl empress. Not long later Empress Dowager Lü Zhi died.

52. THE LÜ FAMILY IS EXTERMINATED

The members of the Lü family thought they'd better stage an armed rebellion. But they were afraid of Premier Chen Ping and General Zhou Bo, so they hesitated to actually make such a move.

When Chen Ping and Zhou Bo got wind that Lü Zhi had died, they decided to take action. Although Zhou Bo was the Han Dynasty's minister for military affairs, he could not command the army on his own because part of the tiger-shaped tally was in the hands of Lü Lu. That tally, the Hufu, had two halves and only when the men who held each half agreed on an important action and brought the halves together could the decision be considered authoritative.

Li Ji, the son of General Li Shang, was a good friend of Lü Lu. Zhou Bo and Chen Ping, after careful discussion with each other, sent some men to kidnap Li Shang and forced him to ask his son Li Ji to persuade Lü Lu to hand over the tiger-shaped tally to Zhou Bo. Li Ji went to see Lü Lu and talked him into it.

When Zhou Bo went into the tent of the commander of the northern army with the tiger shaped tally, Lü Lu had left. So Zhou Bo took command of the army in the north of the capital. Lü Chan did not know that Lü Lu had left the army in the north of the capital. He went to Weiyang Palace intending to kill the Emperor and usurp the throne. Zhou Bo sent Liu Zhang with 1,000 soldiers to protect the Emperor. By the time Liu Zhang hurried to Weiyang Palace with his men and entered the gate, Lü Chan had forced his way into the yard of the palace. Liu Zhang and Lü Chan stood and eyed each other for a long time. At noon Liu Zhang attacked, and the soldiers of the two sides began to fight; finally, Liu Zhang killed Lü Chan.

Zhou Bo issued orders to arrest the members of the Lü family. Lü Lu was executed. Lü Xu was arrested and beaten to death. All the members of the Lü family, no matter old or young, were killed. Zhou Bo sent envoys to the State of Yan to kill Lü Tong, who had been made King there by Empress Dowager Lü Zhi.

Chapter Three: The Reign of Emperor Liu Heng

53. Liu Heng, King of the State of Dai, Ascends the Throne of the Han Dynasty

Liu Heng was Liu Bang's fourth son. His mother was Bo Ji. In 196 BC, he was made King of the State of Dai, and for sixteen years he stayed in the capital of the State of Dai at Zhongdu (now Pingyao, Shanxi Province). After the Empress Dowager died, in Autumn 180 BC, her nephews Lü Lu and Lü Chan staged a rebellion. They were smashed by Chen Ping, the premier, Zhou Bo, the commander-in-chief of the army, and Liu Zhang, Marquis of Zhuxu. They had Lü Lu and Lü Chan killed. Then, after some discussion, they decided to put the King of the State of Dai, Liu Heng, on the imperial throne of the Han Dynasty.

They sent an envoy to invite him to take up this new role. Liu Heng was prudent and asked his officials to debate whether he should accept the honor and responsibility. Zhang Wu, the commander of the palace guards, and others, said, "All the officials in Chang'an were generals under Emperor Gaozu. They are very clever military men. They know all kinds of tricks. They are not sincere in inviting you to ascend the throne. They are only afraid of the power of Emperor Gaozu and Empress Dowager Lü Zhi. After some bloody fighting in the capital, Lü Lu and Lü Chan were killed. The officials are now inviting Your Highness to ascend the throne. This is just not credible. We hope that Your Highness will send word that Your Highness is ill and cannot go. That way, Your Highness may wait and see how the situation shapes up."

漢文帝像

5. Portrait of Liu Heng, Emperor Wen of the Han Dynasty

But Song Chang, the capital garrison commander, said, "Their opinion is wrong. The First Emperor of the Qin Dynasty was known as a cruel ruler. Heroes rose up everywhere against him. All of them thought that they would win and become emperor. But only Emperor Gaozu succeeded; he established the Han Dynasty and ascended the throne. The others did not have a chance. This is the first point.

"Emperor Gaozu made his sons and brothers kings of different states. The states face each other across a zigzag front so as to hold each other up. This makes the rule of the Liu family as firm as a rock. The whole realm was under the rule of the emperor. This is the second point.

"When the Han Dynasty ruled over the whole realm, all the cruel laws of the Qin Dynasty were abolished. New laws are practiced there now. Emperor Gaozu granted favor and kindness to the people, and all the people live in peace. So the rule of the Han Dynasty is unmovable. This is the third point.

"Empress Dowager Lü Zhi was powerful. She made three members of the Lü family kings. They arrogated all powers to themselves and carried out a tyrannical rule. But when Commander-in-chief Zhou Bo entered the camp of the army stationed in the north with the tiger-shaped tally, all the soldiers took off their left sleeves and exposed their left arms to show that they were for the Liu family, and they were all against the Lü family. Then they exterminated all the members of the Lü family. This was the will of the Heaven and could not be changed by human power. Now some officials wanted to launch a rebellion, but the people would not submit to them. How could they gain the ruling power! Marquis of Zhuxu and Marquis of Dongmu are in the capital. They are grandsons of Emperor Gaozu. The State of Wu, the State of Chu, the State of Huainan, the State of Langya, the State of Qi and the State of Dai are very strong. This makes the officials who intend to hold a rebellion afraid. Now the King of Huainan and Your Highness are the only remaining sons of Emperor Gaozu. Your Highness is older than the King of Huainan. The people in the realm all know that Your Highness is virtuous, benevolent and dutiful. So the officials invite Your Highness to ascend the throne. I hope Your Highness will not hesitate."

The King of the State of Dai reported all these opinions to his mother. But still they could not make the decision. Then they made a divination. A lot of Dahuang was drawn which read, "You will be the Heavenly King. And you will bring brilliance to the whole realm." The King of the State of Dai said, "I am already a king. Why does it say I will be a king?" The man in charge of divination said, " 'Heavenly King' means Emperor." Then the young King sent Bo Zhao, his mother's younger brother, to see Commander-in-chief Zhou Bo. Zhou Bo explained clearly why they had decided to invite him to ascend the throne of the Han Dynasty. Bo Zhao went back and explained, "There is no doubt of their sincerity in inviting Your Highness to ascend the throne." The King replied with a smile, "What you have said is true."

Then the King started his journey to Chang'an (now Xi'an or Si'an, in the south central part of Shaanxi Province). He had Song Chang sit with him in the same carriage. Zhang Wu and five other officials accompanied them, in different carriages. When they reached Gaoling (now in the north part of Xi'an, Shaanxi Province), the procession stopped. The King of the State of Dai sent Song Chang to go into Chang'an to observe the situation.

When Song Chang reached the bridge over the Weishui River, about two kilometers away from Chang'an, Premier Chen Ping, Commander-in-chief Zhou Bo and the ministers and generals were already there waiting for them. Song Chang went back to report to the King of the State of Dai. When the King's carriage reached the bridge, all the ministers and generals knelt down on their knees, touched their heads on the ground, and submitted themselves to him. The King stepped down from the carriage and bowed to them. Commander-in-chief Zhou Bo went forward and asked to talk to His Highness alone. But the King said, "If you want to talk about official business, you may say it here and now. If you want to talk about private affairs, a king has no private affairs to talk about." Then Commander-in-chief Zhou Bo knelt down on his knees and presented him the seal of the emperor. The King of the State of Dai thanked him and said, "I will talk with you when we reach my residence."

The King and his entourage arrived in Chang'an in the second September of 180 BC (180 BC was an intercalary year which had two Septembers). They stayed in the residence of the King of the State of Dai. All the officials followed him in, and they said, "Premier Chen Ping, Commander-in-chief Zhou Bo, Grand General Chai Wu, Imperial Secretary Zhang Chang, Royal Household Supervisor Liu Ying, Marquis of Zhuxu Liu Zhang, Marquis of Dongmu Liu Xing Jü, and Minister of Minority Nationalities Affairs Liu Jie are going to present the following words to your Highness: 'Liu Hong is not the son of Emperor Liu Ying. He should not be the emperor.' We invited the Marquis of Yin'an, that is Queen of King Qing, King of Langya, all the marquises, and officials who enjoy 120,000 kg of grain a year for salary, to hold a discussion. We came to agree that Your Highness, as the son of Emperor Gaozu, should succeed to the throne. We hope that you will ascend the throne of the emperor." The King of the State of Dai said, "It is an important task to succeed to the throne of the Han Dynasty established by Emperor Gaozu. I am not a capable man. I am afraid I am unfit for the throne. I think it would be better to invite the King of the State of Chu to ascend the throne. I am afraid I don't deserve this invitation." All the officials knelt down and insisted on inviting the King of the State of Dai to accede to their request. The King of the State of Dai faced west and three times more expressed the view that they should choose a more suitable man, then he faced south to express the same idea two times. Premier Chen Ping and other officials said, "We all think Your Highness is the most suitable to succeed to the throne of the Han Dynasty established by Emperor Gaozu. All the marquises and people in the realm think Your Highness is most suitable. We think that it is highly important to choose a suitable man to ascend the throne. We dare not treat it lightly. We hope that Your Highness will accept our invitation. Now please accept the seal of the emperor." Finally the King of the State of Dai said, "Since all the members of the royal clan think that I am most suitable for the throne, I will ascend the throne." And he did. The officials went up batch by batch according to their ranks to express their congratulations to the new emperor.

Then Emperor Liu Heng sent Xiahou Ying, the carriage driver for the emperor, and Liu Xing Jü, Marquis of Dongmu, to clear the palace. They drove Liu Hong, the boy who had been made emperor by Empress Dowager Lü Zhi, out of Weiyang Palace. That evening Xiahou Ying carried Liu Heng, the new emperor, in a carriage for the emperor from the residence of the King of the State of Dai to Weiyang Palace. That night, Emperor Liu Heng appointed Song Chang as the General of the Guards to command the army stationed south of the capital and the army stationed north of the capital. He appointed Zhang Wu as Commander of the Palace Guards in charge of palace security. Then Emperor Liu Heng sat on the throne in the front hall of the palace. He issued an imperial edict which read, "Not long ago, the members of the Lü family were in power. They planned to hold a rebellion. They intended to overthrow the rule of the Liu Family. Now Premier Chen Ping, Commander-in-chief Zhou Bo, the marquises, the members of the royal clan and the officials have killed them. The members of the Lü family have gotten what they deserved. I have now ascended the throne. I will be benevolent to all the people in the realm. I will grant titles to the men, and grant meat and wine to the men's wives. I will allow the people to gather together to eat meat and drink wine for five days."

54. Emperor Liu Heng Grants Awards to the Officials and Generals Who Have Established Great Contributions in Putting Him on the Throne

On 2 October 179 BC, Emperor Liu Heng went to the Temple of Emperor Gaozu. He sent Bo Zhao, as General of Chariots and Cavalry, to escort Empress Dowager Bo Ji to Chang'an from the State of Dai. Then he issued an imperial edict that recounted the recent events and rewarded those who had made this great change possible. "Not long ago Lü Chan made himself the premier, Lü Lu was made commander-in-chief of the army. They sent General Guan Ying with troops to attack the State of Qi. They intended to usurp the power of the Liu family. When Guang Ying reached Xingyang, he stopped there. He united with the marquises to fight against the Lü family. Lü Chan intended to hold a rebellion. Premier Chen Ping and Commander-in-chief Zhou Bo made a plan to get back the power to command the army from Lü Chan. Liu Zhang, Marquis of Zhuxu, rose up first and caught Lü Chan and killed him. Commander-in-chief Zhou Bo led Ji Tong, Marquis of Xiangping, into the camp of the army in the north with the tiger-shaped tally. Liu Jie, Minister of Minority Nationalities Affairs, persuaded Lü Lu to give the tally to Zhou Bo and confer on him the authority to command the army. Now I grant the tax of 10,000 peasant households and 2,500 kilograms of gold to Commander-in-chief Zhou Bo; the tax of 3,000 peasant households and 1,000 kilograms of gold to Premier Chen Ping; the tax of 3,000 peasant households and 1,000 kilograms of gold to General Guan Ying; the tax of 2,000 peasant households and 500 kilograms of gold to Liu Zhang, Marquis of Zhuxu; the tax of 2,000 peasant households and 500 kilograms of gold to Ji Tong, Marquis of Xiangping. And I hereby make Liu Jie Marquis of Yangxin, and grant five hundred kilograms of gold to him."

In December 179 BC, Emperor Liu Heng made Liu Sui King of the State of Zhao. Liu Sui was the son of Liu You, King You of the State of Zhao. He changed Liu Ze, King of the State of Langya, to King of the State of Yan. All the places of the State of Qi and the State of Chu that had been taken by the members of the Lü family were returned to the State of Qi and the State of Chu.

Emperor Liu Heng then abolished the Qin Dynasty law that if one person committed a crime, all the members of his family should be taken and made into slaves.

55. EMPEROR LIU HENG NAMES A CROWN PRINCE

In January 178 BC, the officials suggested to Emperor Liu Heng that he should appoint his eldest son as crown prince so as to show his respect for the Ancestral Temple. Emperor Liu Heng issued an imperial edict which read, "I am not virtuous. The gods have not yet granted me blessings. The people of the realm have not yet shown their satisfaction to me. I wanted to find a virtuous man to whom I would abdicate the throne. But I can't find such a man. Now you suggest me to appoint the crown prince. This will increase my immorality. How shall I face the people of the realm? It would be better not to consider this for now." The officials said, "By appointing the crown prince, Your Majesty will show your respect to the Ancestral Temple and the country, and to show that Your Majesty is very concerned about the realm." Emperor Liu Heng said, "The King of the State of Chu is my uncle. He is old. He knows the principles of righteousness and the ways to rule over the state. The King of the State of Wu is my elder brother; the King of the State of Huainan is my younger brother. They are much more virtuous than I am. They should have a chance to be the emperor! The kings and marquises, and members of the royal clan, have made important contributions to the success of the realm. They are virtuous and righteous. If a man who is more virtuous and more righteous than me is selected, it would be a blessing for the realm and the people. But this way, the virtuous and righteous man is not selected. The crown prince must be selected from my sons. People will think that I give up the virtuous and righteous man but only choose my sons. This is not for the benefit of the realm. I will not do that."

The officials insisted on their suggestion and said, "In ancient times, the Yin Dynasty and Zhou Dynasty lasted for a thousand years. These dynasties existed for really a long time. The kings of these dynasties adopted this practice. The successor to the throne must be selected from the sons of the kings. This regulation existed long ago. Emperor Gaozu brought peace to the whole realm. He made kings of different states and marquises. Emperor Gaozu is the ancestor of the whole realm. The kings of different states who were first made kings by Emperor Gaozu are the ancestors of the kings of different states. The sons and grandsons of the emperor succeed to the throne. The throne is succeeded generation after generation, never ending. This is the way for the existence of the dynasty. So Emperor Gaozu made this regulation to keep the peace in the whole realm. Now if the successor is not selected from the sons of Your Majesty but is selected from the kings of different states and members of the royal clan, this is against Emperor Gaozu's regulation. Liu Qi is the eldest son of Your Majesty. He is honest, sincere and kind hearted. We suggest that he should be made crown prince." Then Emperor Liu Heng accepted their suggestion and made Liu Qi crown prince. Emperor Liu Heng granted titles to all the men who were fathers in the whole realm. He made General Bo Zhao Marquis of Zhi (now Zhicheng Town, Jiyuan, Henan Province).

In March 178 BC, the officials suggested to Emperor Liu Heng that he should name an empress. Empress Dowager Bo Ji said, "Lady Dou, the Crown Prince's mother, should be the empress."

56. Emperor Liu Heng Grants Benefits to the People of the Whole Realm

Emperor Liu Heng issued an imperial edict which read, "In spring time, trees, grass and all kinds of living things grow freely and happily. But among my people, the widows and widowers, orphans and the poor are at death's door. Now, no one is worried about them. Since I am the emperor of the people, I have decided to provide benefits for them." It also read, "The old people need thick clothes to keep them warm; and they need meat to eat. At the beginning of this year, officials were sent to check on the elderly. But they did not give them clothes, cotton, wine or meat. How shall we help the sons and grandsons in the realm to provide for their parents and grandparents? Now I am told that officials provided porridge to the old people. But they didn't use fresh rice to cook porridge. Is this the right way to provide for our elderly? I order: all levels of officials to provide people over eighty years old with 60 kilograms of rice, 10 kilograms of meat, and 32 kilograms of wine every month. For those who were over ninety years old, apart from the things mentioned above, 26.6 meters of cloth and 1.5 kilograms of cotton will be provided. The high ranking officials at the county level must examine the rice provided to the old people and make sure it is fresh. After that, the low ranking officials must districute the rice. For those elderly who are not yet ninety years old, officials at the village level will send the rice to them. The head of the prefecture should send out agents to make an inspection to the counties. If an official in the county level is incompetent, the inspectors may denounce him. This order does not apply to those who have been punished for their crimes and to those who have been sentenced to jail for over two years for their crimes."

In January 178 BC, Emperor Liu Heng issued another imperial edict conferring public benefits. "Agriculture is the foundation of the whole realm. I will personally till the land and grow crops to be offered as sacrifices in the Ancestral Temple. If people borrow seeds and food grain from the county government but they cannot pay back — or cannot pay back sufficiently — they are exempt from paying for the seeds and food grain they borrow."

Then in September, he added: "Agriculture is the foundation of the whole realm. All the people depend on agriculture to survive. Some people leave the land untilled and occupy themselves otherwise. So they live in poverty. I am worried about them. This is the reason why I personally lead the officials in tillig the land and growing crops. I want to persuade those people to come back to do farm work. Now I order that the land tax be reduced by half."

57. EMPEROR LIU HENG PUTS DOWN A REBELLION

In March 177 BC, the officials suggested that Emperor Liu Heng make his sons kings. The Emperor issued an edict announcing, "King You of the State of Zhao was starved to death during the reign of Empress Dowager Lü Zhi. I feel pity for him. I have made his son, Liu Sui, King of the State of Zhao. Liu Sui's younger brother Liu Pi Jiang, Liu Zhang, Marquis of Zhuxu, and Liu Xing Jü, Marquis of Dongmu, have made great contributions. I will make them kings, too." Then Emperor Liu Heng made Liu Pi Jiang King of Hejian (now in Hebei Province); Liu Zhang King of Chengyang (now Chengyang District, in Shandong Province); Liu Xing Jü, King of Jibei (now the areas of the northwest part of Shandong Province and the southeast part of Hebei Province). He also made his son Prince Liu Wu King of the State of Dai (now in Shanxi Province and Hebei Province), his son Prince Liu Can King of the State of Taiyuan (now in Taiyuan, Jinzhong and Lüliang, Shanxi Province), and his son Prince Liu Ji King of the State of Liang (now in Henan Province and the north part of Anhui Province).

The Huns lived in the grasslands of Mongolia. The area known today as Mongolia is an independent republic; Inner Mongolia is an Autonomous Region of China, and the population is largely Han Chinese. For centuries various Mongol nomadic tribes competed to dominate the entire area. From here on, we will refer to Inner Mongolia Autonomous Region of China the area simply as Inner Mongolia.

In May 177 BC, the Huns invaded the areas of Beidi (now Qingyang, in the northeast part of Gansu Province) and Henan (by the Great Bend of the Yellow River, in southern Inner Mongolia). Emperor Liu Heng went to Ganquan (now in northern Shaanxi Province), and he sent Premier Guan Ying to fight the Huns. Premier Guan Ying set off at the head of 85,000 cavalrymen. The Huns retreated to their home territories, and then Emperor Liu Heng stationed some foreces in Chang'an.

Emperor Liu Heng went from Ganquan to Gaonu (now Yinjiagou, in Yan'an, northern Shaanxi Province), then to Taiyuan (now in Shanxi Province). He received the men who had been officials of the former State of Dai when Liu Heng was the king. He rewarded the officials according to the contributions they had made. He granted meat and wine to the people in Taiyuan. He exempted all the people in Jinyang (now in Taiyuan City) and Zhongdu (now Pingyao, in the middle of Shanxi Province) from paying tax for three years. He stayed in Taiyuan for more than ten days.

Now, when Liu Xing Jü, King of the State of Jibei, heard that Emperor Liu Heng had gone to the State of Dai and intended to personally command an expedition against the Huns, he held a rebellion. He planned to send troops to attack Xingyang (now in Henan Province). Then Emperor Liu Heng ordered Premier Guan Ying to turn back, with his troops. He appointed Chai Wu, Marquis of Jipu, as Grand General, and had him take four generals and a great army of a hundred thousand men to launch an attack against Liu Xing Jü. He appointed Zeng He, Marquis of Qi, as general to station an army in Xingyang. In July 177 BC, Emperor Liu Heng came back to Chang'an from Taiyuan. He issued an imperial edict which read, "The King of the State of Jibei has violated morality and has staged a rebellion. He has misled the officials and people to follow him in the rebellion. I will pardon those people and soldiers who surrender before my army arrives. I will restore their original titles to the officials, and I also pardon those who are close to Liu Xing Jü." In August 177 BC Liu Xing Jü, the King of the State of Jibei, was captured. He committed suicide. Emperor Liu Heng pardoned those who had joined in Liu Xing Jü's rebellion.

58. Emperor Liu Heng Gives Orders to Arrest Zhou Bo, and Then Releases Him

Zhou Bo, Marquis of Jiang, had made great contributions in exterminating Lü Lu and Lü Chan and putting Liu Heng on the throne of the Han Dynasty. When Liu Heng ascended the throne, he made Zhou Bo the Right Premier and granted him 2,500 kilograms of gold and the tax on 10,000 peasant households. Ten months later, someone remarked to Zhou Bo, "You got rid of the members of the Lü family and put the King of the State of Dai on the throne. You have won resounding fame throughout the country. You have been rewarded handsomely. You have occupied this highly respected position for a long time. If you don't resign from your position soon, you will face imminent disaster." Zhou Bo was afraid. He, too, sensed the danger. So he asked permission to resign from his position and return the premier's seal to the Emperor. Emperor Liu Heng accepted his resignation.

A year later, Premier Chen Ping died. Emperor Liu Heng appointed Zhou Bo premier again. Ten months later, Emperor Liu Heng said to Zhou Bo, "Some time ago I issued an imperial edict ordering the kings and marquises to go back to the places where they were made kings or marquises. But they do not go. Now you ought to take the lead and go back to Jiang, so as to set an example." Zhou Bo graciously resigned from the position of premier and dutifully returned to Jiang (now Jiangxian, situated in the south part of Shanxi Province).

Even so, from then on, every time when the governor or the commander of Hedong Prefecture came by on an inspection visit, Zhou Bo, as Marquis of Jiang, was afraid that he would be killed. He started to wear a suit of armor and he ordered his family members to carry weapons when meeting officials on these visits. But this backfired. Someone presented a memorial suggesting to the Emperor that Zhou Bo might be planning an uprising. He ordered an investigation. The Grand Justice arrested Zhou Bo and interrogated him. Zhou Bo was so upset that he did not know how to handle the questions. The jailors insulted him. Zhou Bo gave one of the jailors 500 kilograms of gold; this put the man in the mood to be helpful. The jailor obligingly wrote on the back of a wooden book: "The Princess can be your witness," and showed it to Zhou Bo. He was referring to the Emperor's daughter, who was married to Zhou Bo's eldest son Zhou Sheng. She could handily serve as a witness to prove that he was innocent. In the past Zhou Bo had given all the money and gold he was granted by the Emperor to Bo Zhao.

Now Bo Zhao told Empress Dowager Bo that Zhou Bo had been arrested and interrogated. The Empress Dowager found it preposterous to imagine that Zhou Bo would hold a rebellion. When the Emperor went to see his mother, she angrily threw her hat at him and said, "The Marquis of Jiang once held the official seal, so that he commanded the army in the north, but he didn't hold a rebellion then. These days, he lives in a small place; how can you think he would mount a rebellion now!?"

After Emperor Liu Heng read the statement Zhou Bo had given under examination, he ordered the officials to set him free. The Emperor restored Zhou Bo's title of Marquis of Jiang and all the gifts and privileges he had granted to him. When Zhou Bo came out of the jail, he exclaimed, "I once commanded an army of a million men, but I never knew how much power the officials of the jail had!"

59. EMPEROR LIU HENG FOILS LIU CHANG'S PLOT

Liu Chang, King of the State of Huainan, was Emperor Gaozu's seventh son. His mother Zhao Ji was originally a concubine of Zhang Ao, King of the State of Zhao. In 199 BC, Emperor Gaozu traveled to the State of Zhao. In keeping with tradition, Zhang Ao offered Emperor Gaozu some pleasant company for the night — in this case, Zhao Ji. She became pregnant in this encounter. From then on, Zhang Ao did not dare to let Zhao Ji stay in his palace but gave her a house outside his palace.

Meanwhile Guan Gao, the ambitious premier of the State of Zhao, was conspiring to kill the Emperor. But his conspiracy was found out. Zhang Ao was involved in this case. All his family members were arrested and put in jail, including Zhao Ji. She told the head of the prison, "I spent a night with the Emperor and now I am pregnant." The official reported this to Emperor Gaozu. At that time, the Emperor was so angry with the King of Zhao that he ignored the fact that Zhao Ji was carrying his child.

Zhao Ji's younger brother Zhao Jian begged Shen Yi Ji, Marquis of Piyang, to tell Empress Lü Zhi that Zhao Ji was carrying Emperor Gaozu's child; but Empress Lü Zhi was jealous of her and would not tell the Emperor; and Shen Yi Ji did not insist. After the child was born, Zhao Ji was so upset that she committed suicide. The head jailer carried the child to see the Emperor. Emperor Gaozu regretted his neglect and asked Empress Lü Zhi to take care of the child.

In July 196 BC, Ying Bu mounted a rebellion. Emperor Gaozu stripped him of his title of King of the State of Huainan, and he personally led an army to defeat Ying Bu and kill him. He made his son Liu Chang King of the State of Huainan. Liu Chang became king of four prefectures: Jiujiang Prefecture (now in northern Jiangxi Province), Lujiang Prefecture (in southern Anhui Province), Hengshan Prefecture (eastern Hunan Province) and Yuzhang Prefecture (now Nanchang, Jiangxi Province). The State of Huainan covered the areas of what are now all of Jiangxi Province, the southwest part of Anhui Province and the east part of Hubei Province.

Liu Chang's mother had died when he was very young. He was brought up by Empress Lü Zhi. He was very close to Lü Zhi and Emperor Liu Ying. So during the reign of Empress Dowager Lü Zhi, he did not meet with any trouble. He had a grudge against Shen Yi Ji, Marquis of Piyang. But he did not dare to do anything against him. When Liu Heng ascended the throne, Liu Chang considered that he was the closest relative of the Emperor, so he was very arrogant and often acted against the laws. And indeed, Emperor Liu Heng often pardoned him because Liu Chang was his closest relative.

In 177 BC Liu Chang went to the Emperor's court. He was very pretentious and rude to the courtiers. When he accompanied Emperor Liu Heng to the royal hunting ground, he sat in the same carriage with him. He often called the Emperor "elder brother" instead of "Your Majesty".

Liu Chang was so strong that he could lift up a ceremonial bronze three-legged cauldron or ding, a symbol of the power of the ruling dynasty. (They were modeled on ancient cooking vessels, and could weigh over 1000 pounds.) One day he went to the house of Shen Yi Ji, the Marquis. When Shen Yi Ji came out to meet him, he pulled a sledge hammer from his sleeve and whacked Shen Yi Ji. Then he ordered his follower Wei Jing to cut Shen Yi Ji's throat. And Liu Chang jumped on a horse and rode to the palace.

He went before Emperor Liu Heng, took off his outer clothes, and made the following staements. "My mother should not be regarded to have been involved in the case of the King of the State of Zhao. At that time the Marquis of Piyang could have persuaded Empress Dowager Lü Zhi to save my mother. But he did not do it. This is his first crime. Liu Ru Yi, King of the State of Zhao, and his mother did not commit any offences, but Empress Dowager Lü Zhi killed them. Shen Yi Ji did not do anything to protect them. This is his second crime. Empress Dowager Lü Zhi, Lü Lu and Lü Chan tried to harm the Liu Family. Shen Yi Ji did not do anything against them. This is his third crime. Now I must tell you, I have killed the Marquis of Piyang for the sake of the whole realm and to avenge my mother. I await my proper punishment by Your Majesty." Emperor Liu Heng sympathized with him, and, as we know, Liu Chang was indeed his close relative. He granted him pardon.

Understandably, at that time, Empress Dowager Bo, the princes and the officials were afraid of Liu Chang. Liu Chang went back to the State of Huainan. He became even more arrogant and willful. He did not apply the laws of the court of the Han Dynasty in the State of Huainan. When he came out of his palace, he ordered soldiers to stand guard along the way as if he were an emperor. He called his orders "imperial edicts" and he made laws as if he were emperor.

In 174 BC Liu Chang organized a group of 70 men and they made a plan with Chai Qi, the eldest son of Chai Wu, the Marquis of Jipu. They conspired to transport 70 cartloads of weapons to Gukou County, northwest of Chang'an (present-day Xi'an), and then hold a rebellion there. He sent envoys to contact the State of Minyue (now Fujian Province) and the Huns. But this scheme was found out, and those who were involved were punished. Emperor Liu Heng sent envoys to summon the King of the State of Huainan to come to Chang'an.

Premier Zhang Cang, Feng Jing (Minister of Minority Nationality Affairs), Liu Yi (Royal House Supervisor and Acting Imperial Counselor), He (Supreme Magistrate), and Fu (Capital Garrison Commander), all presented a memorial to Emperor Liu Heng which read, "Liu Chang, King of the State of Huainan, has abolished the laws made by Emperor Gaozu. He did not obey the imperial edicts issued by Your Majesty. He leads a dissipated life and takes liberties: the top of his carriage is covered in yellow silk — which is reserved for use on the emperor's carriage. He has adopted all the formalities which were only to be adopted by an emperor when leaving and returning to his palace. He has made his own laws and abandoned the laws made by the court of the Han Dynasty. He has appointed Chun, the Head of the Palace Guards of the State of Huainan, as premier. He has harbored fugitives and criminals who have run away from other areas under the reign of the Han Dynasty or the kingdoms. He lets them hide in the State of Huainan and gives them shelter. He helps them to set up families. He grants them properties, titles, land and houses. He even makes them marquises. He gives the marquises 100,000 kilograms of grain a year as salary. Fugitives and criminals should not be given the title of marquises and such rich income.

"Why has he rewarded them so generously? Liu Chang wants them to do something. Dan, Liu Chang's adviser, Wu Kai Zhang, an official who has committed crimes and has been deposed from his position, and 70 other persons have colluded with Qi, the eldest son of Marquis Jipu, to plot a rebellion. They intend to do great harm to the Ancestral Temple of the Han Dynasty and the realm. They sent Wu Kai Zhang to tell their plans to Liu Chang secretly and they also plan to ask the State of Minyue and the Huns to send troops to attack the Han Dynasty. Wu Kai Zhang went to the State of Huainan to see Liu Chang. Liu Chang talked with Wu Kai Zhang several times and invited him to dinner. Liu Chang helped him to take a wife and establish a family and provides him 100,000 kilograms of grain a year as salary. Wu Kai Zhang sent a man to tell Dan that he has told their plan to Liu Chang. Chun, the Premier of the State of Huainan, also sent an envoy to report this to Dan. The officials of the court have detected their conspiracy. They sent Qi, Chang'an Garrison Commander, and others to arrest

Wu Kai Zhang. Liu Chang hid him and would not hand him over to the government. Liu Chang talked with Jian Ji, the commander of the guards of the palace of the State of Huainan, and they decided to kill Wu Kai Zhang to prevent their secrets being divulged. Then they had Wu Kai Zhang killed. They put his dead body in a coffin and buried it in Feiling (now Shouxian, Anhui Province). Then Liu Chang told the officials who had come to arrest Wu Kai Zhang that he did not know where he was. Later Liu Chang killed an innocent man. He ordered his officials to sentence six innocent persons to death and executed them. He acquitted those fugitives who had been sentenced to death for their crimes. He arrested those criminals who did not run away to substitute for those who have run away. He accused innocent persons at will and they had no recourse to appeal for justice. Liu Chang has arrested more than 14 persons and sentenced them to hard labor, the men guarding the city wall in the daytime and repairing it at night, with the women husking rice with mortar and pestle. He pardoned 18 criminals who had been given death penalty and 68 criminals who had been sentenced to hard labor. He granted titles to 94 men.

"Some time ago Liu Chang fell ill. Your Majesty was worried about him and sent envoys to take a comfort letter and dried dates to him. But Liu Chang did not want to accept the letter and the dried dates granted by Your Majesty. He refused to meet the envoys. Some people of the State of Nanhai who live in Lujiang area held a rebellion. King of the State of Huainan sent some officers and soldiers to suppress the rebellion. Thinking that the people in the State of Huainan are poor, Your Majesty granted 5,000 rolls of cloth to Liu Chang and ordered him to give it to the officers and soldiers who are poor. Liu Chang did not want to accept the things Your Majesty gave him. He deceived Your Majesty by saying that there were no poor officers or soldiers in his army. Zhi, the King of the State of Nanhai, sent a letter and a jade disk with a hole in its center [a "bi" disk, a sign of respect] to Your Majesty. Jian Ji burned the letter so that it could not be presented to Your Majesty. The officials wanted to summon Jian Ji and punish him, but Liu Chang did not hand him over. He deceived the officials by telling them that Jian Ji was ill.

"Liu Chang should be sentenced to death. We hope that he will be punished according to the law."

Emperor Liu Heng could not bring himself to do it. He told them to take up the question with the marquises and the top-level officials.

The counsellors agreed that Liu Chang was a law-breaker; he refused to accept imperial edicts; he secretly joined forces with criminals and others to conspire in a rebellion; he provided generous care to fugitives; and he intended to enroll them in his rebellion. They recommended he should be punished according to the law.

Emperor Liu Heng still held back; and he exemptedLiu Chang from the death penalty; but he did strip him of his title of King.

Premier Zhang Cang and the other officials presented another memorial, emphasizing that "Liu Chang has committed a serious crime. He deserves the death penalty.... We suggest sending Liu Chang into exile in Yandao County of Shu Prefecture (Sichuan Province). His sons and wife should go with him. The government of Yandao County should build houses for them and provide food, vegetables, salt and cooking utensils, mats and mattresses for them. We suggest that this decision should be made public and let all the people know this."

Emperor Liu Heng concurred, and he issued an edict to this effect. "The local government should provide 2.5 kilograms of meat and 1.3 kilograms of wine every day to Liu Chang. Ten of his concubines will go with him. I ratify all the suggestion put up by the officials."

All those who had been part of the conspiracy were killed. Then the King of the State of Huainan was sent into exile. He was put into a covered wagon, and the door was sealed. The local officials were held responsible for seeing to it that the wagon moved properly from one county to another. At that time Yuan Ang, a court official, said to Emperor Liu Heng, "Your Majesty has treated the King with excessive indulgence and did not appoint strict grand tutor and guardian to guide him. This is the reason why he has wound up in exile. The King of the State of Huainan is not a tough man. Now he is being treated so roughly. I am afraid he might catch cold and die on the way. Then people will think that Your Majesty has killed your younger brother. This is not a right thing to do!" Emperor Liu Heng said, "I just want to let him suffer a little. Later I will let him come back."

The county officials passing Liu Chang from one county to the next did not dare to take off the seal and open the door of the wagon. But the King had fallen into a depression. During the journey, he said to his servant, "In the past people said that I am a brave man. But now who will call me a brave man? How can I be brave in such a situation! I have ended up in exile because I have been indulgent and did not realize my mistakes. How can I spend the rest of my life in such a dreary way!" Then he refused to eat anything and starved himself to death.

When the wagon reached Yong County, the officials unsealed the door. Liu Chang had already died. This was reported to the Emperor, who cried bitterly. He said to Yuan Ang, "I ignored your advice and this has led to Liu Chang's death." Yuan Ang said, "Your Majesty can do nothing about it. I hope Your Majesty will not be too sad." Emperor Liu Heng asked, "What shall I do?" Yuan Ang said, "Your Majesty could kill the Premier and the Imperial Counselor so as to assuage the anger of the people." Emperor Liu Heng ignored that suggestion. He ordered Premier Zhang Cang and Imperial Counselor Liu Yi to arrest and interrogate those county officials who had passed the wagon to the next county but had not taken off the seal and provided food for Liu Chang. All these officials were executed. Then Liu Chang was buried in Yong County. Thirty peasant households were sent to guard Liu Chang's tomb.

Two years later, in 172 BC, Emperor Liu Heng still felt bad about Liu Chang. Liu Chang had left behind four sons, just seven or eight years old. Emperor Liu Heng made the eldest son, Liu An, Marquis of Fuling; the second son, Liu Bo, Marquis of Anyang; the third son, Liu Ci, Marquis of Zhouyang; the fourth son, Liu Liang, Marquis of Dongcheng. Later, the Emperor made the eldest the King of the State of Huainan; the second, King of the State of Hengshan; the third, King of the State of Lujiang. They were kings of the original territory of the State of Huainan.

60. Emperor Liu Heng Spreads Peace through Marriage with the Huns

Intermarrying with neighboring peoples is an ancient technique for encouraging fraternal feelings. The policy of seeking peace with the Huns through marriage was initiated by Emperor Gaozu. Back in October 201 BC, the Emperor had personally led a great army against Modu, the king of the Huns. Emperor Gaozu reached Pingcheng (now northeast of Datong City, Shanxi Province) ahead his main force, and Modu was able to trap him in an encirclement for seven days. That was when Emperor Gaozu sent gifts to Modu's wife, who persuaded Modu to let him go. After Emperor Gaozu made his escape, he adopted Liu Jing's advice and made peace with the Huns by marrying a daughter of the royal clan to Modu.

In May 177 BC, the Huns invaded Beidi (now Qingyang, in Gansu Province) and Henan. Emperor Liu Heng went to Ganquan. In June, Emperor Liu Heng announced that, "The Han Dynasty and the Huns have made an agreement to become brothers. The two sides have promised not to breach each other's borders. We have given rich treasures to the Huns. Now the King of the Right Wing of the Huns has left his lands. He has led his people to the area of Henan without any apparent reason. They have come close to the Great Wall. They have killed Han officers and soldiers. They have driven away the people of the local tribes who live by the Great Wall and they cannot go back to their homeland. The Huns bully and humiliate the Han officials of the border area. They come into the Han territory and loot the people. They are haughty, brutal and immoral. They have gone against the agreement. Now I order 85,000 cavalrymen to be stationed in Gaonu. I have sent Premier Guan Ying to lead an army to fight against the Huns." Very soon the Huns retreated.

In June 176 BC, Modu, King of the Huns, sent a letter to Emperor Liu Heng which read, "Some time ago Your Majesty talked about the peace agreement. I agree with what you have said. The officials of the Han Dynasty in the border areas insulted the King of the Right Wing of the Huns. The King of the Ring Wing confronted the Han border officials. This has led to the destruction of the agreement between the Emperor of the Han Dynasty and me, and has led to the breakup of our relationship as brothers. I have punished the King of the Right Wing of the Huns. I have sent him to attack the State of Yuezhi in the west. Thanks to the blessings granted by Heaven, the King of the Right Wing of the Huns, commanding courageous officers and soldiers on strong horses, destroyed the State of Yuezhi. They killed many Yuezhi people and forced many others to surrender. He conquered the State of Loulan, the State of Wusun, the State of Hujie and another 26 states near them. All the people of these states have become slaves of the Huns. He unified all the nomadic peoples as one family. Now that the warring has been stopped in the northern areas, I will halt all military actions and let the soldiers have a good rest. I will give up the hatred between us and resume the agreement so that the people in the border areas can live peacefully. I don't know whether Your Majesty agrees with me or not. Now I have sent envoys to take a letter to Your Majesty. They will take a camel, two horses and two carriages drawn by four horses. If Your Majesty does not want the Huns to get close to the Great Wall, I will order the officials and people of the Huns to move away. When the envoys sent by Your Majesty arrive, I will issue the order."

When this letter was presented to Emperor Liu Heng, he asked the officials to discuss whether they should fight the Huns or resume the policy of peace through marriage. They conferred, and their consensus was this: "The King of the Huns recently defeated the State of Yuezhi. He has won a great victory. Now is not the time for us to fight his victorious army. Furthermore, the places where the Huns live are swampy lands. Even if we occupy these places, we cannot live there. It would be better to resume the agreement." Emperor Liu Heng agreed.

In 174 BC, Emperor Liu Heng sent a letter to Modu to that effect, and he sent Modu a beautiful garment made of finest silk, a long silk garment and a brocade robe, a comb carved from deer horn, belt decorated with gold, a band hook made of gold, ten rolls of silk, thirty rolls of brocade, forty rolls of red silk fabrics and forty rolls of green silk fabric.

Not long later Modu died. His son Ji Yu succeeded him as King of the Huns. Emperor Liu Heng selected a daughter of the royal clan and married her to Ji Yu.

In winter 167 BC, the King of the Huns sent 140,000 cavalrymen to invade the border areas. They attacked Zhunuo Frontier Fortress and Xiaoguan Pass (Ningxia Hui Autonomous Region). Mao, the Commander-in-chief of the Han army in Beidi (now Qingyang, in Gansu Province) was killed. The Huns captured many people and looted many domesticated animals. Then the Huns reached Pengyang. The King of the Huns sent a detachment to Huizhong (in Gansu Province) to burn the temporary imperial palace that stood there for use during inspection tours. The Huns' cavalry scouts reached Ganquan (in Shaanxi Province).

Emperor Liu Heng sent three generals to station troops in Longxi (Gansu Province), Beidi, and Shangjun (Shaanxi Province). He appointed Zhou She, the Capital Garrison Commander, as General of Defense, and Zhang Wu, Commander of the Palace Guards, as General of Chariots and Cavalry. He ordered them to take their troops to the north of Weishui River to defend the capital. There were 1,000 chariots and 100,000 cavalrymen under their command. Emperor Liu Heng personally brought greetings and gifts to the army units. He gave talks before the troops and gave them instructions. He granted awards to the officers and soldiers.

Emperor Liu Heng intended to command the expedition against the Huns personally. The officials tried to talk him out of it, but he would not listen to them. Empress Dowager Bo, too, insisted. At last Emperor Liu Heng gave up his plan. Then he appointed Zhang Xiang Ru, the Marquis of Dongyang, as Grand General, Dong Chi, Marquis of Cheng, as Forward General, Luan Bu as General to fight against the Huns. The King of the Huns stayed within the Great Wall for about a month, and then he went back. The Han Dynasty troops drove the Huns out from behind the Great Wall and then turned back. They did not kill any of the Huns.

From this time forward, the Huns became very proud. They broached the border areas every year and killed many Han people. The people in Yunzhong (now Togtoh, Inner Mongolia) and Liaodong (now Liaoyang, Liaoning Province) suffered the most. More than 10,000 people in Dai Prefecture (now Yuxian, in the northwest part of Hebei Province) were killed by the Huns. Emperor Liu Heng was worried. He sent an envoy to take a letter to the King of the Huns. The King of the Huns sent a return letter to express his thanks to Emperor Liu Heng and suggested to resume the policy of pacification through marriage.

In 161 BC, Emperor Liu Heng sent envoys with a letter to the King of the Huns: "As has been recognized by Emperor Gaozu, the areas to the north of the Great Wall are inhabited by nomadic people. These areas are under your jurisdiction; whereas the areas within the Great Wall are inhabited by the Han people. They are under my jurisdiction. We let our people till the land and grow crops, weave cloth, hunt animals for a living. We do our best to let our people live in peace so that fathers will not have to leave their sons. The ruler and his subjects get on well with each other. There have been no rebellions. Now, I hear that some wicked persons and officials have gone against justice and tried to drive a wedge between you and me. This has happened in the past. You sent me a letter which read, 'The rulers of the two countries have become close relatives by marriage. We have got on well with each other. I will stop all military actions and let the soldiers have a good rest. I will give up the hatred between us and resume the agreement so that the people in the border areas can live peacefully.' I agree with what you said in the letter. The Huns live in the north areas. It is very cold in these areas. So I have ordered officials to send you grain, gold, cloth, silk and cotton every year. Now the whole world is in peace. The people are living happily. You and I should give up the past hatred and become brothers again. We will resume the policy of peace through marriage."

In 158 BC Ji Yu, the old King of the Huns, died. His son Jun Chen ascended the throne. Emperor Liu Heng decided to resume the policy of pacification through marriage with the Huns.

That winter, 30,000 Huns invaded Shangjun (Shaanxi Province), and 30,000 Huns invaded Yunzhong (now Togtoh, Inner Mongolia). Emperor Liu Heng made arrangements to block the attack. He appointed Mian, the Commander of the Guards of the Palace Gates, as General of Chariots and Cavalry to command the troops under him to station in Feihu (now Hebei Province); he appointed Su Yi, the former premier of the State of Chu, as General, to take troops to Gouzhu Mountain (now Yanmen Mountain, in Shanxi Province); he sent General Zhang Wu to take his troops to Beidi (now Qingyang, in Gansu Province); he made Zhou Bo's son Zhou Ya Fu a general and had him take his troops to Xiliu (Shaanxi Province), northeast of the capital; he made Liu Li, the Director of the Royal Clan Affairs, a general and had him station his troops in Bashang (east of Xi'an, Shaanxi Province); he ordered Xu Han, Marquis of Zhuzi, to take his troops to Jimen (Shaanxi Province). Several months later the Huns went away. Emperor Liu Heng ordered the generals to withdraw.

61. Emperor Liu Heng Passes Away and is Given the Posthumous Title Emperor Wen

On 6 July 157 BC Emperor Liu Heng passed away in Weiyang Palace at the age of forty-seven. He left a posthumous edict spelling out how he wished his demise to be handled. First he gave some perspective: "I hear that all living things born in this world will die someday. Nothing can live forever. It is a natural rule that everyone must die. So death should not be regarded as a sorrowful thing.

"Now, the people like life and dislike death. They spend so much money on lavish funerals for the dead that they bankrupt themselves. They put on such heavy mourning robes that they hurt themselves. I don't want them to do that. I am not a virtuous man and have not brought benefits to the people. Now I am dying, and people have to put on heavy mourning clothes to mourn for me for a long time. They will be tortured by the heat of the summer and the cold of the winter. My death will make people suffer. If I impose restrictions on what they eat and prohibit them from worshiping the gods during the mourning period, that will increase my sins. I will feel sorry for the people.

"I have had the good furtune to be given the power to protect the Ancestral Temple. I have sat on the throne of the Han Dynasty for more than twenty years. Blessed by Heaven and Earth, the whole realm has been in peace. There have been no wars in the realm. I am not a clever man. I am afraid that I may have made mistakes and brought dishonor to the virtue of the late emperors. I have been on the throne for a long time. I am afraid that I cannot die a natural death. Now I have lived my full span. My tablet can be kept in the Ancestral Temple. So there is nothing to be sorrowful for.

"Now I order all the officials and people that they should put on mourning robes to mourn my passing for three days. After that they may take off the mourning robes. Don't prevent people from marrying, offering sacrifices to their ancestors, drinking wine and eating meat. Don't put mourning cloths on the carriages and weapons. Don't mobilize people to the palace to mourn for me. Those who are present in the mourning place should not be barefooted. The linen cloths rapped on their heads should not be wider than three inches. Those who should mourn in the palace should wail just fifteen in the morning and in the evening. After my coffin is buried, those who mourn for me should put on mourning robes with red collars for fifteen days, mourning robes with light red for fourteen days and mourning robes made of silk for seven days. After that they don't need to wear mourning robes anymore. Questions that are not covered by this edict are to be handled in the same vein. This edict should be made known to the public so that people may know my intention. Don't carve up the mountain or divert the river in Baling to build an elaborate mausoleum. And send all my concubines back to their homes."

In his posthumous edict, Emperor Liu Heng appointed Zhou Ya Fu, the Capital Garrison Commander, as General of Chariots and Cavalry; Han, the Minister of Foreign Affairs, as the General in Command of the Stationing of Troops; Wu, Commander of the Palace Guards, as General in Charge of Covering the Grave with Soil. Some 16,000 soldiers were sent to Baling from the nearby counties, and the Minister of Personnel sent 15,000 soldiers to Baling. All these soldiers were put under the command of General Wu for the important work of preparing the grave.

On 12 July 157 BC, the coffin containing the late Emperor was buried in Baling (eastern outskirts of Xi'an, Shaanxi Province). It was suggested that the posthumous title for Emperor Liu Heng should be Emperor Wen (文帝, which means "the kind emperor who gave benefits to the people and loved the people."

Emperor Liu Heng came from the State of Dai. He was on the throne for twenty-three years. He led a frugal lifestyle. He did not increase the number of houses, gardens, horses, carriages and robes in the palace. He once wanted to build a terrace in the palace. He summoned craftsmen to calculate how much money should be spent in building the terrace. They said that 50 kilograms of gold was needed. Emperor Liu Heng said, "50 kilograms of gold is equivalent to all the property of ten average families. Now, I am living in the palace left by my father. I don't wish to commit any error that can tarnish the honor of my father. So there is no need to build the terrace."

Emperor Liu Heng often wore clothes made of rough fabric. He did not allow his favorite concubine Lady Shen to wear clothes or skirts which were so long as to reach the floor. He did not allow the use of embroidered fabric to make bed curtains. He preferred to live a simple life. He ordered the use of earthenware to build his tomb in Baling. He did not allow gold, silver, copper or tin to decorate his tomb and there was no grave mound because he wanted to save money and he did not want to bring hardship to the people.

At one point Zhao Tuo, King of the State of Nanyue, declared himself Emperor Wu of Nanyue. His territory included parts of Guangdong and Guangxi Zhuang, a small part of Fujian Province, Hainan Province, Hong Kong, Macao, and the north part of Vietnam. This was quite an impertinent move, but Emperor Liu Heng simply invited Zhao Tuo's brothers to the palace from Zhending (now in Hebei Province) and gave them valuable gifts. Then Zhao Tuo abandoned the title of emperor and declared the State of Nanyue to be a vassal state of the Han Dynasty.

With the Huns, Emperor Liu Heng implemented the policy of pacification through marriage. The Huns broke the agreement and invaded the border areas of the Han Dynasty. He just sent troops to guard these border areas. He did not send troops deeper into the territory of the Huns because he did not want to bring trouble to the people.

Liu Pi, King of the State of Wu, pretended to be ill and would not go to Chang'an to have an audience with Emperor Liu Heng. Emperor Liu Heng sent him a small table and a walking stick. When Yuan Ang and other officials presented their advice to Emperor Liu Heng, they were free to talk frankly and use sharp words. He took their counsel with tolerance.

Zhang Wu and other officials were found to have accepted bribes. Instead of putting them on trial by officials, Emperor Liu Heng gave them money taken from the imperial household so as to make them feel ashamed. He educated the people with morals. So the people of the whole realm lived in plenty and they acted according to propriety and righteousness.

CHAPTER FOUR: THE REIGN OF EMPEROR LIU QI

62. LIU QI, THE CROWN PRINCE, ASCENDS THE THRONE OF THE HAN DYNASTY

On 12 July 157 BC, Liu Qi, the Crown Prince, ascended the throne of the Han Dynasty in the Temple of Emperor Gaozu. On 14 July 157 BC he declared that he had adopted the title of Emperor.

In October 157 BC, Emperor Liu Qi issued an edict. It read, "I hear that in the ancient time, the founder of a dynasty established contributions to the realm, and the successor had virtue. There was a reason for performing rites and making music. The purpose of making music was to propagate virtue. The purpose of performing dances was to express the great contributions the founder of the dynasty had made. In the Temple of Emperor Gaozu, the ceremony of offering sacrifices includes the Martial Morality Dance, the Culture Dance and the Dance of Five Colors. In the Temple of Emperor Hui, the Culture Dance and the Dance of Five Colors are presented.

"Let us consider Emperor Wen. Under the rule of Emperor Wen, the whole realm is in great peace. He abolished the crime of defamation and did away with corporal punishment; he provided benefits for old people and for orphans. He took care of the people all over the realm. He suppressed his own desires. He would not accept articles of tribute presented by officials. He did not do anything for personal gain. He only punished criminals themselves, not their wives and children. He did not allow killing those who had not committed any crimes. He abolished corporal punishment. He let all his concubines go home after he passed away. He never did anything which would leave other persons without offspring. I am not a clever man and cannot understand all that Emperor Wen has done.

6. Portrait of Liu Qi, Emperor Jing of the Han Dynasty

"Emperor Wen carried out reforms which no emperor in the past carried out. He made great contributions. He improved the lot of the people all over the realm. He was as bright as the sun and moon. But the dances and music presented in the Temple of Emperor Wen are not commensurate with his great contributions. This makes me cringe. Now I order that dances should be performed that show the great contributions he had made. Then the great contributions of my ancestors should be written in books and be passed down from generation to generation.

"Now I order the premier, the marquises, officials who enjoy 1,000 kilograms of grain per year for salary and the officials in charge of rites to create ritual norms for the ceremony of offering sacrifice in the Temple of Emperor Wen."

Premier Shentu Jia and the other officials responded by presenting a memorial to Emperor Liu Qi. "Your Majesty always thinks about filial piety. Your Majesty has ordered dances to manifest the great virtues and magnificent achievements of Emperor Wen. We are not capable of creating such dances. This is what we suggest: Emperor Gaozu established the greatest contributions. Emperor Wen had the greatest virtues. The Temple of Gaozu should be the Temple of the First Ancestor for the emperors. The Temple of Emperor Wen should be the Temple of the Second Ancestor for the emperors. All the following emperors should pay their respects to the Temples of the Ancestors. All the kings of the states and marquises should build a Temple of the Second Ancestor for Emperor Wen in their states. The kings and marquises should send envoys to the capital to accompany the Emperor to pay his respects to the Temples of the Ancestors every year. We suggest that this should be written down in the books and be made known to the people all over the realm." Emperor Liu Qi agreed.

63. Emperor Liu Qi Suppresses the Rebellion of the Seven States

Liu Pi, King of the State of Wu, was the son of Emperor Gaozu's elder brother Liu Zhong. In 201 BC Emperor Gaozu made Liu Zhong King of the State of Dai (now the south part of Inner Mongolia and northern Shanxi Province). But in December 200 BC, the Huns attacked the State of Dai. Liu Zhong could not resist the attack. He abandoned the State of Dai and ran away to Luoyang (now in Henan Province), then to the capital to Emperor Gaozu. Emperor Gaozu was not hardhearted enough to punish him according to the laws because he was a close relative. The Emperor stripped Liu Zhong of the title of King of the State of Dai and made him Marquis of Heyang (now in just Shaanxi Province). In 197 BC Ying Bu, King of the State of Huainan, rebelled. He took Jing (now the west part of Hubei Province) in the east. Then he crossed Huai River in the west and attacked the State of Chu.

Emperor Gaozu personally commanded an army to fight against Ying Bu and killed him. At that time, Liu Zhong's son Liu Pi was twenty years old. He was very strong. He, as a general of cavalry, followed Emperor Gaozu to fight against Ying Bu. They defeated Ying Bu in the west of Qi (now Qichun, in southeastern Hubei Province) and Kuaizhui (now Suzhou). Ying Bu escaped. Liu Jia, the King of the State of Jing, was killed by Ying Bu. He had no heirs.

Emperor Gaozu was worried because the people in the areas of Wu and Kuaiji are very nimble and valiant. He could not find a capable man to pacify the people in these areas. His sons were still very young. So he made Liu Pi, his elder brother Liu Zhong's son, King of the State of Wu. Liu Pi became the king of fifty-five cities in Dongyang Prefecture (now Yangzhou and Huai'an, in Jiangsu Province), Zhang Prefecture (in the southeast part of Anhui Province) and Wu Prefecture (in Jiangsu Province and Zhejiang Province).

After Liu Pi knelt down before Emperor Gaozu and accepted the seal of King of the State of Wu from the hands of Emperor Gaozu, the Emperor read Liu Pi's face, and then said, "Your face shows that you will rebel someday." Emperor Gaozu was sad. But he had already made the appointment. So he clapped Liu Pi on the back and said, "Fifty years from now, someone will rebel in the southeast of the realm. Will it be you? But all the people with the same family name of Liu are in one family. I hope you will not rebel." Liu Pi touched his head on the ground and said, "I dare not do that."

During the reign of Emperor Liu Heng, Liu Pi's eldest son Liu Xian went to the capital to have an interview with the Emperor. Then he drank wine and played a gambling game with Liu Qi, the Crown Prince. Liu Xian was a nimble and valiant man. During the game, the two had an argument and Liu Xian was very disrespectful. The Crown Prince was so angry that he lifted the heavy wooden gambling board and struck it on Liu Xian's head, killing him. Then Liu Xian's dead body was carried back to the State of Wu to be buried there. When he saw this, the King of the State of Wu said angrily, "My son bears the same family name with the Emperor. Since my son died in Chang'an, he should be buried in Chang'an. It is not necessary to carry his dead body back here to be buried!" So the body was carried back to Chang'an and was buried there.

In this incident King of the State of Wu did not observe the customs between the emperor and the subjects. The King of the State of Wu did not go to Chang'an to have an interview with the Emperor anymore, on the excuse that he was ill. Emperor Liu Heng understood that King of the State of Wu was staying away only because his son was killed. After an investigation, Emperor Liu Heng knew for certain that the King of the State of Wu was not ill at all. Thus, when envoys from the State of Wu arrived in Chang'an, the Emperor had them arrested and punished. The King of the State of Wu was afraid, and he stepped up his conspiracy. When he sent an envoy to express his best regards to the Emperor in the autumn, Emperor Liu Heng interrogated the envoy. The envoy said, "The King is actually not ill. Your Majesty arrested several of his envoys. So he pretends to be ill. There was a saying in ancient times, 'Those who are sharp-sighted and are able to perceive the fish in deep water will end up in disaster.' Now the King of the State of Wu pretends to be ill. When this is found out and Your Majesty lays the blame on him, he will be so afraid that he does not know what to do. He is afraid that Your Majesty will kill him. Then he will carry out his worst plan. I hope that Your Majesty will let him go and give him a chance to reform."

Then Emperor Liu Heng released all the envoys sent by King of the State of Wu and let them go back to the State of Wu. The Emperor Liu Heng granted a small table and a stick to King of the State of Wu. He allowed King of the State of Wu not to come to the court to have an interview with him, on the grounds that the King was already very old. After King of the State of Wu was pardoned, he backed down on his conspiracy. In the State of Wu, there were rich resources of copper and salt, so the people did not need to pay tax. When it was a man's turn for corvey service, to do conscript labor, he could pay another man to take his plac. When a man was doing conscript labor, Liu Pi, King of the State of Wu, would pay him money twice as much as a man would be paid to do conscript labor for another person. He also expressed his regards and concern for scholars. He gave benefits to the people in the countryside. He did not allow officials sent by other states to catch fugitives hiding in his State of Wu. He ruled over the State of Wu in this way for forty years. So the people of his state were obedient to him and did what he said.

Chao Cuo was the manager of the Crown Prince's household, and he gained the Crown Prince's favor. One day he observed to the Crown Prince that the territory of the State of Wu was too big, and suggested that since the King of the State of Wu had committed some crimes, the court of the Han Dynasty might want to take the opportunity to reduce his territory. He presented several memorials to the Emperor with this suggestion. But Emperor Liu Heng was not hardhearted enough to do that. From then on, thte King of Wu became even more arrogant and imperious.

When Liu Qi ascended the throne of the Han Dynasty, he appointed Chao Cuo Imperial Counselor. Chao Cuo reminded Emperor Liu Qi of recent history. "When Emperor Gaozu pacified the whole realm, his brothers were still young. His sons were young and weak. So he made his bastard son Liu Fei King of the State of Qi, ruling more than seventy cities; he made his younger brother Liu Jiao King of the State of Chu, ruling more than forty cities; he made his elder brother's son Liu Pi King of the State of Wu, ruling more than fifty cities. The territories of these three kingdoms together account for half of the whole territory of the Han Dynasty. In the past there was enmity between the King of Wu and the Crown Prince, and he pretended to be ill and did not come to the capital to have an interview with Emperor Wen. According to the law, he should be executed for that alone. But Emperor Wen was not hardhearted enough to do that. So he granted a small table and a stick to the King of the State of Wu.

"Emperor Wen was very kind to King of the State of Wu. He should correct his errors and make a fresh start. But he has become even more arrogant and conceited. He has attracted renegades from all over the realm to the State of Wu, and has put them to making coins with copper excavated from the mountains, and they are boiling sea water to stock pile valuable salt. These are signs that he is planning a rebellion. Now, if Your Majesty reduces the size of his territory, he will rebel; if Your Majesty does not reduce the size of his territory, he will rebel anyway.

"But if Your Majesty reduces the size of his territory, he will rebel in a hurry. The disaster resulting from his rebellion will be less. If Your Majesty allows him to wait until he is fully prepared to rebel, the disaster will be greater."

In winter 155 BC, Liu Mao, King of the State of Chu, went to the capital to have an interview with Emperor Liu Qi. Chao Cuo told Emperor Liu Qi that a year before, when Liu Wu came to mourn the death of Empress Dowager Bo, he committed adultery in his room for mourning. He suggested that Liu Wu should be executed. But Emperor Liu Qi pardoned Liu Wu. He just cut a few prefectures from the State of Wu (Donghai Prefecture, Yuzhang Prefecture and Kuaiji Prefecture. In 155 BC Liu Sui, King of the State of Zhao, committed some crimes. Emperor Liu Qi cut Hejian Prefecture from the State of Zhao. Liu Ang, King of the State of Jiaoxi was caught selling government positions, and Emperor Liu Qi cut six of his counties.

Finding that the court of the Han Dynasty was planning to cut more land from the State of Wu, Liu Pi, King of the State of Wu, feared that Emperor Liu Qi would cut his holdings endlessly. He wanted to unite with other kings to hold the rebellion. He knew that King of the State Jiaoxi was brave, would act on impulse without due consideration, and liked to fight. The kings in the Qi area (now Shandong Province) were afraid of him. So the King of the State of Wu sent Ying Gao, his adviser, to see the King of the State of Jiaoxi. Ying Gao did not take any letters with him. He just said to King of the State of Jiaoxi, "Now the Emperor is listening to wicked officials and is modifying the laws. He is taking land away from the kings. He is killing good people. The King of the State of Wu and Your Highness are famous kings. When you are under suspicion, you will not be able to sleep in peace. The King of the State of Wu is ill. He has not been able to go to meet with the Emperor for more than twenty years. He is afraid that when the Emperor suspects him, he will not be able to explain to the Emperor. He is very careful, but still he is afraid that the Emperor will find fault with him... I hear that Your Highness has made some mistakes in selling official posts and the Emperor has cut your territory under this excuse." The King of the State of Jiaoxi said, "What you have said is right. What can I do about it?" Ying Gao said, "Now King of the State of Wu thinks that he shares the same worries with Your Highness. He is willing to uphold the principals of righteousness and overthrow the Emperor at the sacrifice of his own life."

The King of the State of Jiaoxi was scared and said, "I dare not do that. If the Emperor presses too hard, I will have to die. I will have to obey his order!" Ying Gao said, "Imperial Counselor Chao Cuo has misled the Emperor. He instigates the Emperor to reduce the territory of the kingdoms. Devoted officials are not allowed to say anything against him. All the officials of the court hate him. All the kings intend to rebel. And now a comet has appeared in the sky. Locusts have come several times. These phenomena rarely appear. Heroes will rise at this time. So the King of the State of Wu will wage a campaign against Chao Cuo. With the assistance of Your Highness, he will be invincible. If Your Highness gives a word of promise, then King of the State of Wu will attack Hanguguan Pass, take the food warehouses in Yingyang, and fight off the troops sent by the Emperor of the Han Dynasty. The King of the State of Wu needs the help from Your Highness. If Your Highness joins in the rebellion, the whole realm can be conquered. Then the two kings will divide the whole realm in two and each king will take one part. Is that a good idea?" The King of Jiaoxi agreed."

Ying Gao went back to report to King of the State of Wu that King of the State of Jiaoxi had agreed to join in the rebellion. The King of Wu was still afraid that King of the State of Jiaoxi would not join in the rebellion, however, so he went there personally and met the king to make an agreement to rebel together.

When the officials of the State of Jiaoxi got to know that their king had decided to join in the rebellion, they remonstrated with him, saying; "It is good to serve only one emperor. Now Your Highness has decided to march westward with the King of the State of Wu. If you succeed, the two kings will fight against each other for more territory. Then disaster will begin. The territories of the kings are less than twenty per cent of the whole territory of the Han Dynasty. Your rebellion will make worry the Empress Dowager. That is not a good plan."

The King of Jiaoxi would not listen to them. He sent envoys to the State of Qi (northern Shandong Province) to see the king, Liu Jiang Lü; to the State of Zichuan (Shandong Province) to see the king, Liu Xian; to the State of Jiaodong (Shandong Province) to see the king, Liu Xiong Qu; to the State of Jinan (central Shandong Province) to see the king, Liu Pi Guang. The envoys persuaded all these kings to join in King of the State of Wu's rebellion. They all agreed.

One day in January 154 BC a very bright star appeared in the west. A fire caused by heaven burned the halls in the Eastern Palace in Luoyang (now in Henan Province). On the same day Liu Pi, King of the State of Wu, Liu Wu, King of the State of Chu, Liu Sui, King of the State of Zhao, Liu Ang, King of the State of Jiaoxi, Liu Pi Guang, King of the State of Jinan, Liu Xian, King of the State of Zichuan, and Liu Xiong Qu, King of the State of Jiaodong, held their rebellion.

They marched their troops westward, demanding Emperor Liu Qi to kill Chao Cuo. Emperor Liu Qi accepted Yuan Ang's suggestion and had Chao Cuo executed. Then he sent Yuan Ang to the State of Wu to tell Liu Pi that he had executed Chao Cuo in accordance with his requirement. But Liu Pi and the other kings did not stop their rebellion. They marched their troops westward to surround the State of Liang (Henan Province and Anhui Province). Emperor Liu Qi sent Grand General Dou Ying and Commander-in-chief Zhou Ya Fu with troops to put down the rebellion.

In June 154 BC the Emperor issued an edict pardoning fugitive soldiers of the rebellion army and Liu Yi, the son of King of the State of Chu, and some others who had taken part in the rebellion. He made Grand General Dou Ying Marquis of Weiqi. He made King of the

State of Chu's son Liu Ping King of the State of Chu. He made his son Prince Liu Rui King of the State of Jiaoxi. He made his son Price Liu Sheng King of the State of Zhongshan. He transferred Liu Zhi, King of the State of Jibei, to be King of the State of Zichuan. He transferred Liu Yu, King of the State of Huaiyang, to be King of the State of Lu. He transferred Liu Fei, King of the State of Runan, to be King of the State of Jiangdu. By that time Liu Jiang Lü, King of the State of Qi, and Liu Jia, King of the State of Yan, had already died.

Before Commander-in-chief Zhou Ya Fu started marching eastward to put down the rebellion of the State of Wu and the State of Chu, he went to see Emperor Liu Qi and discuss his strategy. He said, "The soldiers of the State of Chu are nimble and valiant. It is difficult to fight face to face with them in battlefield. I plan to let the enemies attack the State of Liang while I lead some troops to cut the enemy's food transportation routes. Then we can defeat the enemies." Emperor Liu Qi ratified his plan.

Commander-in-chief Zhou Ya Fu took his great army to Yingyang (northern Henan Province) when the Wu troops were attacking the State of Liang. Liu Wu, King of the State of Liang, was very worried. He asked for help. Zhou Ya Fu commanded his troops to march northeastward to Changyi (Shandong Province) and pitched camps there to defend themselves. The King of the State of Liang sent envoys to ask Zhou Ya Fu for help every day. But Zhou Ya Fu refused to go to save the State of Liang.

The King of the State of Liang presented memorials to incriminate Zhou Ya Fu for not coming to save him. Emperor Liu Qi sent envoys with imperial edicts to Zhou Ya Fu ordering him to save the State of Liang. But Zhou Ya Fu refused to accept the order. He defended his camps resolutely and would not go out. He sent light cavalrymen to penetrate to Sikou (in Huaiyin, Jiangsu Province) where the Si River and Huai River met. They cut the food transportation route of the armies of the State of Wu and the State of Chu. The troops of the State of Wu ran short of food. They were starved. The Wu troops challenged Zhou Ya Fu's troops to battle, but they refused to go out of their camps to fight. The Wu forces went to the southwest corner of the camps, but Zhou Ya Fu ordered his troops to prepare to defend the northwest corner. And some time later, the elite troops of the army of the State of Wu really did go to the northwest corner of the camps to launch their attack — but they could not enter the camps. The Wu soldiers were hungry, so they retreated.

Zhou Ya Fu sent his best troops to pursue and attack them. They inflicted a crushing defeat. Liu Pi, King of the State of Wu, abandoned his army and ran away with several thousand men. They fled to Dantu (now inZhenjiang City, Jiangsu Province) south of the Yangtze River. The Han Dynasty troops followed up their victory with hot pursuit. They killed more than 100,000 enemy soldiers. Many Wu soldiers surrendered.

Emperor Liu Qi offered 500 kilograms of gold to those who could capture King of the State of Wu. A month later King of the State of Wu was killed in Dantu. Liu Ang, King of the State of Jiaoxi, Liu Wu, King of the State of Chu, Liu Sui, King of the State of Zhao, Liu Pi Guang, King of the State of Jinan, Liu Xian, King of the State of Zichuan, and Liu Xiong Qu, King of the State of Jiaodong, committed suicide.

Emperor Liu Qi made Liu Li, the son of Liu Jiao (Emperor Gaozu's younger brother), King of the State of Chu. He made his son Prince Liu Rui King of Jiaoxi and made his son Prince Liu Sheng King of the State of Zhongshan (the areas around Beijing).

The war against King of the State of Wu lasted for three months. The State of Wu and the State of Chu were defeated and conquered. All the generals thought that Zhou Ya Fu had adopted a very good strategy. But from then on the King of the State of Liang hated Zhou Ya Fu.

64. Emperor Liu Qi Makes His Son Liu Che the Crown Prince

In summer 153 BC, Emperor Liu Qi made his eldest son Liu Rong the Crown Prince, and made his tenth son Liu Che King of the State of Jiaodong.

Liu Rong's mother was Concubine Li. Liu Che's mother was Lady Wang. Lady Wang married Liu Qi when he was the Crown Prince. When she was carrying Liu Che, she dreamed that the sun went into her belly. She told her dream to Crown Prince Liu Qi. The Crown Prince said, "This is an excellent sign." Emperor Liu Heng passed away before Lady Wang gave birth to the child. After Liu Qi had ascended the throne, Lady Wang gave birth to a boy. At that time Empress Bo did not have any child. Several years later Emperor Liu Qi made Concubine Li's son Liu Rong Crown Prince, and he made Lady Wang's son Liu Che King of the State of Jiaodong.

Princess Liu Piao was Emperor Liu Qi's elder sister. She had a daughter named Chen Jiao. She wanted to give Chen Jiao to Liu Rong as his concubine. Concubine Li did not want her son to take Princess Liu Piao's daughter Chen Jiao as his concubine. She hated Princess

Liu Piao because she had recommended many beautiful women to Emperor Liu Qi, and he liked them. This meant that Concubine Li was in less favor with the Emperor. Of course, she was angry. So she rejected Princess Liu Piao's offer.

Then Princess Liu Piao asked Lady Wang. Lady Wang accepted her offer and Princess Liu Piao's daughter Chen Jiao became Liu Che's concubine. Princess Liu Piao was angry with Concubine Li and in front of Emperor Liu Qi, she accused Concubine Li, saying, "When Concubine Li meets with the ladies and concubines of Your Majesty, she often asks the servants to spit on their backs. She practices witchcraft." This made Emperor Liu Qi dislike Concubine Li.

Once Emperor Liu Qi felt he was ailing, he wanted Concubine Li to take care of all his sons, and he said to her, "When I die, please take good care of all my sons and treat them as your own sons." Concubine Li was angry and refused to do that. She made some impertinent remarks. Emperor Liu Qi was very unhappy. He cherished resentment of her in his heart but he did not express it.

Princess Liu Piao praised Lady Wang's son Liu Che in front of Emperor Liu Qi, and Emperor Liu Qi also thought that Liu Che was a virtuous and able person. And he remembered that Lady Wang had told him that when she was carrying Liu Che, she dreamed that the sun went into her belly. So he hesitated to make any decision. Lady Wang secretly asked the officials to ask Emperor Liu Qi to make Concubine Li empress. The Minister of the Minority Nationality Affairs said to Emperor Liu Qi, "It is written in the book that 'the son is prized because of his mother; the mother is prized because of her son'. So the mother of the Crown Prince should be made empress." Emperor Liu Qi said angrily, "It is not right, you should not say that!" Then he ordered to have the Minister of Minority Nationality Affairs executed.

In winter 150 BC Emperor Liu Qi deprived Liu Rong of his title of Crown Prince and made him King of the State of Linjiang (in Hubei Province). Concubine Li was depressed. She could not see the Emperor anymore. She died in sorrow. One day in April 150 BC Emperor Liu Qi made Lady Wang Empress. Twelve days later he made Empress Wang's son Liu Che Crown Prince.

Then in 146 BC Liu Rong committed a crime. He took the land outside the wall of a temple to build his palace. Emperor Liu Qi summoned him to the capital. The carriage was at the north gate of Jiangling (in Hubei Province). When Liu Rong went up the carriage, the carriage axle broke and the carriage became useless. The people of Jiangling shed tears for him and said, "Our king will not come back any more!" When Liu Rong arrived in the capital, he was escorted to the office of the Capital Garrison Commander, Zhi Du, who interrogated him. Liu Rong was so scared that he committed suicide. He was buried in Lantian (Xi'an City, Shaanxi Province). More than 30,000 swallows carried soil in their beaks to the tomb of Liu Rong. The people had pity on him. Liu Rong had no heirs. So after he died, the land of the State of Linjiang was taken back by the Han Dynasty and was made Nan Prefecture.

65. Emperor Liu Qi Continues the Policy of 'Pacification through Marriage' towards the Huns

In May 156 BC, the Huns entered the area of Dai (now Yuxian, Hebei Province). Emperor Liu Qi continued the policy of pacification through marriage towards the Huns and sent envoys to escort a daughter of the royal clan to marry Junchen, the King of the Huns.

In February 148 BC, the Huns invaded Yan (the area around Beijing). That was too much, and Emperor Liu Qi stopped sending brides to the Huns.

The next spring, two kings of the Huns came to surrender. Emperor Liu Qi made them marquises.

In January 142 BC, Emperor Liu Qi dispatched Zhi Du to fight the Huns. He made Zhi Du the head of Yanmen Prefecture (now in Shanxi Province). He granted Zhi Du the right to make decisions by himself. The Huns knew that Zhi Du was an honest and upright man, so they just stayed in the border area for some time. Then they went back. The Huns even made life-size figures of Zhi Du for target practice. They rode on horseback and shot arrows at the figures, but none of them could hit the target. This showed that the Huns were very afraid of Zhi Du. So during his lifetime, the Huns dared not get close to Yanmen.

But Empress Dowager Dou hated Zhi Du very much because her grandson Liu Rong had died when he was interrogated by Zhi Du. Empress Dowager Dou ordered to arrest Zhi Du and intended to put him to death according to the laws. The Emperor Liu Qi objected, saying, "Zhi Du is a devoted official." He wanted to release him, but Empress Dowager Dou said, "Was the King of Linjiang not a devoted official?" Then Zhi Du was executed. Soon after, the Huns entered Yanmen.

Emperor Liu Qi went back to the policy of sending wives to the Huns. He allowed the Huns go into the passes of the Great Wall and do business in the markets. He provided many rolls of cloth and silk, a lot of gold and silver and other valuable objects to the Huns. He sent daughters of the royal clan to marry the king of the Huns. During the lifetime of Emperor Liu Qi, the Huns did not carry out large-scale invasions into the border areas of the Han Dynasty.

66. EMPEROR LIU QI PASSES AWAY

In October 142 BC, both a solar eclipse and lunar eclipse happened. In December there was thunder. The days were gloomy. The sun was purple. The stars and the moon were visible in the daytime.

On 29 December 142 BC Emperor Liu Qi held a capping ceremony for Crown Prince Liu Che, and on 9 January 141 BC, Emperor Liu Qi passed away at the age of forty-eight. He was on the throne for sixteen years. He left a posthumous edict according to which each of the kings and marquises was granted two carriages drawn by four horses; each of the officials who enjoyed 120,000 kg of grain a year for salary was granted one kilogram of gold; ordinary officials and people were granted a hundred coins; all the maids in the palace could go back to their own homes and their families were exempted from tax in their lifetime. On 28 February 141 BC, Emperor Liu Qi was buried in Yangling (in Weicheng District, Xianyang City, Shaanxi Province).

Emperor Liu Qi was given the posthumous title of Emperor Jing (景帝), which means "the Emperor who upholds righteousness and takes firm action."

CHAPTER FIVE: THE MAGNIFICENT REIGN OF EMPEROR LIU CHE

67. LIU CHE, THE CROWN PRINCE, ASCENDS THE THRONE OF THE HAN DYNASTY

On 9 January 141 BC Liu Che, the Crown Prince, ascended the throne of the Han Dynasty at the age of sixteen. He paid his respects to Empress Dowager Dou, making her Grand Empress Dowager; and his mother Empress Wang became Empress Dowager. In March 141 BC, he made the Grand Empress Dowager's half-brothers Tian Fen and Tian Sheng marquises.

When Liu Che ascended the throne, the Han Dynasty had existed for more than sixty years. The whole realm was at peace. All the officials hoped that Emperor Liu Che would hold the ceremony of Worshiping Heaven and Earth on Mount Tai (Shandong Province). They hoped that he would publish new calendar and change the colors of the clothes for court officials.

Emperor Liu Che advocated Confucianism. He invited those who were able and virtuous to be court officials. Zhao Wan and Wang Zang were good at literature and they both were appointed as high ranking officials at court. They suggested Emperor Liu Che to build a hall in the south of the capital from which he could issue his policies and orders, and hold interviews with the kings and marquises. And they suggested to Emperor Liu Che that he might take actions by himself without any need to ask permission from Grand Empress Dowager Dou.

But at that time, Grand Empress Dowager Dou believed in Taoism and she did not like Confucianism. In October 138 BC she sent officials to carry out a secret investigation of Zhao Wan and Wang Zang. It was found that Zhao Wan and Wang Zang had done some unlawful things for their private interests, so Grand Empress Dowager Dou had them arrested and put in jail. They committed suicide. Premier Dou Ying and Commander-in-chief Tian Fen were dismissed from their posts. And then all the power was in the hands of Grand Empress Dowager Dou.

68. Emperor Liu Che Appoints Educated Men to Important Positions

In 135 BC Grand Empress Dowager Dou died. FInallly, Emperor Liu Che was really in power. In October 134 BC, Emperor Liu Che held a policy question-and-answer meeting with more than one hundred scholars. The Emperor wrote, "I want to have my orders carried out by using the force of social customs and habits education so that the punishment to the criminals can be reduced and the crafty and evil persons will reform themselves; I want to let my people live in harmony and peace. I want to carry out enlightened politics. What shall I do to rectify politics so that sweet dew will fall all over the realm and the people will have a rich harvest of the crops, and the people in the whole realm may enjoy the grace I grant to them, and even the grass and trees are moistened by the sweet dew I grant them? What shall I do so that solar eclipse and lunar eclipse will not occur; the stars will appear in the night time; the cold season and the warm season occur properly and the people will receive the blessings granted by the heaven? What shall I do so that my grace will spread abroad and let all the people in the world enjoy my grace?"

Dong Zhong Shu, a scholar of Confucianism, wrote his answer to the Emperor's question as follows. "Your Majesty has issued a brilliant imperial edict looking for the answers of the life given by Heaven and the temperament of human beings. I am not in a position to answer these two questions. I have studied the interrelationships between Heaven and human beings in accordance with the records in Spring and Autumn Annals and what the previous dynasties did. I find that things were terrible. When moral corruption occurred in a dynasty or a state, Heaven would punish or warn them by sending natural disasters. If they did not shape up and correct the mistakes, Heaven would send monstrous phenomena to warn or intimidate them. If the dynasty or state still did not repent and mend its ways, they would suffer great harm and fall.

"From this we can see that Heaven is kind to the ruler of a dynasty or a state. It tries to help the ruler to get rid of disasters and disorder.

If the ruler is not really very brutal and immoral, Heaven will do its best to help him and let him survive. The most important thing is that the ruler must work hard and do his best. He must study hard and read many books. Then he will became a learned man and become a talented and wise ruler. He will do his best to rule wisely and he will become more and more virtuous. And he will achieve more success. All these can be obtained in a short time, and they will bring good results very soon. It is written in the Spring and Autumn Annals, 'Work from morning till night; never slacken your effort.' It is written in the Book of Documents, 'Work hard! Work hard!' These words inspire people to be industrious and work diligently.

"The Spring and Autumn Annals lay stress on integration. This is an eternal principle. But now different teachers teach different doctrines. People hold different opinions. The scholars follow different schools of thought. They hold different ideas. So the ruler cannot establish a stable and unified legal system. The legal system changes frequently. The officials and the people do not know which laws they should follow. I suggest that all the theories and schools of thought which are not within the doctrines of Book of Rites, Classic of Music, Classic of Poetry, Book of Documents, Book of Changes and Spring and Autumn Annals, or the theories and schools of thought which do not belong to the doctrine of Confucianism, should be banned and should not be developed the same way as Confucianism. The heterodox and perverse theories will die out. Then integration can be realized. The unified legal system will become clear and the people will act in accordance with the unified legal system."

Emperor Liu Che accepted Dong Zhong Shu's suggestion and made him premier of the State of Jiangdu. The king of the State of Jiangdu was Liu Fei, Emperor Liu Che's elder brother. Liu Fei was proud and brave. He harbored an intention to rebel. Dong Zhong Shu suggested that Liu Fei should follow the doctrine of rites and righteousness. Then Liu Fei gave up his wicket ideas and transformed himself into a good king. Liu Fei had great respect for Dong Zhong Shu.

Another scholar of the Doctrine of Confucianism was Gongsun Hong. In August 130 BC, Emperor Liu Che initiated a search for virtuous and worthy scholars. He raised the following questions for the scholars to answer: "What is the basis for the principle of the Heaven and the principle of human beings? Can the influences of good fortune and bad fortune be predicted? What were the reasons for the flood during the reign of Yu and the drought during the reign of Tang? How will benevolence, righteousness, the system of ritual norms and propriety, and the ability to see what is right and fair be practiced? What about the succession to the throne and passing the throne to the later generations; life and death; the signs of the will of the Heaven; and the rise and fall of the dynasties? You have learned the records of astronomy, geography and human affairs. You know their true meanings. You may answer my questions in detail and write an essay. I will read all your answers."

Gongsun Hong wrote as follows. "I hear that in ancient times, Emperor Yao and Emperor Shun did not pay much attention in granting titles, but the people behaved properly; they did not focus on punishment, but the people seldom committed crimes; they acted correctly and treated the people with good faith. When a dynasty was in decline, the ruler was attentive in granting titles and handsome rewards, but the people did not behave properly; he applied severe punishment, but that could not keep the people from doing evil things. This is because the ruler did not act properly and he did not treat the people with trust. Since severe punishment and handsome rewards will not be able to inspire people to act properly and prevent bad actions, a ruler must treat the people with trust. Let him appoint officials to suitable positions according to their ability; in this way the officials are able to perform their duties properly. He must ignore useless suggestions, then he may accomplish the work he intends to do. He must avoid launching useless prjoects, so as to reduce the tax burden of the people. He should not do anything that would make the peasants miss the farming seasons or do anything that would diminish the manpower of the people; then the people will become prosperous. He should promote virtuous officials and dismiss those lacking in virtue; then the court will be respected. He should promote those who have made contributions and demote those who have not; then the officials will yield and will not scramble for power and positions. He should give appropriate punishments to those who have committed crimes; then misdeeds will be stopped. He should reward virtuous men; then officials will be encouraged to be virtuous.

"These eight points are the basic principles to rule the people. If the people have jobs to do, they will not fight with each other for jobs. If their problems can be solved reasonably, they will not complain. If the people are educated to be courteous and righteous, they will not be violent. If the ruler loves his people, the people will be close to the ruler. These are of top priority for a ruler. So the legal system should not violate righteousness. Then the people will obey the laws and will not go against them. People will live in harmony and will not violate the ritual norms. Then the people are friendly and will not be violent. So the acts which are punished by laws are rejected by righteousness; acts which are praised by harmony are accepted by ritual norms. People obey ritual norms and righteousness. If rewards and punishments are applied in accordance with ritual norms and righteousness, the people will not violate the laws. So in ancient times, the rulers just had the criminals wear special hats and clothes to distinguish them from the public; that was enough to punish them. In this way, the people will not violate the laws. This is because ritual norms and righteousness were practiced at that time."

More than one hundred scholars presented their answers to Emperor Liu Che. The Minister of Ceremonies reported to Emperor Liu Che that Gongsun Hong's answer was ranked in last place. But after Emperor Liu Che had read all the answers, he put Gongsun Hong's answer in first place. Emperor Liu Che made him a court academician. Later Emperor Liu Che appointed him Minister of Personnel.

69. Emperor Liu Che's Plan to Beat the Huns

Junchen, the King of the Huns, sent an envoy to ask Emperor Liu Che to send a princess to be his wife so as to keep peace between them. Emperor Liu Che asked the court officials to discuss this matter. Wang Hui, the Minister of Minority Nationality Affairs, had been an official in the border area, and he knew the Huns very well. He said, "The Huns and the Han Dynasty maintain peace through the policy of pacification through marriage. But not long after receiving a royal bride, the Huns will violate the peace treaty. It is better not to give such a promise. I suggest that we should raise a great army instead and defeat the Huns."

Han An Guo, the Imperial Counselor, said, "If we fight a battle five hundred kilometers away, it will be unfavorable for us. Now, the Huns are all well-armed and have sufficient horses to figh. They move very quickly, like birds. It is very difficult to get them under control. If we occupy their lands, our territory will not be expanded by much; if we conquer their people, we will not become much stronger. Since ancient times, the Huns have not submitted to Central China. And if the army of the Han Dynasty is sent to a place more than one thousand kilometers away to fight, the soldiers and the horses will be exhausted. The Huns will take advantage of this. Then our army will be in great danger. I think it would be better to keep peace with the Huns through marriage." Most of the court officials agreed with Han

An Guo. Emperor Liu Che took this advice and gave consent to the requirement of the King of the Huns.

In 133 BC Nie Yi, a rich businessman in Mayi (now in Shanxi Province), asked Wang Hui, the Minister of Minority Nationality Affairs, to convey his words to Emperor Liu Che: "Now the Huns have made peace with us. They are now relaxed. We may lure the Huns to come, by promise of gain. If we lay an ambush and start a sudden attack, we will certainly defeat them." Emperor Liu Che asked the high ranking officials, "I married a princess to the King of the Huns as his wife, and sent gold, silver, cloth and silk to him. But the King of the Huns has become much more arrogant. The Huns have invaded our territory many times. The people in the border areas have suffered a lot. I have pity on them. Now I intend to raise an army to attack the Huns. What do you think?"

Wang Hui, the Minister of Minority Nationality Affairs, said, "I have thought about this before. I agree with Your Majesty. I hear that in the past the King of the State of Dai had to deal with the strong Huns in the north while his army was fighting with the army of the Central China. He had to provide for the old people and the young children of his state. He called on his people to grow crops on time. So the granaries of the State of Dai were always full. The Huns did not dare to invade the territory of the State of Dai. Now Your Majesty is powerful. The whole country has been unified. The people are united. Your Majesty has sent troops to defend the border areas. Much food has been transported to the troops defending the border. Much preparation has been made against the invasion by the Huns. But still, the Huns have invaded our territory many times. The reason is that they think they are more powerful and they do not feel afraid. I think we should give them a hard blow."

Han An Guo, the Imperial Counselor, said, "I don't think so. I hear that Emperor Gaozu was surrounded by the Huns in Pingcheng. Emperor Gaozu and his troops were hungry for seven days. But after the siege was raised, Emperor Gaozu came back to the capital. He was not angry with the Huns. He only thought of the interest of the realm. He did not want to vent his personal spite in the sacrifice of the interest of the whole realm. So he sent Liu Jing to present five hundred kilograms of gold to the King of the Huns and promised to make peace by marrying a princess to the King of the Huns. I think it is better not to beat the Huns."

Wang Hui said, "Emperor Gaozu did not take revenge on the Huns after the siege in Pingcheng because he wanted the people to have a rest. Now the Huns have invaded our border areas frequently and the people in the border areas cannot live in peace. Many soldiers defending the border areas have been killed. I think it is better to strike the Huns."

Han An Guo said, "The Huns are light cavalrymen. They move very quickly. They would come like the wind and go away like lightning. They raise livestock. They hunt animals with bows and arrows. They are nomadic people and do not live in one place. It is difficult to get them under control. So I think it is better not to attack them."

Wang Hui said, "I don't think so. Anyone who has done harm to the other cannot be spared. Anyone who has committed a crime is not allowed to run away. The Huns have invaded our territory many times and they should be punished. I don't mean to send troops to go deep into the territory of the Huns. The King of the Huns is very greedy. We may lure him to the border. We may select brave cavalrymen to lay an ambush in secret places and let them get ready to fight. Then we can have full control of the situation. We may order the troops to attack the right wing or the left wing, the vanguards or the rear guards of the Huns. Then we may catch the King, and we will surely win."

Emperor Liu Che thought that made sense, and he adopted Wang Hui's suggestion. He secretly sent Nie Yi to reconnoiter. Nie Yi pretended that he had committed a crime and ran away into the territory of the Huns. He offered to the King of the Huns, "How about I kill the magistrate of Mayi and surrender to you with the city? You can get all the properties and treasures of Mayi." The King of the Huns believed him and agreed with his plan. Nie Yi went back to Mayi, and he had them execute a criminal who had been sentenced to death. He hung the head on the city wall of Mayi. The envoy sent by the King of the Huns saw the head hanging there, and he believed that Nie Yi had really killed the magistrate. Nie Yi told the envoy, "The magistrate of Mayi has been killed. Tell your king that he may come right away." The envoy went back and then the King of the Huns, with a hundred thousand cavalrymen, passed the Great Wall and entered Wuzhou Fortress (in the west of Datong City, in the north part of Shanxi Province).

At that time more than 300,000 infantrymen with chariots and cavalry lay in ambush in the mountain valley beside the City of Mayi. Li Guang, the Commander of Palace Guards, was General of Chariots and Cavalry; Gongsun He, Official in Charge of Emperor's Carriages and Horses, served as General of the Light Chariots;

Wang Hui, the Minister of Minority Nationality Affairs, served as General Commanding Stationing Troops; Li Xi, Official in Charge of Discourse, served as General of Infantry; Han An Guo, the Imperial Counselor, served as Commanding General. All the generals were put under the command of Han An Guo. They were ordered that when the King of the Huns entered Mayi, they should command their troops to attack, with Wang Hui and Li Guang to attack the troops escorting the Huns' supplies and gear.

When the King of the Huns was about fifty kilometers away from Mayi, he noticed that herds of livestock were wandering all around the area, grazing in the fields, but he could not see any herdsman. That seemed strange. He saw a stronghold nearby. He ordered his soldiers to attack it. At that time an officer from Yanmen (now Youyu, Shanxi Province) Military Command was making an inspection to Mayi and was staying in that fortress. When he saw the approaching Huns, he ordered the soldiers to defend the fortress. But very soon the Huns took the fortress and caught him. He was brought before the King of the Huns. The King was about to kill him with his sword, but the officer told the King that he knew the plans of the Han army. He was set free, and he told all the details of the Han plan. The King of the Huns was greatly frightened, and realized that this was why he felt such foreboding.

Then he commanded his troops to retreat. When he reached a safe place, the King of the Huns said, "It is the will of the Heaven that I caught the officer." He made the officer Heavenly King.

In accordance with the plan, the Han troops would come out to fight with the Huns when they saw the troops commanded by the King of the Huns. But the King of the Huns did not appear, so the Han troops did not come out to fight and they got nothing. General Wang Hui should attack the Hun troops escorting the supplies and gear of the Hun army. But when he saw the King of the Huns retreating with his army, there were many Hun soldiers. So he did not dare to come out to attack.

Emperor Liu Che was very angry with Wang Hui because he had not come out to attack the supplies and gear. Wang Hui reminded him of the whole plan and said, "The King of the Huns did not reach the place where we planned to start the attack; he turned back. I only had thirty thousand men under me. I could not fight against one hundred thousand Hun troops. If I fought, I would certainly be defeated. I know very clearly that I would be executed when I came back. But I have brought back thirty thousand men to Your Majesty."

Nonetheless, Wang Hui was handed over to the Supreme Magistrate for trial, and he was sentenced to death for hesitating, taking no action, and avoiding the enemy.

Wang Hui bribed Premier Tian Fen with five hundred kilograms of gold. But Tian Fen did not dare to beg Emperor Liu Che to spare Wang Hui. He went to see Empress Dowager Wang and said, "Wang Hui was the first one to put up the suggestion of fighting against the Huns in Mayi. But now the plan was a failure and Wang Hui will be executed. This is a way of allowing the Huns to take their revenge." When Emperor Liu Che went to see his mother, Empress Dowager Wang conveyed Tian Fen's words to him. Emperor Liu Che said, "Wang Hui is the first one who put forward the plan of attacking the Huns in Mayi. I raised three hundred thousand troops in accordance with his plan. But the King of the Huns ran away. If Wang Hui had commanded his troops to attack the Hun troops escorting the supplies and gear of the Hun army, we still could get some war trophies. And this would give some comforts to the people and officials. If Wang Hui is not executed, how can we express our apologies to all the people for the failure in Mayi?" When Wang Hui heard this, he committed suicide.

70. Wei Qing Wins the First Victory over the Huns for the Han Dynasty

Wei Qing was from Pingyang County (now in Shanxi Province). His father was Zheng Ji, a low ranking official in Pingyang County. Zheng Ji worked for Cao Shou, the Marquis of Pingyang. Cao Shou married Princess Yangxin, who was Emperor Liu Che's elder sister. After Princess Yangxin married the Marquis of Pingyang, she became Princess of Pingyang.

Zheng Ji had slept with a housemaid named Wei who served in the house of Marquis of Pingyang. Housemaid Wei was pregnant and gave birth to a baby boy. He was named Zheng Qing. Housemaid Wei had several children: eldest daughter Wei Jun Ru, second daughter Wei Shao Er, third daughter Wei Zi Fu, son Wei Bu and son Wei Guang. Zheng Qing was brought up by his mother in the Marquis of Pingyang's house. In his childhood, Zheng Qing was brought back to his father. His father sent him to herd the sheep. His father's other sons did not treat Zheng Qing as their brother. Zheng Qing once went to Ganquan Palace, an imperial palace for short stays away from the capital, in Ganquan (in Yan'an City, Shaanxi Province) with others. A criminal with an iron yoke round his neck read Zheng Qing's face carefully and then said, "You will be a very noble man. You will be made a marquis." Zheng Qing said with a smile, "I am a bondservant. I will be very happy if I am not beaten or scolded. It will not be possible for me to be made a marquis!"

When Zheng Qing grew up, he worked on the estate of the Marquis as a servant to protect Princess Pingyang when she was riding out on a horse. In spring 139 BC, after attending a ceremony to ward off disaster and pray for happiness in Bashang (in Xi'an City), Emperor Liu Che went to Pingyang to visit his elder sister Princess Pingyang. Princess Pingyang gathered a dozen beautiful young girls in Pingyang County to attend to him, but the Emperor did not like any of them. After he drank some wine, the dancers and singers came up to present their dances and songs. Wei Zi Fu was among the dancers. When Emperor Liu Che saw Wei Zi Fu, he liked her. That day Wei Zi Fu assisted Emperor Liu Che in changing clothes in a changing room, and they were intimate. After that, Emperor went back and sat by the table. He felt happy. He granted Princess Pingyang 500 kilograms of gold. Princess Pingyang sent Wei Zi Fy into the palace. When Wei Zi Fu was getting up into the carriage, Princess Pingyang patted her on the back and said, "Now you are leaving for the palace. When you gain favor with the Emperor, don't forget us."

After his elder sister Wei Zi Fu gained the favor of Emperor Liu Che, Zheng Qing changed his surname to Wei. So Zheng Qing became Wei Qing. At that time the empress was Chen Jiao. She was the daughter of Liu Piao, Emperor Liu Che's aunt. Empress Chen did not have any children. But not long after Wei Zi Fu had entered the palace, she was pregnant. When Liu Piao heard about this, she hated Wei Zi Fu very much. She sent some servants to catch Wei Qing. At that time Wei Qing was working in Jianzhang Palace. Liu Piao intended to kill him.

Gongsun Ao, an officer of the cavalry, was Wei Qing's friend. He and several brave men rushed into the place where Wei Qing was kept and saved him. When Emperor Liu Che heard about this, he summoned Wei Qing and appointed him as the Commander of the Guards of Jianzhang Palace. Soon, Wei Qing became Palace Attendant. His half-sister Wei Jun Ru married Gongsun He, Official in Charge of Emperor's Carriages and Horses. His half-sister Wei Shao Er's husband Chen Zhang was summoned by Emperor Liu Che to the palace and was made an official. Gongsun Ao was appointed as a high ranking official because he had saved Wei Qing. Wei Qing was named Official in Charge of Discourse.

In spring 129 BC, the Huns entered Shanggu (Hebei Province). They killed the officials and people there. Emperor Liu Che sent Wei Qing, the General of Chariots and Cavalry, with his troops to march out from Shanggu; he sent Gongsun Ao, General of Cavalry to march out from Dai Prefecture (Hebei Province); he sent Gongsun He, General of Light Chariots, to march out from Yunzhong (now Togtoh, Inner Mongolia); he sent Li Guang, General of Valiant Cavalry, to march out from Yanmen (Youyu, in Shanxi Province). Each general had ten thousand cavalrymen.

Wei Qing marched a long way northward to Longcheng (on the upper reaches of Orkhon River, in Mongolia). Longcheng was the place where the Huns held the ceremony of offering sacrifices to the Heaven. There Wei Qing and his troops had a battle with the Huns. They killed 700 Hun officers and soldiers. So they won the first victory over the Huns for the Han Dynasty.

Gongsun He, General of Light Chariots, set out from Yunzhong, but they did not meet the Huns. So they turned back. Gongsun Ao, General of Cavalry, lost 7,000 cavalrymen in the battle. Li Guang, General of Valiant Cavalry, set out from Yanmen and they met the Hun army, but they were greatly outnumbered by the Huns and were defeated.

Li Guang was captured by the Huns. The King of the Huns knew that Li Guang was a good general, and he had already instructed his troops, "When you catch Li Guang, you must bring him before me alive." Li Guang had been wounded, so they put him on a kind of stretcher, a net that they carried between two horses. They transported Li Guang this way for about five kilometers. Li Guang lay there, pretending that he had died. Suddenly, he saw a Hun boy riding a very good horse. He jumped from the net to the horse. Then he held the boy and used the whip to urge the horse to ride very quickly southward for more than ten kilometers. Several hundred Hun cavalrymen ran after him. Li Guang used the boy's bow and arrows to shoot and he killed many of them. So Li Guang escaped and came back. Since Gongsun Ao and Li Guang had been defeated, they were arrested and put in jail and were tried by the Supreme Magistrate.

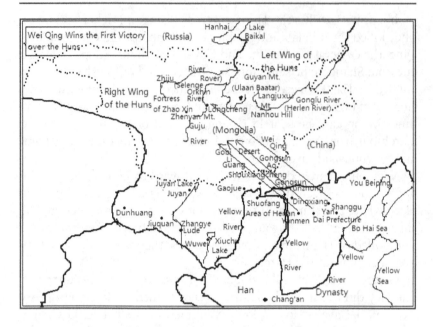

Wei Qing Wins the First Victory over the Huns

Emperor Liu Che wrote, "The tribes in the north have no sense of righteousness. Recently the Huns invaded our border areas several times, so I sent troops to fight them. However, in ancient times emphasis was put on training the soldiers and raising the moral of the troops. But our officers and soldiers were recently grouped together and put under the generals. They did not know each other very well and they did not cooperate with each other very well. The commanders under General Gongsun Ao and General Li Guang were not capable enough to command the troops under them. The high ranking officers under them went against the principle of righteousness. They left the troops under and ran away. The low ranking officers went against the laws. According to Art of War, if the officers and men relax their will to fight and they are not trained to be ready to fight, it is the fault of the general; if the general has issued strict orders and requirements but the officers and soldiers do not fight to the best of their ability, that is the misconduct of the officers and soldiers. Now the generals have been sent to be tried by the Supreme Magistrate. They will be punished according to the laws. If both the generals, and officers and soldiers as well, are punished, that is not what I want to do. I am sorry for the ordinary officers and soldiers. I hope they will outlive this disgrace and reform themselves. If they are sentenced to severe punishment, there will be no way for them to start over again. I will pardon those officers and soldiers sent to fight in Yanmen and Dai Prefecture who did not act according to laws."

After the trials, Gongsun Ao and Li Guang were sentenced to death. They paid ransoms for the redemption of their lives, so they escaped death penalty but became common persons. Emperor Liu Che granted Wei Qing, who had won the first victory over the Huns in Longcheng, the title of Secondary Marquis.

71. Emperor Liu Che Makes Wei Zi Fu Empress

After Wei Zi Fu entered the palace, Emperor Liu Che did not go to her room and sleep with her for more than a year. At that time Emperor Liu Che decided to send home those concubines who had not given birth to any child for him. Wei Zi Fu went to see Emperor Liu Chu. She wept and begged the Emperor to let her leave the palace too, and go home. After that, Emperor Liu Che felt sorry for her and often went to her room, she became a favorite. She gave birth to three daughters. In December 130 BC she gave birth to a baby boy. The boy was named Liu Jü.

When Liu Che was still the Crown Prince, he married Chen Jiao, the daughter of Princess Liu Piao who was the elder sister of Emperor Jing, Liu Che's father. When Liu Che ascended the throne of the Han Dynasty, he made Chen Jiao Empress. But Empress Chen did not give birth to any children. Still, she enjoyed great favor from Emperor Liu Che because her mother Liu Piao had contributed a lot in Emperor Jing's decision to make Liu Che the Crown Prince. When she learned that Emperor Liu Che often went to Wei Zi Fu's room, she was very jealous. She asked Chu Fu, a sorceress, to curse Wei Zi Fu. It was an act of treason and heresy. This was found out by Emperor Liu Che. He was in a rage; he deposed her from the position of empress. In March 129 BC he made Wei Zi Fu Empress, and soon after, he made Liu Jü the Crown Prince.

72. Zhufu Yan's Advice to Emperor Liu Che to Be Moderate in the War against the Huns

Zhufu Yan was from Linzi (now in Zibo City, central Shandong Province) of the State of Qi. He was a learned man. He first studied Political Strategies. Later he studied the Book of Changes, Spring and Autumn Annals and the books of different schools of thought. He travelled to the State of Yan (now Beijing), the State of Zhao (now Handan, Hebei Province) and the State of Zhongshan (now Dingzhou, Hebei Province). He hoped that the rulers of these states would adopt his ideas and put him in a high ranking position. But he was not noticed by any of these rulers. In 134 BC he went westward to Xianyang, the capital of the Han Dynasty. He went to see General Wei Qing. The General was impressed, and talked about Zhufu Yan before Emperor Liu Che several times. But still Emperor Liu Che did not notice him. One day in 127 BC, Zhufu Yan submitted a written statement to the court in the morning. In the afternoon the same day, he was summoned by Emperor Liu Che to the court. Zhufu Yan talked about nine matters, eight of which were about laws and one of which was to counsel the Emperor to be moderate in the war against the Huns.

The counsel read: "I hear that a wise emperor will read all counsel given, even if some are very frank, so as to have a broader view of matters. A loyal courtier will present his frank advice even if he would be severely punished for his frankness. So he should present all the strategies without any reservation and the contribution he has made will be remembered by many generations to come. Now I will suggest some strategies even if I could be punished for this. I hope Your Majesty takes into consideration the strategies I present and pardon to me if there are mistakes in my suggestions.

"It is written in Military Science of Sima Rangju: 'If the ruler of a nation is a warmonger and carries out wars frequently, this nation will perish even if it is a big nation. When the world is in peace, if the ruler of a nation is not prepared for war, this nation will be in great danger.' When the army of a state defeats the enemy and returns triumphantly, the ruler will order the musicians to play the victory marches. The ruler of a state organizes the peasants and his troops to hunt animals in spring and autumn, so as to let his peasants and troops have military exercises. The rulers of different states train their troops in spring and order them to make weapons in autumn. They do all these to stay prepared for war. If a ruler starts a war out of anger, he acts against the principle of virtuousness. Weapons are used for killing. Fighting is an immoral act. In ancient times, when a ruler of a state was very angry and started a war, thousands of soldiers were killed and the blood flowed like streams. So a wise king would consider the matter carefully before deciding to start a war. He must be certain that he would surely win. A king who indulges in wars will surely regret in the end.

"In the past the First Emperor of the Qin Dynasty had a strong army and they always won. He attacked all the states and conquered them. He unified the whole realm. He made great contributions in the unification of China. He won many victories. He wanted to attack the Huns. However, Premier Li Si said, 'I suggest that Your Majesty better not attack the Huns. The Huns do not live in places with city walls. They do not have supply storage houses. They move frequently like birds. It is very difficult for us to control the Huns. If Your Majesty sends forth soldiers carrying light loads to go a long distance, they will run out of food very soon. If the soldiers carry heavy loads of food, it would be very difficult for them to march forward. In the best case, the Huns' lands are useless. The Hun people, they will not submit to us. Your Majesty would only have to abandon what was won after hard battles. That will not be in the interests of the people. That will make China tired and that will let the Huns gain advantage. This is not a good policy.' The First Emperor of the Qin Dynasty did not take his advice. He sent Meng Tian to attack the Huns. He took a vast area, and the Yellow River became the border line. But the land they had taken from the Huns was saline and alkaline. Crops cannot grow on such land. Then the First Emperor of the Qin Dynasty sent all the able-bodied men in the realm to guard the Bei River. The soldiers stayed there for more than ten years. Many of them died there. The Qin Dynasty army never crossed the Bei River and marched northward. Is that because there were not enough soldiers and there were not enough weapons? The reason is it was an impossible task. Food was gathered from the whole realm, from as far away as the eastern region by the sea, a long way to the Bei River. Out of 400 kg of food sent out, only 68 kg of food could reach the Bei River. The men worked very hard on the farms, but the crops they produced were not sufficient to feed the army; the women worked very hard to spin and weave, but the cloth they produced was not enough to make tents for the army. The people lived in great hardship. No one took care of the elderly people with no family. Many people died. Then the people of the realm rebelled against the Qin Dynasty.

"When Emperor Gaozu brought peace, he ordered his army to capture the border areas. When he got the information that the Huns had gathered in Daigu area, he intended to attack them there. Imperial Counselor Cheng tried to persuade Emperor Gaozu to give up the idea. He said, 'We'd better not do that. The Huns sometimes gather together like animals and sometimes scatter like birds. It is very difficult to predict their movement.' Emperor Gaozu ignored Imperial

Counselor's advice. When he reached Daigu, he was surrounded by the Huns in Pingcheng. Emperor Gaozu regretted his error. He sent Liu Jing to made peace with the Huns by marrying a princess to their King. From then on there have been no wars between the Han Dynasty and the Huns.

"It is written in the Art of War, 'If an army of 100,000 men is raised, the daily expenditure will amount to a thousand ounces of silver.' The Qin Dynasty always kept an army of more than 300,000 men. Although they could defeat enemy troops and kill their generals and capture the King of the Huns, what they had done increased the great enmity and deep hostility of the opponents. What the army gained could not make up for the cost of supporting the army. The Huns are known for robbing, looting and invading. These are their natural instincts. In ancient times, in the periods of Yu Dynasty, Xia Dynasty, Yin Dynasty and Zhou Dynasty, the Huns were not required to act according to the laws and moral principles because they were regarded as animals but not human beings. Now people do not look back to tradition in dealing with the Huns but only follow the mishandling of the Huns in recent times. This makes me worried. It has made the people suffer enormously. If the war lasts for a long time, unexpected events will occur. If a man works in difficult conditions for a long time, he will change his views. If the people in the border areas live in great hardship, the generals and officials there will be suspicious of each other and will collude with the foreigners. This is the reason why Zhao Tuo and Zheng Han were able to realize their ambition to establish their independent states. The policies of the Qin Dynasty could not be carried out because the power had been in the hands of these two persons. So it is written in the Book of Zhou, 'Policies and orders issued by the ruler affect the national security; the survival of a nation depends on the generals and officials appointed by the ruler.' I hope Your Majesty may consider my advice."

At that time Xu Le and Yan An also presented their thoughts to the same effect. Emperor Liu Che summoned Zhufu Yan, Xu Le and Yan An to the court and said, "Where were you? I should have met you earlier!" Then Emperor Liu Che appointed them as Imperial Attendants.

73. Emperor Liu Che Carries Out the Order of Expending Favors Suggested by Zhufu Yan

Zhufu Yan said to Emperor Liu Che, "In ancient times the land for a king was only fifty square kilometers. It was easy for an emperor to keep the kings under control because they were not strong. But now a king may have dozens of cities and the land of more than five hundred square kilometers. If they are treated in a free and easy way, they will become conceited and extravagant and commit all kinds of immoral acts. If they are treated strictly, they will collude with each other and rebel against the central government. If we reduce their land by law, they will rebel. That was what Chao Cuo had done in the past. Now each king has more than ten sons and brothers. But only the eldest son is heir to the kingdom. The rest of the sons do not have an inch of land. This does not conform to the principles of benevolence and filial piety. I suggest that Your Majesty order the kings to give favors to all their sons and brothers. A king should divide his land among his sons and brothers and Your Majesty may make them marquises. Then everyone would be happy to have got what he desires. Your Majesty may order the kings to distribute favors to their sons and brothers, and the actual effect will be that the states of the kings will be carved up and become weak. The power of the states will be reduced." Emperor Liu Che accepted Zhufu Yan's suggestion.

In January 127 BC Emperor Liu Che issued an edict which read, "King of the State of Liang and King of the State Chengyang have deep feelings to their younger brothers. They want to divide the land of their states and distribute their land to their younger brothers. I grant them my rectification. If any king intends to distribute his land to his sons and brothers, I will grant his sons and brothers titles." Then the kings expended their favors to their sons and brothers and distributed land to them. Emperor Liu Che granted them titles and put them under the jurisdiction of prefectures. From then on the kingdoms became divided and much weaker.

74. Wei Qing Wins More Victories over the Huns

In winter 129 BC several thousand Huns invaded the border areas. The people in Yuyang Prefecture (now Miyun, Beijing) suffered the most. Emperor Liu Che sent General Han An Guo to station his army in Yuyang to prevent further invasions. In autumn 128 BC, 20,000 Hun cavalrymen entered Liaoxi Prefecture (Yixian, Liaoning Province) and killed the prefecture chief. They captured more than 2,000 people. Then they marched to Yuyang Prefecture (now Miyun, Beijing) and defeated more than 1,000 men under the prefecture chief of Yuyang. At that time General Han An Guo took his troops to Yuyang. The Huns surrounded them there.

General Han An Guo commanded 1,000 cavalrymen to fight with the Huns. After a battle, nearly all his 1,000 cavalrymen were killed and General Han An Guo himself was wounded. The army in Yan (now Beijing) arrived and saved General Han An Guo. When the Huns saw that new forces had come, they ran away. Not much later the Huns invaded Yanmen (Shanxi Province) and killed more than 1,000 people there.

In autumn 128 BC, Emperor Liu Che appointed Wei Qing as General of Chariots and Cavalry and had him lead 30,000 cavalrymen to march from Yanmen (now Youyu, in the northwest part of Shanxi Province); he sent Li Xi and his troops to march out from Dai Prefecture (now Yuxian, Hebei Province). They marched right out through the Great Wall to attack the Huns. And they killed several thousand Hun officers and soldiers.

In 127 BC Emperor Liu Che sent General Wei Qing to set out from Yunzhong (now Togtoh, Inner Mongolia). Wei Qing marched his army westward to Gaoque (now in Hanggin Houqi, Inner Mongolia). Then he took his troops across the Yellow River and occupied Henan (the Great Bend of the Yellow River). His army marched to Longxi (Gansu Province). They battled with the Hun troops under the King of Baiyang and the King of Loufan in Henan. They killed and captured several thousand Hun officers and soldiers. They got more than 1,000,000 cows and sheep. The King of Baiyang and the King of Loufan escaped.

From then on, there were no Huns in Henan. The Han army took the area and Emperor Liu Che made it into Henan Shuofang Prefecture. He ordered the soldiers to build a city named Shuofang City and to repair the fortresses built by General Meng Tian during the Qin Dynasty (221 BC–207 BC). The area of Shuofang Prefecture was protected by the Yellow River. At the same time the Han Dynasty gave up the area of Zaoyang (now the area of Zhangjiakou, in the northwest part of Hebei Province) in Shanggu, which was a remote place, to the Huns.

Emperor Liu Che made Wei Qing Marquis of Changping and granted him the tax of 3,800 peasant households. Su Jian, a high ranking officer under Wei Qing, established contributions in this action against the Huns. Emperor Liu Che made Su Jian Marquis of Pingling and granted him the tax of 1,100 peasant households. He sent Su Jian to supervise the building of the city of Shuofang. Zhang Ci Gong, a high ranking officer in Wei Qing's army, also made major contributions in these battles. Emperor Liu Che made him Marquis of

Antou. Emperor Liu Che summed up these events, saying, "The Huns go against the will of the Heaven and all ethics and morality. They are brutal to old people. They rob other people. They deceive the people of the loca ltribes and borrow soldiers from them. They have invaded our border areas many times. So I raised a great army and put it under the command of the generals to fight against the Huns. It is written in the Book of Songs, 'In an expedition the army of Xianyun was driven to Taiyuan' and 'Many soldiers and carriages were sent to the north to build the city of Shuofang'. Now Wei Qing, General of Chariots and Cavalry, marched his army westward to Gaoque. They killed and captured 2,300 Hun officers and soldiers. They captured many carts full of supplies and gears of the army and loads of livestock as booty. I have made Wei Qing Marquis of Changping. The troops under him pacified area of Henan in the west. They went past the old fortress of Yuxi, climbed over Zi Mountain, and built a bridge over the Bei River and went across it. They captured the Fortress of Puni and the Fortress of Ful. They killed many Hun cavalrymen. They caught 3,071 spies. They interrogated the captives and got information about the Hun army. They won a great victory. They got more than 1,000,000 cows and sheep. Wei Qing came back with his whole army triumphantly. I will add the tax of three thousand peasant households to Wei Qing."

In winter 127 BC, King Junchen of the Huns died. His younger brother Yizhixie made himself Kin. He attacked Yuchan, Junchen's son and Crown Prince, and defeated him. Yuchan ran away and surrendered to the Han Dynasty. Emperor Liu Che made him Marquis of She'an. But several months later Yuchan died.

In summer 126 BC,, King Yizhixie commanded the Huns to strike the area of Dai Prefecture; they killed Gong You, the prefecture chief. They invaded Yanmen and killed more than a thousand people. In 125 BC the Huns invaded the areas of Dai Prefecture, Dingxiang Prefecture (now Horinger, in Inner Mongolia), and Shang Prefecture (now Yulin, in Shaanxi Province). They killed several thousand Han people. In autumn the same year they invaded Yanmen prefecture again. They killed more than one thousand Han. In 124 BC 30,000 Hun cavalrymen invaded Dai Prefecture; 30,000 Hun cavalrymen invaded Dingxiang Prefecture (Horinger, Inner Mongolia); 30,000 Hun cavalrymen invaded Shang Prefecture (now Yulin, Shaanxi Province). They killed several thousand Han people of these prefectures. The King of the Right Wing of the Huns had a grudge against the Han Dynasty because the Han army had occupied Henan (the area of the Great Bend of the Yellow River) which was under his jurisdiction and had built the City of Shuofang there. So he commanded his troops to invade the border areas and Henan and Shuofang. They killed many people in these areas.

In spring 124 BC, Emperor Liu Che had Wei Qing take his 30,000 cavalrymenfrom Gaoque (now Hanggin Houqi, Inner Mongolia) to the north. He appointed Su Jian, Commander of the Palace Guards, as Guerrilla General, Li Jü, the Metropolitan Superintendent, as General of Crossbow Troops, Gongsun He, Official in Charge of Emperor's Carriages and Horses, as General of Cavalry, Li Cai, the Premier of the State of Dai, as General of Light Chariots. All these four generals were put under the command of Wei Qing. This route of the army would march out from Shuofang City (in the northwest of Hanggin Qi, Inner Mongolia) to the north.

He made Li Xi, Minister of Minority Nationality Affairs, and Zhang Ci Gong, Marquis of Antou, generals. Emperor Liu Che ordered them to march out from You Beiping Prefecture (now Lingyuan, in the west part of Liaoning Province) to the north.

The King of the Right Wing of the Huns thought that the Han troops could not make it as far as his location. He drank a lot of wine and got drunk. The Han troops marched out of the Great Wall and continued northward for 350 kilometers. They reached the place where the King of the Right Wing of the Huns was at night and surrounded him. He was greatly frightened. He made a breakthrough and ran away to the north, in the dark, with one of his concubines and several hundred cavalrymen. Guo Cheng, the Commander of the Light Cavalry, and others of the Han army ran after the King of the Right Wing of the Huns for more than a hundred kilometers but could not catch up with them.

The Han army won a great victory. They captured more than ten minor kings under the King of the Right Wing of the Huns, more than 15,000 men and women, about a million domestic animals. Then Wei Qing commanded his army to return.

When the army reached the Great Wall, Emperor Liu Che sent an envoy to take the seal of the Grand General to the army under Wei Qing, to make Wei Qing the Grand General. All the generals were put under his command. After that Wei Qing went back to Xianyang, the capital of the Han Dynasty.

Emperor Liu Che said, "Grand General Wei Qing personally commanded the officers and soldiers to fight the Huns and won a great victory. They captured more than ten kings of the Huns. I grant him the tax of 8,700 peasant households." Emperor Liu Che made Wei

Qing's three sons marquises: Wei Kang Marquis of Yichun, Wei Bu Yi Marquis of Yin'an and Wei Deng Marquis of Fagan. Wei Qing said, "I have the luck to serve in the army. Under the blessing of Your Majesty our army won a great victory. The officers have established great contributions in this battle. Your Majesty has granted me the tax of more peasant households. My sons are still very young. They have not established any contributions but they have been made marquises. I don't think this is the right way to inspire the officers and men of the army under me to fight bravely in battles. My three sons do not dare to accept the titles granted to them."

Emperor Liu Che said, "I have not forgotten the contributions made by the officers and men under your command. I have decided to reward them as well." Then Emperor Liu Che issued an imperial edict to the Imperial Counselor which read, "Gongsun Ao, Protector of the Army, has followed Grand General three times to fight against the Huns. He has done his best to protect the officers and men of the army. I hereby make Gongsun Ao Marquis of Heqi. Commander Han Yue went out of Tianhun Pass with the army and reached the court of the King of the Right Wing of the Huns. He fought bravely and captured the minor kings under the King of the Right Wing of the Huns. I have decided to make him Marquis of Longdou. He, General of the Cavalry, followed the Grand General to fight against the Huns and captured the minor kings under the King of the Right Wing of the Huns. I have decided to make him Marquis of Nanpiao. Li Cai, General of Light Chariots, followed the Grand General to fight against the Huns and captured the minor kings under the King of the Right Wing of the Huns. I have decided to make him Marquis of Le'an. Officers Li Shuo, Zhao Bu Yu, and Gongsun Yong have followed the Grand General to fight against the Huns for three times and they captured the minor kings under the King of the Right Wing of the Huns. I have decided to make Li Shuo Marquis of Zhizhi, Zhao Bu Yu Marquis of Suicheng, and Gongsun Yong Marquis of Congping. General Li Jü, General Li Xi, Commander Dou Ru Yi and Wan, General of the Palace Guards, have established military contributions in this battle. I have decided to grant them the titles of marquis. I will grant each of them the tax of 300 peasant households."

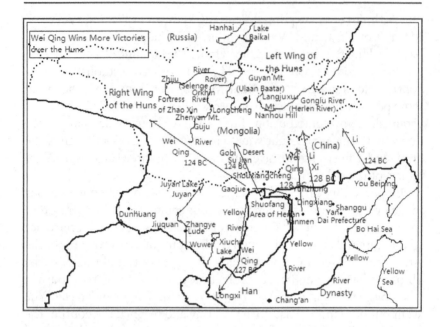

Wei Qing Wins More Victories over the Huns

75. Zhang Qian's Mission to the Western Regions and the Opening Up of the Silk Road

Zhang Qian was born in Chenggu (now in Hanzhong, Shaanxi Province). During the period of Jianyuan (140 BC–135 BC) of the reign of Emperor Liu Che, Zhang Qian was an officer of the Imperial Guards. At that time, Emperor Liu Che talked with the Huns who had surrendered. They told Emperor Liu Che that the Huns had defeated the State of Yuezhi (Gansu Province). The King of the State of Yuezhi was killed. The King of the Huns used his skull as a wine container. The people of the State of Yuezhi moved westward. They hated the Huns very much. But they could not find any other states to form an alliance with, to attack the Huns.

At that time Emperor Liu Che was planning to attack the Huns. When he got this information, he decided to send envoys on a mission to join with the State of Yuezhi to attack the Huns. The envoys had to cross through Hun territory. Then in 139 BC Emperor Liu Che issued an imperial edict to recruit those who would carry out the mission. Zhang Qian responded to the call for recruits. He was appointed to go on a mission to the State of Yuezhi, and Ganfu, a servant of the family of Tangyi, went with him. Ganfu was a Hun. Zhang Qian and his team went out of Longxi (Gansu Province). They went into the territory of the Huns. Unluckily they were captured. They were escorted before King Junchen of the Huns. King Junchen said, "The State of Yuezhi is north of my territory. How can the Emperor of the Han Dynasty send envoys there? If I want to send envoys to the State of Yue, will the Emperor allow my envoys to go through the territory of the Han Dynasty to the State of Yue?" Zhang Qian and his team were detained on the territory of the Huns for more than ten years. The King gave Zhang Qian a Hun woman as his wife, and she bore him a son. All throughout the time he was detained by the Huns, Zhang Qian carried the imperial staff with a yak's tail, the symbol of a diplomat of the Han Dynasty.

After Zhang Qian and his team had been kept by the Huns for this long, the Huns relaxed their watch. Then Zhang Qian and his team took their chance and escaped. They went westward for weeks, and finally reached the State of Dayuan in the Ferghana Valley in Central Asia. The King of the State of Dayuan had heard that China was a prosperous country with rich products. He wanted to do business with China but merchants from his State could not get to China because the way was blocked by the Huns. When Zhang Qian showed up, the King of the State of Dayuan was very glad and asked him where he intended to go. Zhang Qian said, "I am on a mission to the State of Yuezhi for the Emperor of the Han Dynasty. The road to Yuezhi is blocked by the Huns and we were captured by them. Now we have escaped. I hope Your Highness will deputize someone to guide us to Yuezhi. If I can get there and complete my mission, I will go back to China and tell the Emperor that Your Highness has given me great help. The Emperor will surely send many precious materials to Your Highness."

The King of the State of Dayuan agreed with him. He sent guides and interpreters to go with Zhang Qian, and they reached the State of Kangju which was situated further west. Then they headed southward and reached the State of the Greater Yuezhi. The King there had been killed by the Huns and the Crown Prince had become King. The people of Yuezhi had conquered the State of Daxia and settled down there. The King of Greater Yuezhi became the ruler. The land of Daxia was fertile. There were very few invasions from other states. The people led a comfortable life. The King of the State of Greater Yuezhi considered that the Han Dynasty was very far away, and he did not have any desire to take revenge on the Huns. Zhang Qian conveyed Emperor Liu Che's intention to form an alliance with the State of Greater Yuezhi to fight against the Huns, and then he travelled onward to the State of Daxia (Bactria, in what is now Afghanistan and part of Southern Tajikistan and Uzbekistan). But when Zhang Qian came back from the State of Daxia, the King of the State of Greater Yuezhi still did not give an answer to his proposal.

Zhang Qian and his team stayed in the State of Greater Yuezhi for a year. Then they began their return trip, navigating past some of the highest mountains in the world — the Pamir Mountains (in eastern Tajikistan and southwestern Xinjiang, China), the Kunlun Mountains, the Altun Mountains, then to the Qilian Mountains. Zhang Qian intended to go back to Chang'an through the area populated by the Qiang People (now Qinghai Province). But again they were captured by the Huns. They stayed in Hun territory for more than a year. Finally, in 126 BC King Junchen of the Huns died. King Luli of the Left Wing of the Huns attacked the Crown Prince and he declared himself King of the Huns. The State of the Huns was in complete disarray, and Zhang Qian with his Hun wife and son and Ganfu made a break for it and sped away back to the lands of the Han Dynasty.

Emperor Liu Che appointed Zhang Qian Official in Charge of Discourse and he granted Ganfu the title of Fengshijun (Official on Mission).

Zhang Qian's First Mission to the Western Region

Zhang Qian was a strong-minded man. He was kind to the people. The people of the local tribes liked him. Ganfu was a Hun. He was good with a bow and arrow. When Zhang Qian and his team were short of food, Ganfu would hunt for the team. When Zhang Qian started out on his mission from Chang'an in 139 BC, there were more than a hundred persons in the team. But after thirteen years, only Zhang Qian and Ganfu came back.

Zhang Qian had been to Dayuan, Greater Yuezhi, Daxia (Bactria) and Kangju (now Uzbekistan and Tajikistan). He learned that there were five or six big states near these states. He presented a report to Emperor Liu Che as follows:

> Dayuan is situated southwest of the State of the Huns and west of the Han Dynasty. It is about 3,500 kilometers away. The people live in fixed abodes. They till the land and grow rice and wheat. They make wine with grapes. There are many good horses in Dayuan. The horses sweat blood. They are the descendants of the horses from Heaven. There are more than seventy cities in the State of Dayuan, and they have city walls and many houses. There are several hundred thousand people in this state. The soldiers ride horses and use bows and spears. The State of Kangju is situated north of Dayuan. The State of Greater Yuezhi is to the west of Dayuan. The State of Daxia is situated south of Dayuan. The State of Wusun is situated to the northeast, and to the east of Dayuan are the State of Jumi (in Xinjiang Uygur Autonomous Region) and the State of Yutian (in Hotian, also in Xinjiang Uygur Autonomous Region). All the rivers to the west of Yutian flow westward into the West Sea (the Caspian Sea, in western Central Asia). The rivers to the east of Yutian flow eastward into Yanze (Salt Lake) (now Lop Nur, in southeastern Xinjiang). The water of the Yanze flows underground southward then flows to the ground and becomes the source of the Yellow River. Jade stones can be found in this place. The rivers flow into China. The State of Loulan and the State of Jushi are situated in the area of Yanze. There are cities with city walls in these states. Yanze is 1,750 kilometers away from Chang'an. The right wing of the Huns live in the area east of Yanze and the territory of the Huns extends to the Great Wall in Longxi (in Gansu Province). The south border of the Huns is in the area where the Qiang People lives (Gansu Province and Qinghai Province). So the road from the Han Dynasty to the Western Regions is blocked.

> The State of Wusun is situated northeast of the State of Dayuan about 700 kilometers away (between Lake Balkhash of Kazakhstan and the Tian Mountains in the western part of Xinjiang Uygur Autonomous Region, China). The people there are nomads. They migrate with their domesticated animals. They have the same customs and living habits as the Huns. There are tens of thousands of soldiers in this state. The soldiers are brave. In the past the people of the State of Wusun submitted to the Huns. Now that the State of Wusun has become

strong, the people do not submit to the Huns anymore. The King of the State of Wusun refused to go to the court of the Huns to have an interview with the King of the Huns.

The State of Kangju is northwest of Dayuan about 700 kilometers away (within Uzbekistan and Kazakhstan). The people of this state are nomads, with the same customs and living habits as the Yuezhi. There are eighty thousand or ninety thousand soldiers in this state. It is adjacent to Dayuan. This state is weak. The people of Kangju submit to the State of Yuezhi in the south and submit to the Huns in the east.

The State of Yancai (possibly related to the Alan people) is northwest of Kangju, about 700 kilometers away. The people of this state are nomads. They have the same living habits with the people of Kangju. There are more than a hundred thousand soldiers in this state. This state is adjacent to a lake so big that it seems to have no opposite bank. It is said that this is the North Sea (Caspian Sea).

The State of Greater Yuezhi is situated to the west of the State of Dayuan about 700 kilometers or 1050 kilometers away. The people of the State of Greater Yuezhi live on the north bank of the Gui River (Amu Darya, which flows through Tajikistan and Uzbekistan, then into the Aral Sea). The State of Daxia is to the south of it. The State of Anxi (Parthian Empire) is to the west. The State of Kangju is to the north. The people of the State of Greater Yuezhi are nomads who move with their domesticated animals; their customs and habits are the same as the Huns'. There are about a hundred thousand or two hundred thousand soldiers in this state. In the past, when the State of Yuezhi was strong, the people looked down upon the Huns. When Modu became King of the Huns, he led an attack on the State of Yuezhi and defeated it.

King Laoshang of the Huns killed the King of the State of Yuezhi and used his skull as a wine goblet. The people of the State of Yuezhi originally lived in the area of Dunhuang and Qilian Mountains (Gansu Province). After the State of Yuezhi was defeated by the Huns, most of the people moved far west, past the State of Dayuan. They attacked the State of Daxia and conquered it. Then the people of Yuezhi set their capital on the north bank of the Gui River and established the court of the King of the State of Greater Yuezhi. A small part of the people of the State of Yuezhi still stay in the area of the original State of Yuezhi; they have established the State of Lesser Yuezhi in the area south of the Qilian Mountains.

The State of Anxi (Parthian Empire) is situated to the west of Greater Yuezhi about 1500 kilometers away (it stretched from the Euphrates in central eastern Turkey to Eastern Iran). The people of this state live in fixed abodes. They till the land and grow rice and wheat. They make wine with grapes. The cities are as big as those in the State of Dayuan. There are several hundred cities in this state. The territory of this state stretches for about 1500 kilometers. It is the biggest state in the Western Regions. There are markets by the Gui River (Amu Darya). Carts and boats of the people and merchants move about for more than 1500 kilometers. They make silver coins. The figure of the face of the king is stamped on the coins. When the king dies, the coins will be changed. Then new coins will be made with the face of the new king on the new coins. They make horizontal marks on leather as a form of writings. The State of Tiaozhi is situated to the west of the State of Anxi. The State of Yancai and the State of Lixuan are north of the State of Anxi.

The State of Tiaozhi (Daqin) is west of the State of Anxi about 1050 kilometers away. This state is located by the West Sea (Caspian Sea). The weather is hot and wet. The people there till the land and grow rice. There are very big birds in this state. The eggs of these birds are as big as pots. There are many people in this state. There are lesser rulers. This state is under the rule of the State of Anxi and is regarded as an outlying state of the State of Anxi. The people of the State of Tiaozhi are good at performing magic tricks. The old people of the State of Anxi said that the Ruoshui River and Heavenly Queen Mother are in the State of Tiaozhi. But they have never seen them.

The State of Daxia is situated southwest of the State of Dayuan, on the south bank of Gui River (Amu Darya). The people live in fixed abodes. There are cities and houses in this state. The customs and living habits of the people of this state are the same with those of the people of the State of Dayuan, but they have no supreme ruler. There is a minor ruler in each city. The army is weak. The soldiers are afraid of fighting. The people of this state are good at commerce. When the people of the State of Yuezhi moved west, they defeated the State of Daxia and ruled over this state. This state is heavily populated; there are about a million people. The capital is Lanshi City. There is a market there in which all kinds of commodities are traded. The State of Shendu (India) is situated to their southeast.

Zhang Qian said, "When I was in the State of Daxia, I saw sticks made of bamboo produced in Qionglai of Shu and cloth produced in Shu. I asked the local people, 'Where did you get those things?'

The people of Daxia told me that their merchants bought them from Qiantuok, about 700 kilometers southeast of Daxia. The people live in fixed abodes. Their customs and living habits are the same with those of the people of Daxia. The weather is hot and humid there. The soldiers ride on elephants to fight. This state is situated by a big river. I think Daxia is about 4,200 kilometers away from the Han Dynasty, to the southwest. Shendu is about 1,500 kilometers southeast of Daxia, and products from Shu can be found there. So Shendu is not far from the Shu area. When our envoys go on a mission to the State of Daxia, if they take the route through the area of Qiang, the way is dangerous; the people of Qiang hate Han envoys. If the envoys take a northerly route, they will be caught by the Huns. I think it would be better for any envoys to go through the area of Shu. There are no enemies along this route."

From what Zhang Qian had said, Emperor Liu Che came to understand that Dayuan, Daxia and Anxi were big states, and there were many strange things, the people lived in fixed abodes and had the same customs and living habits as the Chinese people; the armies in these states were weak and the people liked the things produced in China. To the north of these states there were the State of Greater Yuezhi and the State of Kangju; the armies of these states were strong. Zhang Qian suggested that they could induce the kings of these states to send envoys to come to have an interview with Emperor Liu Che by promise of gain and get these states submit to the Han Dynasty by righteousness. Then the territory of the Han Dynasty could be expanded for more than 3,500 kilometers. Through translation from language to language they could understand more languages and cultures and learn different customs and living habits. Then the virtuousness and power of the Emperor might spread far and wide.

Emperor Liu Che agreed with Zhang Qian's idea. Then he dispatched Zhang Qian to Jianwei (now Yibin, Sichuan Province) to send out secret envoys from four different places: the first batch from Ran and Mang (now in northern Sichuan), the second batch from Xi (in the south central part of Sichuan), the third batch from Qiong (Qionglai, west-central Sichuan), and the fourth batch from Bo (now Aba, northwestern Sichuan Province). Each of them travelled for about 700 kilometers. But the envoys going northward were blocked by the tribes of the Di and Zuo peoples; the envoys going southward were blocked by the Xi and Kunming people. There was no ruler in the area of the Kunming. There were plenty of robbers and thieves. They robbed and killed the envoys of the Han Dynasty.

The envoys heading west learned that about 300 kilometers west of the Kunming territory there was a state where the people rode on the back of elephants. The name of this state was Dianyue (now in east-central Yunnan Province). Some merchants from the Shu area (now Sichuan Province) who secretly dealt in commodities had been to this state. So in order to find a way to the State of Daxia, the officials of the court of the Han Dynasty began to get in contact with the State of Dianyue. In the past, the court of the Han Dynasty had invested in major efforts to find a route through the southwest but failed. But when Zhang Qian said they could get to the State of Daxia by going through those area, they began again to work on the local tribes in the southwest.

76. Liu An, King of the State of Huainan, Secretly Plans to Rebel

Liu An, King of the State of Huainan (now north-central Anhui Province), liked to read books and play the zither. He did not like hunting or riding horses. He wanted to do good for the people so that his name would be known far and wide. Several thousand learned men of all fields came to serve him. Liu An compiled "Nei Shu (內書) (Inner Book)" which contained twenty-one articles, "Wai Shu (外書) (Outer Book)" which contained many articles, and "Zhong Pian (中篇) (Middle Volume)" which contained eight volumes about the technologies of alchemy. There were more than two hundred thousand Chinese words in Zhong Pian. At that time Emperor Liu Che liked arts and literature. He regarded Liu An as one of his uncles and respected him very much. When Emperor Liu Che granted Liu An any imperial edict, he himself drafted the edict first, then summoned Sima Xiang Ru, the great writer of the time, to go over the draft before it was sent out to Liu An.

Liu An went to the court to present his book "Nei Pian" to Emperor Liu Che. The Emperor was impressed and asked him to write "On Li Sao (離騷) (The Lament by Qu Yuan)". Liu An got the imperial edict in the morning and finished compiling the book by lunchtime and presented it to the Emperor. He also presented his writings "Song De (頌德) (Eulogy Virtues)" and "Chang'an Du Guo Song (長安都國頌) (Ode to Chang'an, the Capital)" to Emperor Liu Che. When the Emperor invited Liu An to a banquet or to have an interview, Liu An would talk freely about gains and losses, arts of necromancy, astrology and medicine. They would talk till very late.

When Liu An first went to the court, he became a good friend of Tian Fen, Marquis of Wu An, the Commander-in-chief of the Army. Once Tian Fen met Liu An in Bashang (east of Xi'an, Shaanxi Province). He said to Liu An, "His Majesty still has no Crown Prince. Your Highness is the grandson of Emperor Gaozu. You have practiced benevolence and righteousness. All the people of the realm know that. When His Majesty passes away, Your Highness will be the one who will succeed to the throne." Liu An was very glad to hear that. He gave a lot of gold to Tian Fen.

The officials in the State of Huainan and their guests often reminded him how his father Liu Chang had died, so as to stir up his hatred against the Emperor of the Han Dynasty. One day in 135 BC, the comet appeared. Liu An wondered what would happen. Someone told him, "In the past when the army of the State of Wu rose in rebellion, the comet appeared. It was only a meter long, but the blood of the soldiers flew for more than three hundred kilometers. Now the comet is as long as the whole sky; there will be much more bloodshed." Liu An thought about the fact that Emperor Liu Che had not appointed a Crown Prince. If anything unexpected happened, the kings of different states would rise up to compete for the throne. So he stepped up his preparations for war. He bribed the prefecture chiefs and other kings with gold and silver. Liu An's guests tried in every way to please him. Liu An was glad and gave them a lot of money.

Liu An had a daughter named Liu Ling, who was clever and could talk persuasively. He gave Liu Ling a big expense allowance and sent her to Chang'an to collect information and to associate with the people around Emperor Liu Che. In 127 BC, the Emperor granted a stick and a small table to Liu An and allowed him not to go to the capital to meet face-to-face. Tu, Liu An's queen, gave birth to a son named Liu Qian who was made Crown Prince of the State of Huainan. When Liu Qian grew up, he married Xiu Cheng Jun's daughter. Xiu Cheng Jun was the son of the daughter of Empress Dowager Wang. Since Liu An was preparing a rebellion, he was afraid that his son's concubine might hear about the conspiracy, so he planned with the Crown Prince. Then Crown Prince Liu Qian pretended that he did not like his concubine anymore and he did not sleep with her concubine for three months. Liu An pretended to be very angry with the Crown Prince and shut him up with his concubine in the same room. But the Crown Prince did not get close to her. Then the concubine begged to leave. Liu An wrote a letter to apologize to the girl's father and then sent her back home. Later Queen Tu, Crown Prince Liu Qian and Liu

Ling became so bold as to take the houses and land of the people by force. They arrested people at their own will.

Crown Prince Liu Qian practiced swordsmanship and he thought that he was the best man in using the sword. But he heard that Lei Pi, a palace guard, was very skillful. He summoned Lei Pi to have a match with him. Lei Pi politely declined several times but Liu Qian insisted. During the match, Lei Pi struck the Crown Prince with his sword. Lei Pi was very afraid. At that time, many people who wanted to join the army went to Chang'an, the capital of the Han Dynasty. Lei Pi wanted to join the army to fight against the Huns. Crown Prince Liu Qian spole ill of Lei Pi in front of Liu An, who ordered the commander of the palace guards to dismiss Lei Pi; this would be a warning to the other palace guards. In 124 BC, Lei Pi ran away to Chang'an. He presented a memorial to Emperor Liu Che to explain the matter. Emperor Liu Che ordered the Supreme Magistrate and the Chief of Henan Prefecture to investigate into the case.

The Chief of Henan Prefecture issued an order to arrest and to interrogate Liu Qian, the Crown Prince of the State of Huainan. Liu An, the King of the State of Huainan, and his queen would not send their son Liu Qian to be interrogated. Instead, they planned to rise up in rebellion. But they could not make the final decision. They hesitated for more than ten days. At that time Emperor Liu Che issued an imperial edict to interrogate the Crown Prince of the State of Huainan. The premier of the State of Huainan was angry with the chief of Shouchun County because he had withheld the order to arrest the Crown Prince and escort him to Chang'an to be interrogated. He accused him of disrespecting the Emperor. Liu An begged the premier not to accuse the chief of Shouchun County but the premier would not listen to him.

Then Liu An asked an official to present a memorial to Emperor Liu Che leveling accusations against the premier. Emperor Liu Che ordered the Supreme Magistrate to follow the case. Liu An was involved; he sent somebody to get information about the decisions of the investigating officials. The officials suggested to arrest Liu An and punish him. Liu An was afraid and wanted to rebel. Crown Prince Liu Qian said, "If the Emperor sends an envoy to arrest Your Highness, Your Highness may order some guards holding spears to stand by Your Highness. If the envoy has come to arrest Your Highness, the guards may immediately kill him. I will also send somebody to kill the Capital Garrison Commander of the State of Huainan. Then it would not be too late for us to rise in arms."

At that time Emperor Liu Che did not agree with the officials' suggestion to arrest Liu An and punish him. He only sent Hong, the Capital Garrison Commander, as his envoy to question Liu An. Liu An saw that the Capital Garrison Commander came with an amiable manner and he only inquired about the matter regarding Lei Pi. Liu An thought there was nothing serious afoot, so he did not take any action against the envoy.

The Capital Garrison Commander came back to the capital and reported everything to Emperor Liu Che. The officials who insisted on punishing Liu An said, "King Liu An of Huainan prohibited Lei Pi, who wanted to fight against the Huns, from coming to the capital. This is an act against the imperial edict issued by Your Majesty. He should be executed." Emperor Liu Che did not ratify their suggestion. Some officials suggested stripping Liu An of the title of king, but Emperor Liu Che did not ratify this suggestion either. The officials suggested taking five counties from the State of Huainan. Emperor Liu Che agreed to take two counties. Then he sent Hong, the Capital Garrison Commander to pardon Liu An of the crimes he had committed and only to punish him by taking away two counties.

Before the Capital Garrison Commander arrived, Liu An only heard that the officials had suggested putting him to death. He did not know that the Emperor would only take two away counties from the State of Huainan. So he was afraid that the envoy was coming to arrest him. After a discussion with the Crown Prince, he decided to carry out the plan. But when the Capital Garrison Commander reached the State of Huainan, he declared that Emperor Liu Che had pardoned Liu An of his crimes. So Liu An did not carry out his plan. But later he felt unhappy and said, "I have practiced benevolence and righteousness but the Emperor has taken two of my counties back. I feel ashamed." Then he stepped up his conspiracy of rebellion.

Liu An studied the maps with his officials Wu Pi and Zuo Wu and they planned their strategies. Liu An said, "Now the Emperor has not appointed any Crown Prince. When His Majesty dies, the officials will invite the King of the State of Jiaodong or the King of the State of Changshan. By that time all the kings will rise to compete for the throne of the Han Dynasty. So I must make preparations for that. I am a grandson of Emperor Gaozu. I have practiced benevolence and righteousness. For now His Majesty has treated me gently; I will wait. After His Majesty passes away, I will certainly not serve the new emperor!"

Liu Bu Hai was Liu An's eldest son, not the son of the queen but the son of a concubine. Liu An did not like him. The queen did not regard him as a son and the Crown Prince did not regard him as his elder brother. By now, Liu Bu Hai had a son of his own, Liu Jian, and he was a capable man. He saw that the Crown Prince did not regard his father as a brother, and he was offended. By that time the Emperor had issued his imperial edict to carry out the Order to Extend Favors, indicating that all the kings should distribute land to their sons and brothers. Liu An had two sons: one was the Crown Prince, who would succeed the whole State of Huainan, but his eldest son Liu Bu Hai did not have an inch of land.

Liu Jian secretly colluded with some officials and they planned to kill the Crown Prince and put his father Liu Bu Hai on the seat of the crown prince. The Crown Prince got word of this. He arrested Liu Jian and gave him a good beating. Liu Jian had been tipped off that the Crown Prince had planned to kill the Capital Guard Commander sent by Emperor Liu Che. So in 123 BC, Liu Jian asked his good friend Yan Zheng, an official in Shouchun (now Shouxian, in Anhui Province), to present a memorial to Emperor Liu Che which read, "Just as bitter medicine cures sickness, so unpalatable advice benefits conduct. Now Liu Jian, the grandson of the King of the State of Huainan, is a very capable man. Tu, the Queen of the King of the State Huainan, and her son Liu Qian, try to do harm to Liu Jian. Liu Jian's father Liu Bu Hai has not committed any crime. But they arrested him and intended to kill him. Now Liu Jian is still alive. Your Majesty may summon him and question him. Then Your Majesty may know all the conspiracies planned by the King of the State of Huainan." When Emperor Liu Che got the memorial, he ordered the Supreme Magistrate to investigate. Shen Qing was the grandson of Shen Yi Ji, Marquis of Piyang. He was a good friend of Premier Gongsun Hong. Shen Qing always remembered that his grandfather Shen Yi Ji had been murdered by Liu Chang, the former King of Huainan. So he secretly collected all the information about Liu An's secret plans, as the present King of the State of Huainan, and reported all this to Premier Gongsun Hong. From this information, Gongsun Hong deduced that Liu An had been planning to rebel. So he investigated that too. Imperial authorities arrested Liu Jian and interrogated him. From the information provided by Liu Jian, they learned that the Crown Prince of Huainan and his party were involved in the case of the rebellion.

Wu Pi was an official in the State of Huainan. The King of Huainan asked Wu Pi several times whether he should hold a rebellion, and

Wu Pi tried his best to talk him out of it. After Liu Jian was arrested, Liu An was afraid that his conspiracy would be revealed. He stil thought he should hold the rebellion. Then he asked Wu Pi again. This time Wu Pi advised him to go ahead; so Liu An stepped up his planning. He ordered the stone-craftsmen into the palace, and he had them carve the seal of an emperor, the seals for premiers, imperial counselors, generals, and court high ranking officials. He carried out the plan provided by Wu Pi. He let some officers to pretend to have offended him and head out westward to Wei Qing, the Grand General, and Premier Gongsun Hong of the Han Dynasty. When he rose in arms, they would kill Wei Qing and persuade Gongsun Hong to come to the side of the King of the State of Huainan. Liu An wanted to rebel but he was afraid that the premier and his other high ranking officials would not follow him in the rebellion. He discussed this with Wu Pi and made the following plan: a fire would break out in the palace of the King of the State of Huainan; when the premier and the high officials came to fight the fire, all of them would be killed. They also made the following plan: some officers would dress like soldiers catching thieves; they would come from the south with a letter asking for reinforcements, shouting, "The army of the State of Nanyue has come!" Then they would rise in arms.

But before they could make the final decision and launch these plans, the Supreme Magistrate had reported to Emperor Liu Che that Liu Qian, the Crown Prince of the State of Huainan, was involved in the plot to kill the Capital Guard Commander sent by the Emperor. Thus Emperor Liu Che sent the leader of the Supreme Magistrate to the State of Huainan to work with the Palace Guard Commander there to arrest Liu Qian, the Crown Prince. When Liu An heard that the head of the Supreme Magistrate had come, he conspired with the Crown Prince to kill the premier and the high ranking officials and then launch his rebellion. He summoned the premier and the premier came. The Minister of Personnel did not come, on the excuse that he had been out. The Palace Guard Commander said, "I have received an order from the Emperor. I am not allowed to see Your Highness." Liu An thought that if the Minister of Personnel and the Palace Guard Commander did not come, it would be useless to kill the premier. So he let the premier go.

Liu An and the Crown Prince were still hesitating. The Crown Prince thought that his crime was that he had planned to kill the Capital Garrison Commander of the Han Dynasty; now the persons with whom the Crown Prince had made the plan had all died, no one would reveal anything about that. He said to Liu An, "All the officials who can help Your Highness have been arrested. Now no one will help Your Highness to hold the rebellion. If Your Highness holds the rebellion at the wrong time, I am afraid Your Highness will fail. It would be better for me to go forward to let them arrest me." At that time, Liu An also wanted to stop his action and he agreed with the Crown Prince.

The Crown Prince attempted suicide but he did not die. Wu Pi went to the law office and confessed that he had made plotted the rebellion with the King of the State of Huainan. Then the officials arrested the Crown Prince and the Queen. The troops surrounded the palace of the King of the State of Huainan. All the guests of King of the State of Huainan were arrested. The officials in charge of the case found all the weapons and tools for rebellion. They reported all the proof of Liu An's rebellion to Emperor Liu Che. The Emperor ordered his high officials to investigate further; many marquises and high ranking officials of the State of Huainan turned out to have been involved, and they were executed.

Liu Ci, King of the State of Hengshan, was the younger brother of Liu An, King of the State of Huainan. He should have been arrested and punished for being related to Liu An. The officials pointed this out to the Emperor. Emperor Liu Che said, "The kings attend to the affairs of their own states. They should not be punished for being related to Liu An as brothers. This matter should be discussed by the kings and marquises." Liu Peng Zu, King of the State of Zhao, Liu Rang, a marquis, and other forty kings and marquises all said, "Liu An, King of the State of Huainan, has committed high treason. It is very clear that he has planned a rebellion. He should be executed." Liu Duan, King of the State of Jiaoxi, said, "Liu An has ignored the laws and acted perversely. He purposely stirred up trouble so as to send the whole realm into turmoil. He has induced the people to take part in his rebellion. He has betrayed the ancestors. He has spread rumors. It is written in the Spring and Autumn Annals, 'Don't lead the people in a rebellion. The one who leads a rebellion will be executed.' Liu An has committed a crime much more grave than the crime of leading the people in a rebellion. There is no doubt that Liu An has planned to carry out a rebellion. I have examined all the documents for his plan and the maps marking the route for his army to march. He should be executed. The officials of the State of Huainan and the members of the royal clan of the King of the State of Huainan and the close officials who have committed crimes should be punished according to the laws, and those who have not committed any crime should be removed from their posts because they have not done anything to correct Liu An's mistakes, and they should be sent to the army to serve as soldiers and not be allowed to be officials anymore. Those who are not officials should pay 1.5 kilograms of gold to atone for their crime. So that Liu An's crime is known by the people all over the realm, and the people will know the correct behavior for courtiers and no one will do any act of rebellion." Premier Gongsun Hong and Zhang Tang, the Supreme Magistrate, reported the result of the discussion to Emperor Liu Che. Emperor Liu Che sent the Supervisor of the Royal Clan to punish Liu An. But he committed suicide before the Supervisor arrived. The Queen, the Crown Prince of the State of Huainan and his followers were all arrested and executed. The State of Huainan was abolished and was turned into Jiujiang Prefecture.

77. WEI QING WINS STILL MORE VICTORIES OVER THE HUNS

In February 121 BC, Grand General Wei Qing commanded his army to march to the north from Dingxiang (now Heringer, in Inner Mongolia) to attack the Huns. Gongsun Ao, Marquis of Heqi, was the Middle General; Gongsun He, the Official in Charge of Emperor's Carriages and Horses, was the Left General; Zhao Xin, Marquis of Xi, was the Forward General, Su Jian, the Commander of the Palace Guards, was the Right General, Li Guang, the Chief of the Imperial Attendants, was the Rear General, Li Ju, the Minister of Personnel, was the General of Archers; all of them were under the command of Grand General Wei Qing.

The army under Wei Qing met the Huns and killed several thousand officers and soldiers. They returned triumphantly. A month later, they marched north from Dingxiang again. They killed more than ten thousand Hun officers and soldiers. The troops under Su Jian and the troops under Zhao Xin, three thousand cavalrymen in all, met with the main force of the Huns under the direct command of the King of the Huns. They fought against the strong enemy for a whole day. Most of the officers and soldiers of the Han army were killed. Zhao Xin was originally a Hun who had been caught by the Han army and surrendered and had been made Marquis of Xi. The King of the Huns sent an envoy who talked Zhao Xin into surrendering. He took eight hundred men and surrendered to the King of the Huns. Su Jian lost all his men and escaped alone.

He went back to see Grand General Wei Qing. Wei Qing pondered what to do with him, and he asked Zheng Hong, Adviser An, and

Zhou Ba, a staff officer what they thought. Zhou Ba said, "Since you became the commander of the army, you have never punished any general under you by execution. Now Su Jian lost all his troops. He should be executed so as to show your great power." Zheng Hong and An said, "No, we don't think so. It is written in the Art of War, 'Though an obstinate fight may be made by a small force, in the end it must be captured by a larger force.' Now Su Jian led several thousand troops to fight against an army of tens of thousands. They fought for a whole day. None of his soldiers thought of surrendering to the enemy. Now Su Jian has come back. If he is executed, it will be a warning to those devoted men and they will not come back again. So Su Jian should not be executed." Wei Qing said, "I have the luck to serve in the army with the help of my relative. I hold great power in my hands. Just now Zhou Ba advised me to show my power by executing Su Jian. His suggestion is against my will. Even if it is within my power to execute the general, I dare not execute the general outside the borders without authorization. I will take him back to the Emperor and let the Emperor make the decision. I do this because I want to give an example to the officials not to be autocratic." All the officers agreed with him. Then they arrested Su Jian and took him before Emperor Liu Che. The Emperor spared him. Su Jian atoned for his crime by paying a fine.

Zhang Qian also took part in this battle because he had been to the area of the Huns during his mission to the Western Region and had stayed in this area for more than ten years. He knew the geography of the area of the Huns very well. He helped the army to find water and food there, so the troops under Grand General Wei Qing marched forward smoothly and won a great victory. He had made great contributions in this battle. So Emperor Liu Che made Zhang Qian Marquis of Bowang.

78. Huo Qu Bing Establishes Great Contributions in the Fighting against the Huns

Huo Qu Bing was the son of Wei Shao Er, Grand General Wei Qing's elder sister. Huo Qu Bing's father was Huo Zhong Ru. As it happens, Huo Zhong Ru committed adultery with Wei Shao Er and she gave birth to Huo Qu Bing.

Soon after the birth of Huo Qu Bing, Wei Shao Er's younger sister Wei Zi Fu was selected by Emperor Liu Che as one of his concubines and she became distinguished. When Huo Qu Bing was eighteen years old, he became a personal guard of Emperor Liu Che. He was good at riding horses and shooting arrows. In 122 BC Grand General Wei

Qing was ordered to march north to engage the Huns. Huo Qu Bing served in the army commanded by Wei Qing. He was made Captain of Piaoyao. He left the main force behind and led just eight hundred brave cavalrymen forward for several hundred kilometers. They met the Huns and fought bravely and won a great victory. Emperor Liu Che said, "Huo Qu Bing, the Captain of Piaoyao, led his troops to fight with the Huns. They killed 2,028 officers and soldiers. They captured the premier and the high ranking officials of the Huns. They killed Chan, Marquis of Jiruo, who was the grandfather of the King of the Huns; they caught Luogu, who was the uncle of the King of the Huns. Huo Qu Bing has established the greatest contribution all over the whole army. He is the champion of the army. So I have decided to make Huo Qu Bing Marquis of Champions and grant him the tax of 2,500 peasant households. Also, Hao Xian, the Chief of Shanggu Prefecture, has followed Grand General Wei Qing to fight against the Huns four times. He commanded his troops to kill 1,300 Hun officers and soldiers. I have decided to make him Marquis of Zhongli."

Three years later, in spring of 120 BC, Emperor Liu Che made Huo Qu Bing General of Valiant Cavalrymen and ordered him to command ten thousand cavalrymen to go north from Longxi (Gansu Province) to carry out an expedition against the Huns. Huo Qu Bing led his troops past Wuli Mountain (now Maxian Mountain, in the southeast part of Gansu Province). They attacked the Supu Tribe of the Huns. Then they crossed Hunu River (now Shiyang River, in Gansu Province). They went past five kingdoms of the Huns. They did not take anything from the kingdoms which had submitted to the Han army. They nearly caught the son of the King of the Huns. They fought for six days. They went more than 300 kilometers past Yanzhi Mountain (southeast of Shandan, Gansu Province). They fought with the Huns by a mountain pass. They killed the king of the Shelan Tribe and the king of the Luhou Tribe. They killed and captured many Hun officers and soldiers. They captured the son of King Hunxie of the Huns and the premier and other ranking officers. They killed 8,960 Hun officers and soldiers. They captured a gold statue of a Buddha which was used by the Xiuchu Tribe of the Huns. In order to reward these great contributions made by Huo Qu Bing, Emperor Liu Che granted him the tax of 2,200 peasant households.

In summer 120 BC, Huo Qu Bing and Gongsun Ao, Marquis of Heqi, led their troops north from Beidi (now Qingyang, northeast Gansu Province) in two routes; Zhang Qian, Marquis of Bowang, and Li Guang, the Chief of the Imperial Attendants, led their troops to march north from You Beiping (now Lingyuan, Liaoning Province) also in two routes. Li Guang reached the appointed place first with 4,000 cavalrymen. Zhang Qian commanded 10,000 cavalrymen, and they came late. The King of the Left Wing of the Huns, at the command of tens of thousands of cavalrymen, surrounded Li Guang and his troops. Li Guang fought for two days. Half of his troops were killed; but they also killed more than 2,000 Hun officers and men.

When Zhang Qian and his troops came, the Huns left. Zhang Qian had committed the crime of delay. He should be executed. But he paid money to atone for his crime. Huo Qu Bing went out from Beidi and went deep into the territory of the Huns. Gongsun Ao lost his way and could not meet Huo Qu Bing. Huo Qu Bing and his troops walked across Junqi River (now Shandan River, Gansu Province). They crossed Juyan Lake (now Gaxun Nur, in the west part of Inner Mongolia) by boats. Then they marched into the territory of Lesser Yuezhi (Gansu Province) and attacked the Huns in Qilian Mountain. They fought in Lude (now Zhangye, Gansu Province) and won a resounding victory. They caught King Chanheng and King Qiutu of the Huns.

The premiers, generals and commanders of the Huns led 2,500 officers and soldiers to surrender to the Han army. In this battle the troops under Huo Qu Bing killed and captured 30,200 Hun officers and soldiers. They captured five minor kings of the Huns, the mothers of the kings, the wives of the kings and the sons of the kings, fifty-nine persons in all. They captured the premiers, generals and commanders of the Huns, sixty-three persons in all.

Huo Qu Bing Fights against the Huns

In order to reward Huo Qu Bing for his great contributions, Emperor Liu Che granted him the tax of 5,400 peasant households. Emperor Liu Che granted those officers who had followed Huo Qu Bing to the State of Lesser Yuezhi the title of the tenth rank. Zhao Po Nu, a high ranking officer under Huo Qu Bing, killed the King of the Supu Tribe of the Huns, and captured the King of Qiju Tribe of the Huns, King of the Hun Cavalry and his mother and his sons; he captured 3,330 Hun officers and soldiers. Emperor Liu Che made Zhao Po Nu Marquis of Congpiao. Gao Bu Shi, a high ranking commander under Huo Qu Bing, captured King Huyuqi of the Huns, his sons and other members of his family, eleven persons in all; he captured 1,768 Hun officers and soldiers. Emperor Liu Che made Gao Bu Shi Marquis of Yiguan. Gongsun Ao, Marquis of Heqi, did not meet the army under Huo Qu Bing. He was supposed to be executed according to the laws, but he bought his life Huo Qu Bing selected brave commanders and officers. He could go deep into the territory of the Huns. He often commanded the strong cavalrymen to march ahead of the main force to fight against the Huns. The troops under Huo Qu Bing were very lucky. They had never been in a desperate situation. The other generals often hesitated and delayed. Emperor Liu Che highly praised Huo Qu Bing., so Huo Qu Bing was as distinguished as Wei Qing.

Later Yizhixie, King of the Huns, was angry with King Hunxie, because King Hunxie who lived in the west part had been defeated by the Han under Huo Qu Bing several times and had lost tens of thousands of officers and soldiers. He intended to summon King Hunxie and kill him.

King Hunxie and King Xiuchu planned to surrender to the Han Dynasty. They sent an envoy to the border official of the Han Dynasty to announce their intention to surrender. At that time, Li Xi, an official of the border area who was commanding some troops to build a stronghold by the side of the Yellow River, got the information conveyed by the envoy. He immediately sent officers to ride horses quickly to the capital to report to Emperor Liu Che. Emperor Liu Che was afraid that King Hunxie and King Xiuchu would pretend to surrender and carry out a surprise attack on the border area. Then he ordered Huo Qu Bing to take his troops and meet the two kings of the Huns.

King Hunxie killed King Xiuchu along the way and took command of his troops. So the army under King Hunxie became an army of more than forty thousand men. Huo Qu Bing and his troops crossed the

Yellow River and faced King Hunxie. The minor kings and generals under King Hunxie saw the strong Han troops and many of them did not want to surrender. They ran away. Huo Qu Bing rode into the formation of the Hun army and met King Hunxie. They killed 8,000 Hun officers and soldiers who would not surrender. Then Huo Qu Bing ordered some officers and soldiers to escort King Hunxie to Chang'an, the capital of the Han Dynasty, to see Emperor Liu Che. Then tens of thousands of the Huns surrendered.

When King Hunxie was escorted to Chang'an and had an interview with Emperor Liu Che, Emperor Liu Che granted him a great fortune, and the tax of 8,000 peasant households, and made him Marquis of Tuoyin. Huduni, a minor king under King Hunxie, was made Marquis of Xiamo.

Emperor Liu Che highly praised Huo Qu Bing by saying, "Huo Qu Bing led his troops in an expedition against the Huns. King Hunxie in the Western Region and his troops and people all surrendered. They provided food for the Han army. Huo Qu Bing took command of the more than ten thousand men under King Hunxie. They killed 8,000 Hun officers and men who would not surrender. Thirty-two kings of different kingdoms surrendered. No one in Huo Qu Bing's army was killed or wounded. The whole army of a hundred thousand men returned triumphantly. There is peace in the areas of the Yellow River and the Great Wall due to their hard fight against the Huns. I hereby grant the tax of 1,700 peasant households to Huo Qu Bing."

Then Emperor Liu Che reduced by half of the number of troops defending Longxi Prefecture (Gansu Province), Beidi (now Qingyang) and Shang Prefecture (now Yulin, in Shaanxi Province) so as to reduce the burden of conscript labor on the people all over the realm. He let the Huns who had surrendered settle down in Longxi Prefecture, Beidi Prefecture, Shang Prefecture, Yunzhong Prefecture (now Togtoh, Inner Mongolia) and Shuofang Prefecture (now Hanggin Qi, Inner Mongolia). These prefectures were situated outside the Great Wall and on the southern bank of the Yellow River. Emperor Liu Che did not make any changes to the organization of the Huns and let them become vassal states of the Han Dynasty.

In 119 BC the Huns invaded You Beiping (now Lingyang, Liaoning Province) and Dingxiang (now Horinger, in Inner Mongolia). They killed more than 1,000 people there.

79. Wei Qing and Huo Qu Bing Fight the King of the Huns

After Zhao Xin surrendered to the Huns, the King of the Huns made him King of Zici and married his elder sister to him as his wife. He talked with Zhao Xin about how to deal with the Han Dynasty. Zhao Xin suggested retreating to the north of Gobi Desert (which lies betweenMongolia and China) and luring the Han army to pursue them. When the Han were exhausted, they would attack and defeat them. The King of the Huns accepted his suggestion.

In 119 BC, Emperor Liu Che held a discussion with the generals. He said, "Zhao Xin made a plan for the King of the Huns. He thinks that our army will not be able to cross the Desert and stay there north of the Desert. But I will send a great army to go across the Desert and attack the Huns. I am sure we shall win." That spring, Emperor Liu Che ordered Grand General Wei Qing and Huo Qu Bing, General of the Valiant Cavalrymen, each at the head of fifty thousand cavalrymen, to cross the Gobi Desert to fight the Huns. Tens of thousands of soldiers were sent to transport food and army provisions. All the officers and soldiers under Huo Qu Bing were brave men who dared to go deep into the area of the Huns.

At first Huo Qu Bing was to march north from Dingxiang (Horinger). One day the Han troops captured a Hun officer. He told them that the King of the Huns was in the east. Then Emperor Liu Che made a change and ordered Huo Qu Bing to march north from Dai Prefecture (now Yuxian, western Hebei Province). And he ordered Wei Qing to march north from Dingxiang.

Li Guang, the Chief of the Imperial Attendants, was the Vanguard General, Gongsun He, Official in Charge of Emperor's Carriages and Horses, was the Left General, Zhao Yi Ji was the Right General, Cao Xiang, Marquis of Pingyang, was the Rear General. They were all put under the command of Grand General Wei Qing. Zhao Xin said to the King of the Huns, "Now the Han army is ready to go across the great desert. The men and horses of the Han army will be very tired. We may wait and capture them." The Huns moved their provisions to the far north, and their best troops waited north of the Gobi Desert.

Wei Qing marched his troops out of the Great Wall and traveled about five hundred kilometers, and saw that the Huns had already been arranged in battle formation. He ordered his troops to arrange all the carts and chariots around the army to form a camp. He sent five thousand cavalrymen out to fight the Huns. The King of the Huns sent 10,000 Hun cavalrymen to go forward to join battle. By that time the sun was reaching the horizon. A strong wind rose. It blew up sands on the faces of the soldiers and they could not see their enemies. Wei Qing sent men to surround the King of the Huns by the right flank and the left flank. The King of the Huns saw that there were many Han troops and the Han army was very strong. It would be unfavorable for to fight with such strong Han troops. When night fell, the King of the Huns made a breakthrough and fled to the northwest with his six mules and several hundred cavalrymen. At night the Han troops were still fighting with the Huns. The two sides suffered equal casualties. A captured Hun officer told the Han officer that the King of the Huns had already gotten away as night fell. Then Wei Qing sent light cavalrymen to gallop after the King, and Wei Qing himself rode behind them.

The Huns dispersed and escaped. At dawn the Han troops had already ridden for a hundred kilometers but they could not catch up with the King of the Huns. But they had killed and captured more than 10,000 Hun officers and men. They reached the Fortress of Zhao Xin (built by the King of the Huns when Zhao Xin came back from the Han Dynasty) in Zhenyan Mountain (now the Hangayn Mountains, western Mongolia). They found the Hun army's great store of food supplies in the Fortress. The Han army stayed there for one day and then returned. Before they left, they burned all the Hun food supplies. In this battle, the troops under Wei Qing killed 19,000 Hun officers and men.

While Wei Qing was fighting with the King of the Huns, Li Guang, the Vanguard General, and Zhao Yi Ji, the Right General, were marching north along the east route, but they lost their way. After the battle against the King of the Huns, Wei Qing took his troops back south of the desert. Then they met Li Guang and Zhao Yi Ji. Wei Qing intended to send an envoy back to Chang'an to report this to Emperor Liu Che. He sent an officer to question Li Guang, who drew out his sword and killed himself. Zhao Yi Ji paid money to atone for his crime.

At that time, Yizhixie, the King of the Huns, was missing for more than ten days. King Luli of the Right Wing of the Huns made himself king of the Huns, but when Yizhixie got back to his men, King Luli gave up any pretensions to the title.

Meanwhile, the cavalrymen, the chariots and the equipment in Huo Qu Bing's army marched north from Dai Prefecture (now Yuxian, Hebei Province). They were equal to those in Wei Qing's army. Huo Qu Bing commanded the light cavalrymen to ride forward quickly. He let the troops transporting supplies and equipment go behind. They marched across the desert for 700 kilometers. They met with the

Hun troops under the King of the Left Wing of the Huns and fought a major battle. They captured many high ranking Hun officials. They killed King Beijuqi. Then they attacked the Hun army under the grand general of the Left Wing of the Huns and defeated them. They killed the grand general of the Left Wing of the Huns and captured all the army flags and drums.

Battles against the Huns North of the Gobi Desert

They went past Nanhou Hill (eastern Mongolia) and crossed the river. They caught King Tuntou and King Han of the Huns of the Left Wing; they captured the generals, premiers, high ranking officials and high ranking officers, eighty-three persons in all. They held a ceremony to offer sacrifices to Heaven on top of Langjuxu Mountain (now Hentiyn Mountain, east of Ulaan Baatar) and offered sacrifices to the Earth at the foot of Guyan Mountain (now Asaralt Hayrhan, north of Ulaan Baatar). The army under Huo Qu Bing reached Hanhai (now Lake Baikal, in southern Siberia). They captured 70,443 Hun officers and soldiers. The casualties of Huo Qu Bing's army were about 10,000 officers and soldiers. They got food from the enemy. So they marched for a long way but they still had sufficient food supplies.

When Huo Qu Bing returned to Chang'an triumphantly, Emperor Liu Che granted him the tax of 5,800 peasant households. Lu Bo De, the Chief of You Beiping Prefecture, was under the command of Huo Qu Bing. He joined forces with Huo Qu Bing's army on their way north at the appointed time. He followed Huo Qu Bing to Chouyu Mountain (a branch of Hentiyn Mountain, central Mongolia). He and the troops under him fought with the Huns there and killed and captured 2,800 Hun officers and soldiers. Emperor Liu Che made him Marquis of Pili. Wei Shan, a high ranking officer, followed Huo Qu Bing to fight with the Huns. He captured a king of the Huns. Emperor Liu Che made him Marquis of Yiyang. Fulizhi, a former minor king of the Huns who had surrendered to the Han Dynasty, and Yijijian, also a former minor king of the Huns who had surrendered to the Han Dynasty, followed Huo Qu Bing to the north to fight with the Huns; and he made major contributions to the realm. Emperor Liu Che made Fulizhi Marquis of Du, and made Yijijian Marquis of Zhongli.

Zhao Po Nu, Marquis of Congpiao, and An Ji, Marquis of Changwu, also followed Huo Qu Bing to the north and played a great role in fighting the Huns. Emperor Liu Che increased the tax of 300 peasant households to each of them. Jie, the Chief of Yuyang Prefecture (now Miyun, Beijing), and Gan, a high ranking officer, captured the flags and drums of the Huns' army. Emperor Liu Che granted them the title of marquis. He granted Jie the tax of 300 peasant households and Gan the tax of 200 peasant households. Many officers and soldiers under Huo Qu Bing were promoted and were granted rewards. Emperor Liu Che created the position of Grand Marshal. He made both Wei Qing and Huo Qu Bing Grand Marshals. And he ordered to let Huo Qu Bing enjoy the same emolument as that for Wei Qing.

But there were certainly losses, and not only of men. When the army under Wei Qing and the army under Huo Qu Bing marched out of the Great Wall, they had 140,000 horses. But when they came back, only 30,000 horses were left. This was a strategic loss that would have long-lasting consequences.

Now, Huo Qu Bing was a taciturn man. But he was courageous and had the confidence to fight. Emperor Liu Che wanted to teach him *The Art of War* by Sun Tzu. But he declined, saying to the Emperor Che, "The most important thing is the general plan formulated in accordance with the evolving situation. It is not necessary to learn the ancient art of war." Emperor Liu Che ordered a residence built for Huo Qu Bing. When it was ready, Emperor Liu Che asked him to have a look at the grand house. But Huo Qu Bing said, "The Huns have not yet been eliminated, why I should start a family?" From then on Emperor Liu Che liked Huo Qu Bing all the more.

Huo Qu Bing became very noble when he was young. He did not understand the hard life of the soldiers in his army and he did not sympathize with them. When Huo Qu Bing went out to fight with the Huns, the Emperor sent many cooks with tens of carriages to prepare food for Huo Qu Bing. When he came back with his army, there was still a lot of food and meat left in the carriages. But the soldiers were all very hungry for lack of food. When Huo Qu Bing's troops were outside the Great Wall, they were short of food and became very weak. But Huo Qu Bing still ordered his soldiers to build a playground to play Taju, a kind of football game.

By that time, about 90,000 Hun officers and men were killed by the Han troops. And tens of thousands of Han officers and soldiers were killed by the Huns. After these battles the Huns removed to a place far to the north of the desert. They did not maintain any court south of the desert. The Han army occupied the areas north of the Yellow River; 60,000 Han troops were garrisoned in the area from Shuofang (Inner Mongolia) west to Lingju (Gansu Province) to reclaim wasteland for cultivating grain.

This part of the territory of the Huns became the territory of the Han Dynasty. But since there were so few horses left in the Han army, they did not carry out military operations on a large scale against the Huns anymore.

80. THE DEATH OF HUO QU BING

Li Gan was Li Guang's son. He served in Huo Qu Bing's army as a high ranking officer. In the battle against the King of the Left Wing of the Huns, he fought bravely. He captured the flags and drums of the King of the Left Wing of the Huns and killed many Hun officers and soldiers. Emperor Liu Che granted him the title of ailing marquis and the tax of 200 peasant households. He appointed Li Gan as the Chief of the Imperial Attendants, the position Li Guang was once appointed by the Emperor.

Li Gan hated Grand General Wei Qing because his father Li Guang had committed suicide when Wei Qing sent him to be questioned for his failure to meet the main force. So Li Gan seized an opportunity and injured Wei Qing. But Wei Qing was generous; he had pity on Li Gan and did not reveal the fact that Li Gan had injured him. Not long later, Li Gan accompanied Emperor Liu Che to Ganquan Palace (in Chunhua, in the central west part of Shaanxi Province) to hunt animals. Huo Qu Bing hated Li Gan because Li Gan had injured his uncle Wei Qing. So during the hunt, Huo Qu Bing shot an arrow at Li Gan and killed him. At that time Huo Qu Bing enjoyed the favor of Emperor Liu Che. So Emperor Liu Che concealed the fact that Huo

Qu Bing had killed Li Gan and he told others that a deer had hit Li Gan and killed him.

Huo Qu Bing's father Huo Zhong Ru later married a woman and this woman gave birth to a boy, whom they named Huo Guang. So Huo Guang was Huo Qu Bing's younger brother. In 121 BC, Huo Qu Bing went past Hedong Prefecture (now Yuncheng, in the south part of Shanxi Province) on his way to attack the Huns. The chief of Hedong Prefecture met him in the outskirts of the city and escorted him to the guesthouse of Pingyang County (now Linfen City, in Shanxi Province). The chief of Hedong Prefecture sent an official to invite Huo Zhong Ru to come over, and he did come. When Huo Qu Bing met him, he knelt down and said, "I am so sorry because I did not know sooner that I am your son." Huo Zhong Ru helped him up and said, "It is Heaven's will that I can have you as my son." Huo Qu Bing bought a large amount of land and many houses for Huo Zhong Ru. Then he continued on his way to fight against the Huns. When he came back, he went past Hedong Prefecture again. Then he brought his younger brother Huo Guang to Chang'an, the capital of the Han Dynasty. At that time Huo Guang was a teenager. He was appointed as an Imperial Attendant.

In September 117 BC, Huo Qu Bing died at the age of twenty-four. Emperor Liu Che mourned for him. He ordered the troops of the vassal states, all wearing black armor, to line up along the way from Chang'an to the Maoling, the mausoleum of Emperor Wu of Han (in Xingping, 40 kilometers west of Xi'an, in the south part of Shaanxi Province) to escort Huo Qu Bing's coffin to his tomb. The tomb was built like Qilian Mountain. Emperor Liu Che granted Huo Qu Bing the posthumous title of Marquis of Jinghuan (Jing 景 means "great military achievements"; Huan 桓 means "expanding the territory").

81. Zhang Qian's Second Mission to the Western Region

The Silk Road trade routes through Central Asia were expanded significantly due to Zhang Qian's experiences and the intelligence he brought back led. Emperor Liu Che asked Zhang Qian about Daxia and other states in the Western Region. At that time Zhang Qian had lost his title of marquis because in the battle against the Huns in summer 120 BC, he had arrived late at the battlefield. He said to Emperor Liu Che, "When I was detained in the area of the Huns, I heard that the name of the King of the State of Wusun was Liejiaomi. His father was Nandoumi. The State of Wusun and the State of Greater Yuezhi were originally in the area between Qilian Mountain and Dunhuang. The

State of Wusun was a small state. The State of Greater Yuezhi attacked the State of Wusun and killed Nandoumi. The State of Greater Yuezhi occupied the territory of the State of Wusun. The people of Wusun ran away to the area of the Huns. At that time, Liejiaomi was a newborn baby. Bujiu, the high ranking officer taking care of Liejiaomi, carried him to the wilderness and laid him in the grass. Then he went away to look for food. When he came back, he saw that a female wolf was feeding the baby with its milk, and birds with meat in their bills were flying around him. Bujiu thought that the baby must be a god. So he carried the baby to the Huns. The King of the Huns liked the baby and brought him up. When Liejiaomi grew up, the King of the Huns let him be the head of the people of the former State of Wusun and let him command troops. He performed well.

The Tomb of Huo Qu Bing

"At that time, the State of Yuezhi had been defeated by the Huns. The people of the State of Yuezhi went west and attacked the State of Se. The King of the State of Se went far west. Then the people of the State of Yuezhi settled down in the territory of the State of Se. Since Liejiaomi had become strong, he asked the King of the Huns to let him avenge his father's death. The King of the Huns gave his consent. Then Liejiaomi commanded his army to march west and defeated the State of Greater Yuezhi. The people of the State of Greater Yuezhi went west and took the territory of Daxia and settled down there. Since Liejiaomi had defeated the State of Greater Yuezhi, he occupied their territory and settled down there. His army became strong.

"By that time, the King of the Huns died. Then Liejiaomi would not submit to the Huns. The Huns sent troops to attack Liejiaomi but they were beaten back. This confirmed the Huns' idea that Liejiaomi was a god and they kept away from him.

"Now the King of the Huns has been defeated by our Han army and there are no people living in the original territory of the State of Wusun. The people of the minority nationality tribes miss their old homes. They like the goods of the Han Dynasty. We may present a lot of goods to Liejiaomi and ask him to lead his people to come east to their original home place. A princess of the Han Dynasty could be married to Liejiaomi as his wife. Then Liejiaomi will become a brother of Your Majesty and he will obey the orders of Your Majesty. In this way we may cut off the right army of the Huns. If the State of Wusun is united with the Han Dynasty, the State of Daxia and the other states to the west of the State of Wusun will submit to Your Majesty." Emperor Liu Che agreed. He made Zhang Qing General of the Palace Guards and sent him on a mission to the Western Region. Zhang Qian commanded 300 men, each man with two horses. They drove more than ten thousand cows and sheep to go with them. They brought cartloads of gold and silk with them. Many of the men carried the imperial staff with yak's tail, the symbols for the diplomatic envoys. Zhang Qian sent these deputy envoys to other states.

When Zhang Qian reached the State of Wusun, Liejiaomi, King of the State of Wusun, held a ceremony to pay formal respect to Zhang Qian. The ceremony was similar to that for meeting the King of the Huns. This made Zhang Qian uneasy. He knew that the heads of the minority nationality tribes were greedy. So he said, "Now the Emperor has granted you treasures. If you do not bow to express your respect to our Emperor, I will take the treasures back." Liejiaomi stood up and made a bow to express his thanks to the Emperor of the Han

Dynasty. Then Zhang Qian conveyed the intention of Emperor Liu Che by saying, "If the people of the State of Wusun move east to settle down in the place where King Hunxie of the Huns formerly dwelt, the Emperor of the Han Dynasty will marry a princess to you."

At that time the State of Wusun had been split. Liejiaomi was already old. The Han Dynasty was very far away from the State of Wusun. Liejiaomi did not know how big the Han Dynasty was. He had been subjugated to the Huns for a long time. The State of Wusun was near the territory of the Huns. All the high ranking officials were afraid of the Huns. They did not want to move. Liejiaomi could not make the decision on his own. So Zhang Qian could not get a decisive reply from hin.

Liejiaomi had more than ten sons. One of them was called Dalu. Dalu was a powerful man and good at commanding troops. He led ten thousand cavalrymen to live in another place. Dalu's elder brother was the crown prince; he had a son named Junxumi. The crown prince had died early, but before he died, he had made his father promise to make Junxumi the crown prince. Dalu was very angry at being passed over. He colluded with his younger brothers to revolt. They planned to attack Junxumi and Liejiaomi. Liejiaomi was already old and he was afraid that Dalu would kill Junxumi. So he gave Junxumi ten thousand cavalrymen and let him live in another place. Liejiaomi himself had ten thousand cavalrymen. So the State of Wusun was divided in three parts. But as a whole, the State of Wusun was under the rule of Liejiaomi.

But Liejiaomi did not dare to give an affirmative answer to Zhang Qian. Then Zhang Qian sent his deputy envoys to the State of Dayuan (in the Ferghana Valley in Central Asia), the State of Kangju (now Uzbekistan and Tajikistan), the State of Greater Yuezhi (in Afghanistan), and Daxia (Bactri). The King of Wusun sent guides and interpreters to escort Zhang Qian and his team back to the Han Dynasty. At the same time Liejiaomi sent dozens of envoys of the State of Wusun to go with Zhang Qian. They brought dozens of horses as gifts for the Emperor of the Han Dynasty. They would go to the Han Dynasty to have a look, so as to know how big the Han Dynasty was.

82. EMPEROR LIU CHE AND THE NECROMANCERS

In December 119 BC Shao Weng, a necromancer from the State of Qi (Shandong Province), went to see Emperor Liu Che. At that time Lady Wang, a favorite concubine of Emperor Liu Che, had died. Shao Weng performed necromancy at night to present the figure of Lady

Wang. Emperor Liu Che could see the figure from the curtains. For this, he made Shao Weng General Wencheng and granted him many rich gifts. He treated Shao Weng as a distinguished guest. Shao Weng said, "Your Majesty wants to communicate with the gods. But the houses in the palace and the decorations are not for the gods. So the gods will not come." Then Shao Weng drew a chariot moving in the clouds, and asked Emperor Liu Che to take chariots of different colors on different days so as to avoid meeting devils.

Pushing it further, he suggested the Emperor build Ganquan Palace. In the middle of Ganquan Palace there was a platform with houses on it. Heaven, Earth, gods and devils were drawn on these houses. Sacrifices were kept in these houses to offer to the gods so as to invite the gods from Heaven. But more than a year had passed, and no god came. His method of inviting the gods to come was not effective. Then Shao Weng secretly wrote something on a piece of silk and forced a cow to swallow it. He told Emperor Liu Che that there was something strange in the abdomen of the cow. The cow was killed and the piece of silk was found in the stomach of the cow. The words on the silk were very strange. But Emperor Liu Che recognized Shao Weng's handwriting. He interrogated him, and he admitted that it was his handwriting. Emperor Liu Che gave orders to have him executed secretly.

In spring 113 BC Ding Yi, Marquis of Lecheng, presented a memorial to Emperor Liu Che to recommend Luan Da, a necromancer. Luan Da was working in the palace of King of the State of Jiaodong. He learned necromancy from the same teacher as Shao Weng. At that time Emperor Liu Che regretted having Shao Weng executed, and he was glad when Luan Da arrived. Luan Da was a tall, handsome man. He often talked about strategy. He boasted, "I often travel across the sea. I have met with spiritual beings such as An Qi and Xian Men. They thought that I was low and degrading. So they did not have confidence in me. And they thought that King of the State of Jiaodong was only a local king and they would not present the method of alchemy to him. My teacher once said, 'Gold can be obtain by tempering with fire; the dike of the Yellow River breached by floods may be repaired; the medicine of immortality can be obtained; and the gods will come.' But I am afraid that I will meet the same fate as that of Shao Weng. I dare not talk about the method of alchemy." Emperor Liu Che said, "Shao Weng died because he had eaten the liver of a horse. If you can present the method of alchemy, I will give you anything you want." Luan Da said, "My teachers do not ask for anything from people. It is the people who are asking help from my teachers. If Your Majesty really wants to invite them here, Your Majesty should make your envoy distinguished and treat him politely. Your Majesty should take him as a relative. Then Your Majesty may send him on a mission to invite the spiritual beings." Then Emperor Liu Che asked Luan Da to demonstrate his methods. He put chessmen on a chessboard. Then the chessmen bumped into each other by themselves.

At that time Emperor Liu Che was worried because the dike of the Yellow River had indeed been burst by the floods. And he was also worried about obtaining gold. So he made Luan Da General of Wuli (Wuli, Chinese: 五利，meaning "five benefits"). A month later, Emperor Liu Che granted him three more general seals: General of Tianshi (Tianshi, Chinese: 天士, meaning "Heavenly Scholar"), General of Dishi (Dishi, Chinese: 地士, meaning "Earthly Scholar"), and General of Datong (Datong, Chinese: 大通, meaning "Grand Communicator"). In April 113 BC Emperor Liu Che made Luan Da Marquis of Letong and granted him the tax of 2,000 peasant households. He granted Luan Da grand houses and more than one thousand servants. Emperor Liu Che married his eldest daughter Princess Wei Zhang to Luan Da as his wife. Emperor Liu Che ordered a workman to carve the seal of General of Tiandao (Tiandao, Chinese: 天導, meaning "Heavenly Guide"). Then he sent an envoy wearing clothes made of feathers standing on a cogon at night to present the seal of General of Tiandao to Luan Da, who also wore clothes made of feathers and stood on a cogon to accept the seal. Emperor Liu Che granted Luan Da the seal of General of Heavenly Guide because he hoped that Luan Da would guide him to meet spiritual beings. Luan Da became the most distinguished man in the Han Dynasty.

In autumn 112, BC Luan Da was ready to start his journey. He travelled to the east and declared that he was going to the sea to visit his teachers. But when he reached the shore, he did not dare to go into the water. Then he went up Mount Tai to pay respect to Heaven. Emperor Liu Che had sent a man to follow him secretly to make sure he really dared to go into the sea. He came back and reported that Luan Da had not gone into the sea into the sea at all and had not met with anyone at all. But when Luan Da went back to Chang'an, the capital of the Han Dynasty, he told the Emperor that he had gone into the sea and had met his teachers. Luan Da was exposed as a liar. Luan Da presented methods of alchemy but none of them were effective. He was executed.

83. THE FIGHTING STOPS IN THE STATE OF NANYUE

Zhao Tuo was a high ranking officer of the Qin Dynasty (Qin Dynasty: 221 BC–207 BC). The Qin Dynasty unified China. It stopped the fighting in the southern areas of Yangyue (south of the Yangtze River). The Emperor of the Qin Dynasty established Guilin Prefecture (northern Guangxi Zhuang Autonomous Region), Nanhai Prefecture Guangdong Province) and Xiang Prefecture (southern Guangxi Zhuang and the north part of Vietnam). Many people in Central China were moved to live in these three prefectures. They lived together with the original people of the area of Yue for thirteen years.

Zhao Tuo was the County Magistrate of Longchuan County (Guangdong Province). During the reign of the Second Emperor of the Qin Dynasty, Ren Xiao, the Commander of Nanhai Prefecture, fell ill and was going to die. He summoned Zhao Tuo, the County Magistrate of Longchuan County, to Panyu (now Guangzhou), the capital city of Nanhai Prefecture, and said to him, "I hear that Chen Sheng and Wu Guang have rebelled. The rule of the Qin Dynasty is very cruel. The people of the whole realm are suffering. Now Xiang Yu, Liu Bang, Chen Sheng and Wu Guang are fighting with one another for the ruling power. China is in great chaos. Nanhai Prefecture is a remote place. I am afraid that the rebel army will come here. I want to send troops to cut the routes from which outside armies could come. We will make good preparations and wait for the situation to change. The city of Panyu is protected by a mountain in the north and by the sea in the south. This area is about 1,500 kilometers wide from the east to the west. A state may be established in this area. I cannot entrust the task to any of the officials in the prefecture. I will let you be responsible for this." Then he appointed Zhao Tuo as Commander of the Army in Hainan Prefecture.

After Ren Xiao died, Zhao Tuo sent orders to the officers defending Hengpu Pass, Yangshan Pass and Niehuo Pass to block any armies coming from the north. Then he executed all the high-ranking officials sent by the government of the Qin Dynasty and appointed officials of his party to the positions. When the Qin Dynasty had fallen, Zhao Tuo commanded his troops to attack Guilin Prefecture and Xiang Prefecture. He annexed these two prefectures. Then he declared himself King Wu of the State of Nanyue. When Liu Bang, Emperor Gaozu of the Han Dynasty, had pacified the whole realm, he did not attack the State of Nanyue because he thought that the people of Central China were worn out from fighting. In 195 BC Liu Bang sent Lu Jia as his envoy to make Zhao Tuo King of the State of Nanyue. Lu

Jia presented the seal of King of the State of Nanyue to Zhao Tuo and from then on the Han Dynasty and the State of Nanyue sent envoys to visit each other. The local tribes in the areas of Yue were in blissful peace. The State of Nanyue bordered the State of Changsha (now in Hunan Province).

During the reign of Empress Dowager Lü Zhi, the officials of the Han Dynasty suggested that she prohibit trading tools made of iron to the State of Nanyue. Zhao Tuo said, "Emperor Gaozu made me King of the State of Nanyue. The Han Dynasty and the State of Nanyue send envoys to visit each other and have trade relations. Now Empress Dowager has listened to false accusationand has banned the trade of tools. I think this suggestion must have come from the King of the State of Changsha. He will depend on the strength of the Han Dynasty to defeat the State of Nanyue and annex our state." Then Zhao Tuo declared himself Emperor Wu of the State of Nanyue. He sent troops to attack the border area of the State of Changsha. The troops of the State of Nanyue took several border counties of the State of Changsha, and then they retreated. Empress Dowager Lü Zhi sent Zhou Zao, Marquis of Linlü, to lead a great army to attack the State of Nanyue. At that time the weather was hot and humid. Many soldiers and officers fell ill. The troops could not get past the mountains in the north of Guangdong Province. A year later, Empress Dowager Lü Zhi died; then the troops of the Han Dynasty retreated. So Zhao Tuo sent troops to threaten the border areas of the Han Dynasty. He sent treasures to bribe the State of Minyue (now in Fujian Province), the State of Xi'ou and the State of Luo (both in Guangxi Zhuang Autonomous Region). These states submitted to the State of Nanyue. So the State of Nanyue became a big state with 5,000 kilometers from the east to the west. He adopted all the protocols of an emperor. His carriage had a big yellow umbrella as a cover of his carriage, with a big flag on the left side, like that of the emperor. He issued imperial orders as an emperor would do.

In 180 BC Liu Heng ascended the throne of the Han Dynasty. He sent envoys to the minority nationality tribes in the east, the west, the north and the south, telling them that he had come from the State of Dai to ascend the throne of the Han Dynasty and he would show kindness to the people of all the local tribes. He issued orders to build tombs for Zhao Tuo's father and mother in Zhending (southwestern Hebei Province). He sent peasant households to attend to the tombs of Zhao Tuo's father and mother. Ceremonies of offering sacrifices to Zhao Tuo's father and mother were held every year. He summoned

Zhao Tuo's cousins to Chang'an and appointed them to high ranking positions. He issued an imperial order to Premier Chen Ping to choose officials who could be sent to the State of Nanyue as his envoys. Premier Chen Ping told Emperor Liu Heng that Lu Jia had been sent to the State of Nanyue during the reign of Emperor Gaozu. Then Emperor Liu Heng summoned Lu Jia and made him a high ranking official, and he sent him on a mission to the State of Nanyue.

When Zhao Tuo ascended the throne of the Emperor of the State of Nanyue, he did not send any envoys to the Han Dynasty to report this. When Lu Jia reached the State of Nanyue, Zhao Tuo was very afraid. He wrote a letter to express his apology which read, "I, Zhao Tuo, am an old man of the minority nationality tribe in the south. During the reign of Empress Dowager Lü Zhi, the officials of the Han Dynasty tried their best to isolate the State of Nanyue. I suspected that King of the State of Changsha had put up some false accusation against me. And I heard that Empress Dowager Lü Zhi had all my clansmen killed. The tombs of my parents were destroyed and burned. I was so angry that I attacked the border of the State of Changsha. The weather in the south is hot and wet. Many heads of the minority nationality tribes declared themselves kings. The heads of the State of Xi'ou and the State of Luo also declared themselves kings. So I declared myself Emperor of the State of Nanyue so as to make myself happy. I did not dare to tell this to the Emperor of the Han Dynasty." Then he bowed to express his apology for his offence and said that he was willing to make the State of Nanyue a vassal state of the Han Dynasty. He offered to pay tribute to the Emperor of the Han Dynasty every year. Then he issued an order which read, "I hear that two heroes cannot be made Emperors at the same time. Now the Emperor of the Han Dynasty is a kind and capable Emperor. From here on, I will give up the title of emperor and all the ceremonies, carriage and flags of an emperor." Lu Jia came back to Chang'an and reported all this to Emperor Liu Heng. The Emperor was very pleased. During the reign of Emperor Liu Qi, Zhao Tuo declared himself a vassal to Emperor Liu Qi and followed appropriate conduct. He sent envoys to pay respect to the Emperor. But within the State of Nanyue, Zhao Tuo still kept the title of emperor. In 137 BC Zhao Tuo died at the age of one hundred.

Zhao Hu, Zhao Tuo's grandson, became King of the State of Nanyue. At that time Zou Ying, King of the State of Minyue (in Fujiang Province), raised a great army to attack the border area of the State of Nanyue. Zhao Hu sent an envoy to present a memorial to Emperor Liu Che of the Han Dynasty which read, "The State of Nanyue and the State of Minyue are both vassal states of the Han Dynasty. The two states should not attack each other. Now the State of Minyue has raised a great army to invade my state. I dare not raise an army to fight with the State of Minyue. I hope Your Majesty will issue an imperial order to stop the State of Minyue's invasion." Emperor Liu Che thought that the King of Nanyue was righteous and had kept his promise. Then he raised a great army and appointed two generals to lead the army against the State of Minyue. Before the Han army entered the area, Zou Yu Shan, Zou Ying's younger brother, killed Zou Ying, the King of the State of Minyue, and surrendered to the Han army. Then the Han army turned back.

Emperor Liu Che sent Zhuang Zhu to tell the King of the State of Nanyue that he had sent an army against the State of Minyue. The King of Nanyue knelt down and touched his head to the ground and said, "I will do my best to repay the kindness of His Majesty shown on me." He sent Zhao Ying Qi, the Crown Prince, to Chang'an as a guard of the Emperor. The King of the State of Nanyue said to Zhuang Zhu, "My state recently was attacked by the State of Minyue. After you go back, I will prepare to go to Chang'an to have an interview with His Majesty." After Zhuang Zhu had left, his officials remonstrated with him, saying, "The Han Dynasty has raised a great army against the State of Minyue. This action also serves as a warning to the State of Nanyue. The late King had said that the most important thing in serving the Emperor was not to commit any act of impoliteness to the Emperor. You should not listen to the nice words of the envoy and go to see the Emperor. If you go, you will not be able to come back. Then the State of Nanyue will surely fall." Zhao Hu was persuaded not go to Chang'an to meet with Emperor Liu Che, on the excuse that he had fallen ill. More than ten years later Zhao Hu really fell seriously ill. His son Zhao Ying Qi asked permission from Emperor Liu Che to go back to the State of Nanyue. Soon after, Zhao Hu died. He was given the posthumous title of King of Wen (Wen means culture).

Then Zhao Ying Qi became King of the State of Nanyue. He hid the emperor's seal of his great grandfather Zhao Tuo. When Zhao Ying Qi was serving as a guard of the emperor, he had married a girl of the family by the name of Jiu. She gave birth to a son named Zhao Xing. When Zhao Ying Qi became King of the State of Nanyue, he presented a memorial to ask permission from Emperor Liu Che to make Lady Jiu Queen and his son Zhao Xing the Crown Prince of the State of Nanyue. Emperor Liu Che sent envoys to the State of Nanyue to ask Zhao Ying Qi to go to Chang'an to have an interview with him.

Zhao Ying Qi often killed people at his own will. He was afraid that he would be punished by the Emperor according to the laws of the Han Dynasty. So he said that he was ill and refused to go. He sent his son Zhao Ci Gong to be a guard of the Emperor. Not long later Zhao Ying Qi died. He was given the posthumous title of King of Ming (Ming means brilliant).

Then Zhao Xing became King of the State of Nanyue. His mother became Queen Mother. Before Lady Jiu became the concubine of Zhao Ying Qi, she had committed adultery with a man named Anguo Shao Ji. After Zhao Ying Qi died, in 113 BC, Emperor Liu Che sent Anguo Shao Ji to urge Zhao Xing and his mother to Chang'an to have an interview with him like kings of the other vassal states. He ordered Lu Bo De, the Commander of the Imperial Guards, to station an army in Guiyang (Hunan Province) to wait for Anguo Shao Ji to return from the State of Nanyue.

At that time, King Zhao Xing of Nanyue was still young. His mother was from Central China. When Anguo Shao Ji came to the State of Nanyue as an envoy of the Han Dynasty, Lady Jiu committed adultery with him again. Many officials of the State of Nanyue knew about this. They did not submit to the Queen Mother. The Queen Mother was afraid that they would hold a rebellion. She wanted to be able to count on the power of the Han Dynasty to back her u. So she persuaded her son and the officials to become vassals of the Emperor of the Han Dynasty. Then they asked the envoy of the Han Dynasty to take a letter to Emperor Liu Che to the effect that the King of the State of Nanyue wanted to be regarded as a vassal like the other kings of the vassal states. They said that he would go to the court of the Han Dynasty to have an interview with the Emperor every three years; and he would withdraw all the troops in the passes of the border areas. The Emperor ratified all the suggestions made by the King of the State of Nanyue. He granted a silver seal to Lü Jia, the Premier of the State of Nanyue. He also granted seals to the Minister of Personnel, the Commander of the Palace Guards and the Grand Tutor of the State of Nanyue. He abolished the punishments of making marks on the faces of criminals and cutting off their noses in the State of Nanyue. The laws of the Han Dynasty were applied in the State of Nanyue. The envoys of the Han Dynasty stayed there to help to stabilize the State of Nanyue. Then King Zhao Xing and his mother prepared to go to Chang'an to have an interview with Emperor Liu Che.

Premier Lü Jia was already old. He had been premier for three kings of the State of Nanyue. More than seventy persons of his clan served as high ranking officials of the State of Nanyue. Many men of his clan had married the daughters of the kings of the State of Nanyue, and the daughters of his clan were married to the men of the royal family. He held great power in the State of Nanyue. The people trusted him. The King of the State of Nanyue wanted to present memorials to Emperor Liu Che, but Lü Jia tried his best to persuade the King of Nanyue not to do it. But the King of the State of Nanyue would not listen to him. Then Lü Jia began to plan a rebellion. He would not meet the envoys sent by the Emperor of the Han Dynasty on the excuse that he was ill.

The envoys of the Han Dynasty kept an eye on Lü Jia. At that time the King of the State of Nanyue was not strong enough to get rid of Lü Jia. He and his mother were afraid that Lü Jia would hold a rebellion first. Then the King of the State of Nanyue prepared some wine and invited the envoys of the Han Dynasty to the palace of the State of Nanyue. He intended to kill Lü Jia while the envoys of the Han Dynasty were present. The envoys sat on the west side facing east; the Queen Mother sat on the north facing south; the King of the State of Nanyue sat on the south facing north; Lü Jia and other officials sat on the east facing west. Lü Jia's younger brother was a general commanding some troops to guard outside the palace. When they began to drink wine, the Queen Mother said to Lü Jia, "It is favorable for the State of Nanyue to be a vassal state of the Han Dynasty. But why have you always opposed this decision?" She said this so as to arouse the anger of the envoys of the Han Dynasty against Lü Jia. The envoys did not understand what the Queen Mother had said and they did not take any action against Lü Jia. Lü Jia saw that the situation was unfavorable for him. So he stood up and went out of the hall. The Queen Mother was very angry and wanted to kill him with a spear. The King of the State of Nanyue stopped his mother from doing any harm to Lü Jia. When Lü Jia had gone out of the hall, he let his younger brother and the soldiers to go home. From then on he refused to meet the King of the State of Nanyue and the envoys of the Han Dynasty on the excuse that he was ill. He secretly colluded with the officials and planned to hold a rebellion.

But the King of the State of Nanyue did not have any intention to kill Lü Jia, and Lü Jia knew this. So for several months he did not carry out his rebellion. The Queen Mother had committed adultery. The people of the State of Nanyue would not submit to her. She wanted to kill Lü Jia and the other officials, but she was not powerful enough to do that.

Emperor Liu Che learned that Lü Jia would not submit to the King of the State of Nanyue and that the King and the Queen Mother could not control Lü Jia; and the envoys of the Han Dynasty were timid and could not control the situation. His thinking was that the King of the State of Nanyue and the Queen Mother had submitted to the Han Dynasty; only Lü Jia wanted to hold a rebellion. There was no need for him to raise an army against the State of Nanyue. He intended to simply send Zhuang Can with two thousand men to carry out a mission to the State of Nanyue.

Zhuang Can objected, saying, "If I go as a friendly envoy, several persons would be enough to go with me. If I go to fight, two thousand men are not enough." Zhuang Can would not go. Emperor Liu Che dismissed him. Han Qian Qiu, the former premier of King of the State of Jibei (Shandong Province), said to Emperor Liu Che, "The State of Nanyue is only a vassal state. The King and the Queen Mother will collaborate from within the State of Nanyue. Only Premier Lü Jia would not submit to us. If Your Majesty let me lead two hundred warriors to Nanyue, I will surely kill Lü Jia." So Emperor Liu Che sent Han Qian Qiu and Jiu Le, the younger brother of the Queen Mother, with two thousand troops to the State of Nanyue. When they entered the territory, Lü Jia and the other officials launched their rebellion. Lü Jia issued a statement in the State of Nanyue which read, "The King is still young. The Queen Mother is from Central China. She has committed adultery with the envoy of the Han Dynasty. She intends to make the State of Nanyue submit to the Han Dynasty. She plans to give all the treasures of the State of Nanyue to the Emperor of the Han Dynasty to curry favor with the Emperor. She will take many followers to Chang'an and then sell all her followers and make them servants. She intends to profit by sacrificing the interest of the royal clan of Zhao. She does not care about the interests of the State of Nanyue." Then Lü Jia and his younger brother commanded their troops to attack the palace and they killed the King of Nanyue, the Queen Mother and the Han Dynasty envoys. He sent an envoy of his own to inform the King of the State of Cangwu of all his actions and another envoy to the chiefs of other prefectures and counties. Lü Jia made Zhao Jian De, the grandson of Zhao Ying Qi, King of the State of Nanyue.

Han Qian Qiu and his troops entered the territory of the State of Nanyue; they captured several small counties. They reached a place twenty kilometers away from Panyu (Guangzhou, Guangdong Province), the capital of the State of Nanyue. Then the troops of

Nanyue attacked and killed Han Qian Qiu and his troops. The King of the State of Nanyue ordered a man to hoist the flag of the envoy of the Han Dynasty in the Dayu Mountains (between Guangdong Province and Jiangxi Province). Then he sent a letter to Emperor Liu Che to apologize for the crime of killing the Han troops. But the letter was full of rude words. He sent troops to guard strategic places. Emperor Liu Che said, "Although Han Qian Qiu did not established great contributions, he has led his troops to threaten the enemy. He has been at the head of the whole army." He made Han Yan Nian, Han Qian Qiu's son, Marquis of Cheng'an. He decided to send a great army of a hundred thousand men to carry out an expedition against the State of Nanyue.

In autumn 112 BC, Emperor Liu Che appointed Lu Bo De, the Commander of the Imperial Guards, as The General of Calming the Waves. He ordered him to lead his troops to sail from Guiyang (Hunan Province) to the south; Emperor Liu Che made Yang Pu the General of Storey Warships. He ordered him to sail from Yuzhang (now Nanchang, in Jiangxi Province) to the Zhen Shui River (Guangdong Province). He ordered Yan, a former general of the State of Nanyue who had surrendered to the Han Dynasty, to sail from Lingling (Hunan Province) to the Li Jiang River (now in Guangxi Zhuang Autonomous Region); Emperor Liu Che ordered Jia, also a former general of the State of Yue, to sail to Cangwu (now Wuzhou). He sent Yi, Marquis of Chiyi, another general of the State of Nanyue who had surrendered to the Han Dynasty, to command the troops in the area of Ba and Shu (now Sichuan Province) and Yelang (Guizhou Province) to sail down the Zang Ke River (now the Beipan River). They planned to meet in Panyu, the capital of Nanyue.

In winter 111 BC, Yang Pu, the General of Storey Warships, commanded his elite troops to attack Xunxia Gorge (Guangdong Province) and took it. Then they took Shimen. They took the food stored in the ships of the State of Nanyue. They defeated the troops of Nanyue and waited for the troops commanded by the General of Calming the Waves.

The General of Calming the Waves started from a faraway place and his troops arrived late. After they joined forces, they pressed forward. The troops under the General of Storey Warships went forward ahead of the troops under The General of Calming the Waves. Then they reached Panyu. Zhao Jian De, the King of the State of Nanyue, and Lü Jia commanded their troops in defending the city. The troops under the General of Storey Warships were stationed southeast of Panyu.

The troops under the General of Calming the Waves were stationed northwest of Panyu. In the evening the General of Storey Warships attacked and defeated the troops of Nanyue. They set fire to the city.

The officers and soldiers of the State of Nanyue knew that the General of Calming the Waves was a capable man. It was already very late. They did not know how many Han troops had come. The General of Calming the Waves ordered his troops to make camp. He sent envoys to urge the troops of the State of Nanyue to surrender, and someof the officers did. He gave them seals and then sent them back to summon more officers and soldiers of the State of Nanyue to surrender. The General of Storey Warships set fire to the city. Then the Nanyue defenders were driven to the camps under the General of Calming the Waves. At dawn all the Nanyue officers and soldiers surrendered. Lü Jia and Zhao Jian De, the King of the State of Nanyue, escaped to the sea at night with several hundred men on ships and sailed westward. The General of Calming the Waves interrogated the high ranking Nanyue officials and found out where Lü Jia and Zhao Jian De had gone. He sent troops after them. Ma Su Hong, a high ranking officer, caught Zhao Jian De. Emperor Liu Che made him Marquis of Haichang. Du Ji, an officer of the State of Nanyue, caught Lü Jia. Emperor Liu Che made him Marquis of Guicai.

Zhao Guang, King of the State of Cangwu (Guangxi Zhuang Autonomous Region), heard that the Han army had come. He decided to submit to the Han Dynasty.

Peaace was restored in the State of Nanyue. It was divided into nine prefectures. Since Zhao Tuo had made himself King, the State of Nanyue existed for ninety-three years and at last fell.

84. The Rebellion Held by Zou Yu Shan, King of the State of Dongyue

In 135 BC, an army was sent to attack the State of Nanyue by Zou Ying, King of the State of Minyue (Zhejiang Province, Fujian Province and the northeastern part of Jiangxi Province),. The King of Nanyue kept his promise to Emperor Liu Che of the Han Dynasty and he did not to raise an army to fight against the King of the State of Minyue. He just reported to Emperor Liu Che that the Minyue troops had attacked his state. Emperor Liu Che sent Wang Hui, the Minister of Foreign Relations, to take troops from Yuzhang (Nanchang, Jiangxi Province), and Han An Guo, the Minister of the Ministry of Treasure, to take troops from Kuaiji (Suzhou, Jiangsu Province). Before the

Han troops entered the territory of the Minyue, Zou Ying, King of the State of Minyue, sent troops to push them back.

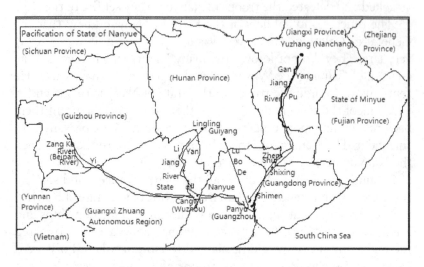

Pacification of State of Nanyue

Zou Yu Shan, the younger brother of King of the State of Minyue, said to his clansmen, "The King has raised an army to attack the State of Nanyue on his own authority. He did not ask permission from the Emperor of the Han Dynasty. So the Emperor has sent troops to punish him. They have many soldiers; the Han army is strong. If we ae lucky enough to defeat them, more Han troops will come. They will not stop until the State of Minyue is destroyed. Now we ought to kill the King so as to express our apologies to the Emperor. Then the Emperor will withdraw his army, and our state will be preserved. If the Emperor refuses to accept our apology, we will have to fight with all our might. If we are defeated, we will run away to the sea." All his clansmen agreed with him.

And Zou Yu Shan killed the King. He had an envoy take his head to Wang Hui, who said, "We have come to kill the King of the State of Minyue. Now he has already been killed and his head has been brought to me. We have won a victory without a battle. This is most favorable to us." Then he sent an officer to inform Han An Guo that the King of the State of Minyue had been killed. At the same time he sent an envoy to take the head of the King of the State of Minyue to report to Emperor Liu Che. The Emperor ordered Wang Hui and Han An Guo to withdraw their troops. The imperial edict read, "Zou Ying was the principal culprit. Only Zou Chou, King Zou Wu Zhu's grandson, has not been involved in the conspiracy." Then Emperor Liu Che sent the Commander of the Imperial Guards to make Zou Chou King of the State of Minyue.

Zou Yu Shan became very powerful in Minyue because he had killed Zou Ying. The officials and the people of Minyue submitted to him, and he styled himself a king. Zou Chou, the official new King of the State of Minyue, could not control him. When the Emperor Liu Che heard this, though, he decided not to send an army; he just said, "Zou Yu Shan has killed Zou Ying. There's no need to raise an army to fight against him." Instead, he made Zou Yu Shan King of the State of Dongyue and let him coexist with King Zou Chou of Minyue.

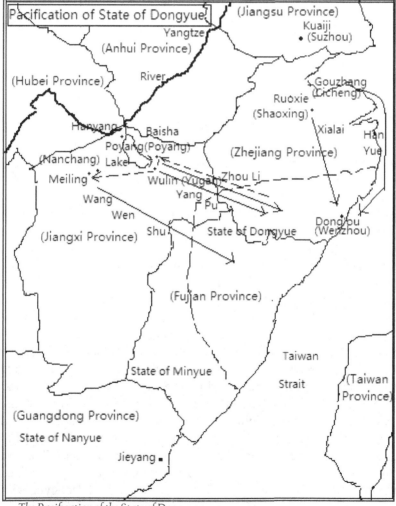

The Pacification of the State of Dongyue

In 112 BC, the State of Nanyue rebelled against the Han Dynasty. Now Zou Yu Shan presented a memorial to Emperor Liu Che, offering to lead eight thousand troops to join forces with the General of Storey Warships to attack Lü Jia, the Premier of Nanyue. When he commanded his troops to Jieyang (Guangdong Province), he paused, saying he couldn't go any further because the wind was too strong and the waves of the sea were too high. He was actually watching to see how the situation shaped up. Meanwhile, he secretly sent an envoy to the King of Nanyue. When the Han army broke into Panyu, the capital of Nanyue, Yang Pu, the General of Storey Warships, presented a memorial to Emperor Liu Che to the effect that he would like to attack Zou Yu Shan's land, the State of Dongyue. But Emperor Liu Che did not agree because he thought that the General of Storey Warships' troops had seen too much action and needed a rest. He ordered him to withdraw, simply leaving some officers stationed in Meiling of Yuzhang (Jiangxi Province).

In autumn 111 BC, Zou Yu Shan got word that the General of Storey Warship had suggested to Emperor Liu Che to kill him; and the Han troops had reached the border of the State of Dongyue and were ready to attack. Then he appointed Zou Li as General of "Swallowing the Han Army". Zou Li commanded his troops to march to Baisha (in Poyang, Jiangxi Province), to Wulin (northeastern Yugan, Jiangxi Province), then to Meiling (west of Nanchang, in northern Jiangxi Province). They killed three high officers of the Han army. At that time, Zhang Cheng, the Minister of the Ministry of Treasure, and Chi Jiang Tun, Marquis of Shanzhou, did not dare to attack the Dongyue army. They commanded their troops to retreat to a safe place. So they committed the crime of cowardice and were executed.

Next, Zou Yu Shan had craftsmen carve a seal for him as Emperor Wu; and he declared that he had ascended an emperor's throne. Emperor Liu Che appointed Han Yue as the General of Crossing the Sea and ordered him to set sail with an army from Gouzhang (now Cicheng, in Zhejiang Province) to attack the State of Dongyue from the east. The General of Storey Warships started from Wulin. Wang Wen Shu, the Commander of the Imperial Guards, started from Meiling, while the Marquis of Yue also took troops by warship and General Xialai started out from Ruoxie (in northern Zhejiang Province) and Baisha. In winter 110 BC, all the Han troops entered the territory of Dongyue. The King of the State of Dongyue sent troops to fend them off. He sent General of Xunbei to defend Wulin.

General Xunbei met several Han officers under the General of Storey Warships and defeated many of them, but another, Yuan Zhong Gu, killed General Xunbei. The Emperor made Yuan Zhong Gu Marquis of Yu'er.

Wu Yang, the former Marquis of Yueyan of the State of Minyue, was in the Han Dynasty. Emperor Liu Che sent him to the State of Dongyue to persuade Zou Yu Shan to surrender. But Zou Yu Shan refused. When the Han army under General Han Yue came, Wu Yang led seven hundred men from his home turf to attack the Dongyue troops in Hanyang (now Hanyang Feng, a mountain on the west side of Poyang Lake, in Jiangxi Province).

Ao, Marquis of Jiancheng of the State of Minyue, got together with Ju Gu, and they killed Zou Yu Shan. They and their troops surrendered to the Han army under General Han Yue. The Emperor made Ju Gu Marquis of Dongcheng and granted him the tax of ten thousand peasant households; he made Wu Yang Marquis of Maoshi; he made Han Yue Marquis of Andao.

Emperor Liu Che acknowledged, "There are many treacherous and rough places in the State of Dongyue. The people of the State of Minyue are ferocious. They change sides frequently." Then he sent troops to force the people of the State of Dongyue and the State of Minyue to move to the area between the Yangtze River and the Huai River (now Anhui Province). So the State of Dongyue and the State of Minyue were completely depopulated.

85. EMPEROR LIU CHE WORSHIPS HEAVEN AND EARTH ON MOUNT TAI

In June 116 BC Jin, a sorcerer, was holding a ceremony in the temple of the Goddess of Earth in Fenyin (now in Wanrong, Shanxi Province). He found that the ground by the temple was concave. He ordered his followers to move the soil with their hands. Then a tripod appeared. This tripod was bigger than the other tripods, and it was decorated with characters and ornamental patterns. He had a very strange feeling about this and reported it to the local official. The local official reported it to Sheng, the Chief of Hedong Prefecture, who in turn reported it to Emperor Liu Che. Then the Emperor sent an envoy to Fenyin to examine the situation and interrogate the sorcerer; the envoy was convinced that the sorcerer had not told any lies in finding the tripod. The envoy and the sorcerer held a ceremony to pay respect to the tripod. Then they escorted the tripod to Ganquan Palace (in Chunhua, Shaanxi Province).

One day when Emperor Liu Che went out on an inspection tour, the tripod was sent along with him. When Emperor Liu Che reached a place called Zhongshan with the tripod, at the time of sunrise, it was very warm and there was a yellow cloud in the sky. A deer ran past. Emperor Liu Che shot an arrow and killed it. Then the deer was used as the sacrifice in the ceremony of offering sacrifices to the Heaven and the Earth. When the tripod was transported to Chang'an, all the officials suggested to Emperor Liu Che that it should be honored.

Emperor Liu Che said, "Recently the Yellow River broke its dike and flooded. There have been bad harvests for several years. So I made an inspection to the temple of Goddess of Earth to pray for good growth of crops. Now the crops are growing very well but it is not yet the harvest time. Why has the tripod appeared?" The officials concerned said, "We hear that in the ancient times, Emperor Tai made one tripod to symbolize the unification of the realm and all the things in the universe. Yellow Emperor made three tripods to symbolize Heaven, Earth and Humanity. Yu the Great collected metal from the nine provinces to make nine tripods to symbolize the nine provinces. The tripods were used to cook for the God of Heaven and the spirits. The three legs of a tripod symbolize three virtues: honesty, steadfastness and gentleness. The tripod enjoys the blessing of Heaven. When the Xia Dynasty fell, the tripods were moved to the Yin Dynasty. When the Yin Dynasty fell, the tripods were moved to the Zhou Dynasty. When the Zhou Dynasty fell, the tripods were moved to the Qin Dynasty. When the Qin Dynasty fell, the tripods disappeared. Now the tripod has been transported to Ganquan. It has become bright, fine and smooth. It changes like a dragon. It will bring endless good fortune. When the tripod reached Zhongshan, there was a yellow cloud in the sky. When the tripod reached Ganquan, there was a yellow and white cloud in the sky in the shape of an animal. And a big bow and four arrows were found under an altar. All these are good omens. Emperor Gaozu acted in accordance with the will of the Heaven. So the tripod should be kept in the Ancestral Temple." Emperor Liu Che accepted their suggestion and kept the tripod in the Ancestral Temple.

The Emperor was very keen to do what he could to bring good fortune to his realm. A man who had gone out to the sea to look for Penglai Island (an imaginary island in legends) informed the Emperor that while Penglai Island was not far away, no one had ever been there because the air stream rising from the island could not be seen. So Emperor Liu Che sent an officer to the sea to keep a watch for the rising of the air stream from Penglai Island. In autumn 116 BC, Emperor Liu Che went up to the highlands in Yong (now Fengxiang, in Shaanxi Province), and held sacrificial rites of worshiping the Heaven.

Gongsun Qing, a man from the State of Qi (now Shandong Province), suggested that Emperor Liu Che should hold the ceremony of worshiping the Heaven and the Earth on a mountain. Emperor Liu Che accepted his suggestion. In January 109 BC Emperor Liu Che made a trip to Goushi (Yanshi, Henan Province). Then he went up Taishi Mountain (art of Songshan Mountains, Henan Province). The officials who had followed him to the mountain heard the shouting of "long live the Emperor" three times. Then Emperor Liu Che ordered that a temple be built on the top of Taishi Mountain for the ceremony of offering sacrifices. He also gave an order to prohibit cutting trees on Taishi Mountain. The people of the three hundred households living at the foot of Taishi Mountain were ordered to attend to the mountain. Then Emperor Liu Che continued his trip eastward to Mount Tai. At that time the leaves of the trees and the grass had not yet sprouted. Emperor Liu Che ordered to have a stone erected on the top of Mount Tai.

Emperor Liu Che went eastward to the sea, and he held a ceremony by the seaside to worship the gods. More than ten thousand people of Qi (now Shandong Province) presented memorials to relate the strange things they had seen. Then Emperor Liu Che ordered several thousand people to go out to sea to look for gods in Penglai Island. Gongsun Qing held the imperial staff with a yak's tail and took the lead. When he reached Donglai (now Yantai, in the east part of Shandong Province), he saw a giant — more than ten meters tall — at night. When he got close, the giant suddenly disappeared. He saw that the foot prints were very big. The officials told Emperor Liu Che that they had seen an old man leading a dog. The old man said, "I want to see the great man." Suddenly the old man disappeared. Emperor Liu Che had seen the big foot prints, but he still did not believe it. When the officials told him about the old man leading a dog, then he believed that the giant man was really a god. He stayed on the sea for the night. He sent several thousand envoys to the sea to look for the gods.

In April 109 BC Emperor Liu Che returned to Fenggao (Shandong Province). He went to the foot of Liangfu Mountain (part of Culai Mountain) where he held a ceremony to worship the Goddess of the Earth. On 19 April, Emperor Liu Che ordered the officials and the scholars to perform the ritual of shooting the oxen. Then an altar was built in the east at the foot of Mount Tai to worship the Emperor of the Heaven. The altar was four meters wide three meters tall. Under the altar a document engraved on pieces of jade was buried. The document was kept secret and no one knew what it was about. After the ceremony, Emperor Liu Che went up Mount Tai only with Huo Shan (Huo Qu Bing's son), the Marquis of Fengchezi, and the Palace Attendant. He also held a ceremony of Worshiping the Heaven on the top of Mount Tai. The next day Emperor Liu Che and his attendant went down Mount Tai. Then they reached Suran Mountain (a branch of Mount Tai, in Shandong Province) where Emperor Liu Che worshipped the Goddess of Earth. In the ceremony Emperor Liu Che knelt down and touched his head to the ground to pay his respect to the Goddess. A band played music during the ceremony. A mattress made of cogon grass was put on the ground. They put the soil of five colors on it and made an altar. Then all kinds of animals and birds were set free. All the animals ran up to the top of Mount Tai and then left. The Temple of Worshiping the Heaven and the Earth was bright at night. In the day time a white cloud rose up from the altar.

When Emperor Liu Che returned to Chang'an from Mount Tai, he sat in the Hall to receive the high ranking officials. They went forward to express their respects batch by batch. Emperor Liu Che said, "In ancient times, the Emperors made an inspection to Mount Tai every five years. All the marquises had their places to stay. Now I order, all the marquises should build residences at the foot of Mount Tai."

Since the time Emperor Liu Che went to worship the Heaven and Earth on Mount Tai, there had not been any natural disaster. The sorcerers said that the gods could be seen on Penglai Island. Then Emperor Liu Che wanted to meet the gods. He made his trip eastward to the sea to look for the gods. One day Huo Shan, Marquis of Fengchezi, suddenly fell seriously ill and died. Emperor Liu Che continued his trip to the sea, and then to Jieshi (Hebei Province). Then he made an inspection to Liaoxi (Liaoning Province), to the north borders and at last to Jiuyuan Prefecture (now Baotou, Inner Mongolia). In May 109 BC, Emperor Liu Che returned to Ganquan (now Chunhua, Shaanxi Province). He had travelled for 9,000 kilometers.

86. The Expedition against Gojoseon

Gojoseon, the ancient Korean Kingdom, was in what is now the east part of Liaoning Province and the north part of the Korean Peninsula. Wei Man, King of Gojoseon, was a man from the State of Yan (now the areas of Beijing, northeastern Hebei Province and western Liaoning Province). In the late 4th century BC, the State of Yan conquered Zhenpan (in northern Korean Peninsula) and Gojoseon. The King of the State of Yan appointed officials to rule over the people in these areas and had fortresses built. When the State of Qin conquered the State of Yan, the areas of Zhenpan and Gojoseon became the outer border areas of Liaodong.

When the Han Dynasty was established, the Emperor considered that the areas of Zhenpan and Gojoseon were far away and difficult to control, so he ordered to have all the fortresses repaired. The border line was the Pai River (now Taedong River). In 195 BC Lu Wan, the King of the State of Yan, rebelled against the Han Dynasty. He was defeated and he ran to the area of the Huns. Wei Man ran away with about a thousand men eastward out of the Great Wall. They crossed the Pai River and stayed in the area to the east of Pai River. They built strongholds to defend themselves. Then they conquered the people in Zhenpan and Gojoseon and the people of the former State of Yan and the former State of Qi. Then Wei Man established his capital in Wangxian (now Pyongyang, in the northwest part of the Korean Peninsula).

During the reign of Emperor Liu Ying and Empress Dowager Lü Zhi, the Chief of Liaodong Prefecture had a talked with Wei Man and they made an agreement that Gojoseon would be a vassal state of the Han Dynasty. According to the agreement, Wei Man was to take care of the people of the local tribes and make sure that they did not invade the border areas of the Han Dynasty; and Wei Man was to prevent the heads of the tribes from going into the area of the Han Dynasty to have interviews with the Emperor of the Han Dynasty. The Chief of Liaodong Prefecture reported this agreement to Emperor Liu Che, and Emperor Liu Che ratified the agreement. Wei Man forced Zhenpan and Lintun (in the east part of the Korean Peninsula) to submit to Gojoseon. So Gojoseon became a big state.

After Wei Man died, his son succeeded to the throne of the King of Gojoseon, followed by his grandson Wei You Qu. More and more Han people were making their way into the area of Gojoseon. Wei You Qu never went to have an interview with Emperor Liu Che. The heads of Zhenpan and the State of Jin (in the south part of the Korean Peninsula) wanted to present memorials to Emperor Liu Che and have an interview with him, but the King of Gojoseon blocked their way. In 109 BC, Emperor Liu Che sent She He as his envoy to take an imperial order to accuse Wei You Qu of his offenses. But Wei You Qu refused to accept the imperial order, so She He went back. When he reached the Pai River, he ordered the carriage driver to kill Chang, a minor king of Gojoseon who was escorting him out of Gojoseon. Then She He crossed the Pai River and ran back to report to the Emperor that he had killed a Gojoseon general. Emperor Liu Che appointed him commander of the army stationed in the east part of Liaodong (Liaoning Province). The King of Gojoseon hated She He. He sent troops to start a sudden attack and killed him.

In autumn 109 BC, Emperor Liu Che sent Yang Pu, the General of Storey Warships, to command fifty thousand men to crossed Bo Hai Sea from Qi (now Shandong Province) to attack Gojoseon; and he sent Xun Zhi, the Left General, to march from Liaodong (now in Liaoning Province) to attack Gojoseon. Wei You Qu sent troops to beat them back. Yang Pu, the General of Storey Warships, reached the city of Wangxian (now Pyongyang, in the northwest part of the Korean Peninsula) with seven thousand men. Wei You Qu defended the city, and found that there were actually few Han troops making the attack. So he commanded his troops to come out of the city to counter-attack. The Han troops under Yang Pu were defeated and ran away. Yang Pu fled to the mountains and hid there for more than ten days. Then he came out to look for his soldiers, and he gathered his troops. Xun Zhi commanded his troops to attack the enemy on the west bank of the Pai River but could not defeat them.

Since the two generals could not defeat the Gojoseon army, Emperor Liu Che sent Wei Shan as his envoy to persuade Wei You Qu to surrender. When Wei You Qu met the envoy, he knelt down and touched his head to the ground to apologize for his offence. He said to the envoy, "I am willing to surrender. I did not surrender before because I was afraid that my generals would kill me if I did. Since you have come, I have made up my mind to surrender." Wei You Qu sent his son, the crown prince, to Chang'an to express his apologies to Emperor Liu Che. He presented five thousand horses to the Han Dynasty and provided food for the Han army.

Ten thousand officers and soldiers of Gojoseon holding weapons escorted the crown prince to the Han Dynasty. When they reached the Pai River, the envoy, Wei Shan, and Left General suspected that the Gojoseon troops would attack them. So they said that since the crown prince had surrendered, the Gojoseon troops should not carry weapons. The crown prince suspected that the envoy and Left General were playing a trick, so he refused to cross the Pai River and turned back. Wei Shan went back to Chang'an and reported this to Emperor Liu Che. Emperor Liu Che ordered to have Wei Shan executed.

Left General defeated the troops of Gojoseon by the Pai River. Then he commanded his troops to advance to the city of Wangxian (now Pyongyang). The Han army surrounded the city on the northwest. Yang Pu, the General of Storey Warships, also headed with his troops to Wangxian. They stationed themselves in the south of the city. Wei You Qu defended the city resolutely. The Han troops attacked for several months but they could not take it.

Left General Xun Zhi had been an imperial guard and attended to Emperor Liu Che for a long time. He won favor from the Emperor. He commanded the soldiers from the areas of Yan (Beijing, northern Hebei Province and western Liaoning Province) and Dai (part of Shanxi Province, and part of Hebei Province). They were very brave. They were filled with pride because they had defeated the Gojoseon troops.

Yang Pu, the General of Storey Warships, took his soldiers from Qi (now Shandong Province) and crossed the sea. They were defeated by the Gojoseon troops commanded by Wei You Qu and many of them ran away. Yang Pu felt ashamed of himself. His soldiers were afraid. When he commanded his troops to surround Wei You Qu, he often held the flag of peace. Left General Xun Zhi attacked the Gojoseon troops commanded by Wei You Qu with great force. The high ranking officials of Gojoseon secretly sent envoys to Yang Pu to convey Wei You Qu's intention to surrender. The envoys went back and forth, but Wei You Qu could not bring himself to actually do it.

Left General Xun Zhi sent officers to Yang Pu to make agreements with him to attack the Gojoseon troops, but Yang Pu would not join forces with Xun Zhi. Xun Zhi sent envoys to persuade Wei You Qu to surrender, but Wei You Qu refused. He only wanted to surrender to Yang Pu. So there were grudges between Xun Zhi and Yang Pu. Xun Zhi thought that Yang Pu had been defeated by the troops of Gojoseon, and now Yang Pu was friendly with Wei You Qu and Wei You Qu would not surrender. So Xun Zhi suspected that there was collusion between Yang Pu and Wei You Qu to hold a rebellion. Emperor Liu Che said, "Now the commanding generals did not dare to march forward. So I sent Wei Shan to persuade Wei You Qu to surrender. Wei You Qu sent his crown prince to Chang'an to express his apology. But Wei Shan could not make his decision resolutely. And there was a misunderstanding between Wei Shan and Xun Zhi. All these ruined the plan of Gojoseon's surrender. Now the two generals are attacking the city. But there are contradictions between the two generals. This is the reason why they cannot take the city." So Emperor Liu Che sent Gongsun Sui to correct their mistakes. Gongsun Sui had the power to act according to the situation. When Gongsun Sui reached the army attacking the city of Wangxian, Left General Xun Zhi said, "We should have conquered Gojoseon long ago. The reason why we have not yet conquered Gojoseon is that Yang Pu has not command his troops to join forces with my troops." He also said to Gongsun Sui, "If we do not arrest Yang Pu now, he will do great harm to us. Yang Pu has colluded with Gojoseon troops to wipe out our troops." Gongsun Sui agreed with his interpretation of the situation, and he sent an envoy to ask Yang Pu to go to the troops under Left General Xun Zhi to discuss military actions. When Yang Pu came, Gongsun Sui ordered Xun Zhi to arrest him. Then Xun Zhi took command of the troops originally under Yang Pu. When this was reported to Emperor Liu Che, the Emperor ordered to have Gongsun Sui executed.

After Xun Zhi took command of Yang Pu's troops, he led his own men and those whoh were originally under Yang Pu in a concerted attack on the Gojoseon. The four high ranking officials of Gojoseon: Lu Ren, Han Tao, Nixi Xiang Can and General Wang Jia, held a discussion. They said, "Originally we planned to surrender to Yang Pu. Now he has been arrested. His troops are under the command of Left General Xun Zhi. Now the troops under Xun Zhi are attacking us fiercely. We cannot resist the attack of such a strong army. But our king would not surrender." Then Han Tao, Wang Jia and Lu Ran went to surrender to the Han army.

In summer 108 BC Nixi Xiang Can sent a man to kill Wei You Qu, King of Gojoseon, and then he went to surrender to the Han army. But the city of Wangxian was not yet taken by the Han army. Cheng Yi, a former official under Wei You Qu, rebelled. He ordered the soldiers under him to kill the officials of Gojoseon. Left General Xun Zhi sent Wei Chang, the son of Wei You Qu, and Zui, the son of Lu Ren, to pacify the people of Gojoseon and they killed Cheng Yi. Then the whole of Gojoseon was conquered by the Han army.Gojoseon was divided into four prefectures: Zhenpan Prefecture, Lintun Prefecture, Lelang Prefecture, and Xuantu Prefecture. Emperor Liu Che made Nixi Xiang Can Marquis of Huoqing, Han Tao Marquis of Qiuju, Wang Jia Marquis of Pingzhou, Wei Chang Marquis of Ji, and Zui Marquis of Juyang. When Left General Xun Zhi was summoned back to Chang'an, he was arrested and executed for the crime of ruining the original plan and fighting for power. Yang Pu, the General of Storey Warships, was to be executed for the crime of attacking the enemy without waiting for the troops under Left General Xun Zhi to arrive, resulting in many soldiers being killed. But he was able to pay hiw way out of it and his life was spared.

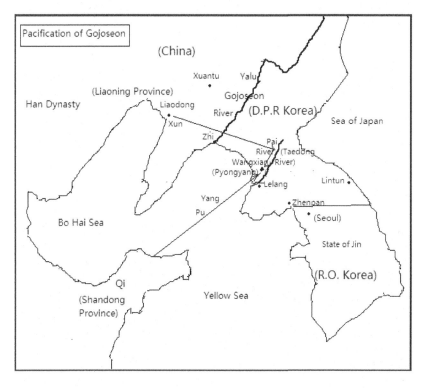

The Pacification of Gojoseon

87. PRINCESS LIU XI JUN AND PRINCESS LIU JIE YOU ARE MARRIED TO THE KINGS OF THE STATE OF WUSUN

When the King of the Huns heard that the State of Wusun had united with the Han Dynasty, he was very angry and wanted to attack Wusun. Han envoys started out from the State of Wusun and went south to the State of Dayuan and the State of Yuezhi. Liejiaomi, the King of Wusun, was afraid that the Huns would attack his state. So he sent envoys to the Han Dynasty, taking some horses to present to Emperor Liu Che. He asked to marry a princess of the Han Dynasty and become a brother of the Emperor of the Han Dynasty. Emperor Liu Che held a discussion with the court officials. The court officials said, "The King of the State of Wusun must send betrothal gifts first. Then the princess will be sent to him." Then Liejiaomi presented one thousand horses as betrothal gifts.

In 105 BC Emperor Liu Che sent Liu Xi Jun, the daughter of Liu Jian, King of the State of Jiangdu, as the princess to marry Liejiaomi, King of the State of Wusun. Emperor Liu Che gave Liejiaomi many gifts. Liejiaomi made Liu Xi Jun the right wife. The king of the Huns also sent one of his daughters to marry Liejiaomi. Liejiaomi made her the left wife.

When Princess Liu Xi Jun arrived in the State of Wusun, she had her palace built and lived there. She met Liejiaomi twice a year. When she met Liejiaomi, she would hold banquets. She gave gifts of money and silk to Liejiaomi's officials and relatives. At that time, Liejiaomi was already old. Princess Liu Xi Jun could not talk with anyone in the State of Wusun because she could not speak the local language. She was sorrowful all the time. She sang the following poem written by herself: "I have been sent to the other end of the world, and married to the King of the State of Wusun; I live in a felt tent with a vaulted roof; the walls of the tent are felt blankets; my main food is meat and my drink is goat milk; I am so sad — I miss my home place; how I long to be a swan and fly back to my home place." When Emperor Liu Che heard about this, he had pity on her. He sent envoys to take curtains and silk to Princess Liu Xi Jun.

Since Liejiaomi, King of the State of Wusun, was so old, he wanted Liu Xi Jun to be the wife of his grandson Junxumi. Princess Liu Xi Jun would not do that. She presented a letter to Emperor Liu Che about this. The Emperor wrote back, saying, "You should follow the custom of the State of Wusun. I want to unite with the State of Wusun to attack the Huns." Then Junxumi took Princess Liu Xu Jun as his wife. When Liejiaomi died, Junxumi succeeded as the King of the State of Wusun. Soon after, Princess Liu Xi Jun gave birth to a baby girl. They named her Shaofu. When Princess Liu Xi Jun died, Emperor Liu Che made Liu Jie You a princess and married her to Junxumi. Liu Jie You was the granddaughter of Liu Wu, King of the State of Chu. At that time, Junxumi's son Nimi was still very young. Before Junxumi died, he appointed Wengguimi, his uncle Dalu's son, to rule over the State of Wusun. He said to Wengguimi, "When Nimi grows up, you should return the power to him."

When Wengguimi became the King of the State of Wusun, he took Princess Liu Jie You as his wife. She gave birth to three sons and two daughters. The eldest son was named Guimi; the second son was named Wannian who was made King of the State of Shache (now Shache, in Xinjiang Uygur Autonomous Region, China); the third son was named Dalel he was made Left Grand General. The first daughter was named Dishi; she was married to Jiangbin, King of the State of Kucha (Xinjiang Uygur Autonomous Region). The second daughter, named Suguang, was married to the Marquis of Ruohuling.

88. LI GUANG LI ATTACKS THE STATE OF DAYUAN

The State of Dayuan was located in the Ferghana Valley in Central Asia. The envoys of the Han Dynasty who had been to the State of Dayuan told Emperor Liu Che that there were very good horses that sweated blood in the State of Dayuan in the city of Osh (now Osh in Kyrgyzstan). But the King of the State of Dayuan hid all the sweating-blood horses and would not let the envoys of the Han Dynasty see them. Emperor Liu Che sent envoys to offer 500 kilograms of gold and a horse made of gold as a gift to the King of the State of Dayuan in exchange for some sweating-blood horses. The King of the State of Dayuan discussed this matter with his officials. He said, "The Han Dynasty is very far away from our state. There is a vast desert between our state and the Han Dynasty. The water in this area is salty. It is very difficult for the envoys of the Han Dynasty to get across this area. Mve any Han envoys died on their way. To the north of this area, there are the Huns. To the south of this area, there is no water or grass, and there are no cities in this area. If several hundred envoys of the Han Dynasty come, half of them will die of hunger on their way. How can a great army get across this arid sand! They can't do us any harm." The horses in Osh were precious. So when the envoys of the Han Dynasty reached Osh, Wugua, the King of the State of Dayuan, refused to give them any. The envoys were so angry that they broke the horse made of gold and turned back.

The King of the State of Dayuan was very angry. He said, "The envoys of the Han Dynasty look down upon me." He ordered King of Yucheng City (in today's Kyrgyzstan) in the eastern border of the State of Dayuan to attack the envoys and killed all of them. They took all the gold and goods sent by the Han Dynasty. When Emperor Liu Che learned about this, he was outraged. Yao Ding Han, who had been on a mission to the State of Dayuan, said to Emperor Liu Che, "The troops of the State of Dayuan are very weak. If we send three thousand men to attack them, they can easily defeat the troops of the State of Dayuan. Your Majesty once sent Zhao Po Nu, Marquis of Zhouye, with seven hundred cavalrymen to attack the State of Loulan.

They successfully captured the King." Emperor Liu Che agreed with him. In August 104 BC, Emperor Liu Che appointed Li Guang Li as General of Osh to lead six thousand Han cavalrymen and more than ten thousand young criminals from different prefectures to attack the State of Dayuan.

Li Guang Li was the elder brother of Lady Li, Emperor Liu Che's favorite concubine, who gave birth to Liu Bo, King of the State of Changyi. The purpose of Li Guang Li's expedition against the State of Dayuan was to go to the city of Osh to get the sweating-blood horses. So he was given the title of General of Osh. Wang Hui, Marquis of Hao, was the guide for the army. The Han army under Li Guang Li went west to cross the lake Lop Nur (in the east part of Xinjiang Uygur Autonomous Region, China). The small states on the way defended their cities resolutely and would not provide food for the Han army. So the Han troops attacked the cities fiercely. They got food when they managed to conquer a city; but when they attacked a city for several days and could not take it, they had to leave it and go forward. When the Han army reached Yucheng City (in today's Kyrgyzstan), only several thousand men still survived. They were all starved and tired. When they attacked Yucheng City, the defenders fought resolutely. The Han troops killed many soldiers of Dayuan but still they could not take the city. Li Guang Li told his generals and officers, "We cannot take Yucheng City. It will be impossible for us to take the capital of the State of Dayuan." So he had his army turn back. It took them two years to go to Yucheng City and come back. By the time they got back to Dunhuang area (in Gansu Province), only ten percent of the men survived.

Li Guang li sent an envoy to present a memorial to Emperor Liu Che which read, "The State of Dayuan is very far away. We did not have enough food for the army. The officers and men are not afraid of fighting. But they are afraid of hunger. There are not enough soldiers in my army. I cannot occupy the State of Dayuan with the remaining troops. I hope Your Majesty will allow me to turn back. When Your Majesty sends me more troops, I will go to attack the State of Dayuan again." When Emperor Liu Che got the memorial, he was very angry. He sent an envoy to Yumenguan Pass (in the west part of Gansu Province) to order the general defending the pass not to let the troops under Li Guang Li enter the pass. The order read, "Kill anyone who is so bold as to enter the pass." Li Guang Li was afraid and had to station his troops in Dunhuang area.

In summer 103 BC, the Han troops under Zhao Po Nu, Marquis of Zhouye, were defeated by the Huns. Twenty thousand of the Han officers and soldiers were killed. All the high ranking officials suggested to Emperor Liu Che to withdraw the troops attacking the State of Dayuan and send them to attack the Huns. But Emperor Liu Che did not agree with them. He had already sent troops to attack the State of Dayuan. The State of Dayuan was only a small state. If the Han troops could not conquer such a small state, the other states such as the State of Daxia would look down upon the Han Dynasty. If the Han troops could not get the precious horses from the State of Dayuan, the State of Wusun and the State of Luntai (Xinjiang Uygur Autonomous Region, China) would look down upon the Han envoys. They would become a laughing stock for the other states. So Emperor Liu Che punished those officials who had suggested giving up the attack of the State of Dayuan.

Then he sent sixty thousand men to the area of Dunhuang to reinforce the troops under Li Guang Li. A hundred thousand cows, thirty thousand horses and many donkeys and camels were used to transport food and weapons for the army. More than fifty high ranking officers were sent to join his army. There were no wells in Guishan City (now Kassansay, Uzbekistan). The water supply came from a river outside the city. Emperor Liu Che sent a water engineering team to dig a channel to divert the flow of the river away. Emperor Liu Che moved one hundred and eighty thousand officers and soldiers from Jiuquan to Juyan (Inner Mongolia) and Xiuchu (Gansu Province) to protect Jiuquan (Gansu Province). Two men who were skilful in herding horses were promoted and put in charge of driving the sweating-blood horses back to the capital when the State of Dayuan was conquered.

Then Li Guang Li, General of Osh, took his reinforced army forward. All the small states on the way welcomed the Han army and provided food for them. When they reached the State of Luntai (Xinjiang Uygur Autonomous Region, China), the local forces put up a stout resistance. After several days' fighting, the Han army at last took the State of Luntai.

Then Li Guang Li marched westward to Guishan City, the capital of the State of Dayuan. There were thirty thousand men in the Han army. The troops of the State of Dayuan came out of the city to repulse their attacks. The Han troops shot arrows at them and defeated them. The Dayuan troops withdrew into the city and continued their resistance. Since the Han army could not readily take Guishan City,

Li Guang Li thought about diverting his army to attack Yucheng City; but he felt that might make the King of Dayuan even more cocky and self-confident. So he decided to continue the attack. He ordered his soldiers to dig a channel to re-direct the river outside Guishan City and here, too, very soon there was no water supply inside the city walls. Then Li Guang Li laid siege to the city.

The Han troops vesieged the city for forty days. The nobles of the State of Dayuan discussed the situation among themselves. One of them said, "King Wugua has hidden all the precious horses. He killed the Han envoys. If we kill King Wugua and give the Han troops the precious horses, the Han troops will raise the siege. If the Han troops do not raise the siege, we will fight till we die." The nobles agreed with him. Then they killed King Wugua.

At that time the Han army had destroyed the outer wall of the city. Jianmi, the brave general of the State of Dayuan, was killed. The troops all ran into the inner city. The nobles sent an envoy carrying the head of King Wugua to see General Li Guang Li. The envoy conveyed the following promise made by the nobles: "If you stop the attack, we will provide you with all the precious horses and let the Han troops take as many as they want. And we will provide food for your troops. If you do not accept this suggestion, we will kill all the precious horses. Relief troops from the State of Kangju are coming. When they arrive, we will attack you from within and they will attack you from without. Now you should make up your mind as to what you will do." At that time the King of Kangju thought that the Han troops were very strong; he did not dare to order his troops to go forward.

General Li Guang Li learned that some men from the Han Dynasty had come to Guishan City to teach the people of the State of Dayuan to dig wells. And there was still a lot of food in the city. The original purpose of the Han expedition was to kill King Wugua, the principal culprit. Now the King's head had been presented to him. If he did not stop the attack, the troops of the State of Dayuan would become even more resolute in defending their city. When the relief forces arrived from the State of Kangju, the Han army would be defeated. General Li Guang Li told his worries to the officers under him; they all agreed with his assessment. So General Li Guang Li gave his consent to the Dayuans' offer.

Then the nobles of the State of Dayuan drove all the horses out of the city and let the Han troops to choose as many as they wanted. And they provided food for the Han troops. The Han selected more than thirty precious horses, and three thousand second-rate horses, male and female. General Li Guang Li made Mocai, a noble of the State of Dayuan, who had treated the envoys of the Han Dynasty well, King of the State Dayuan. A ceremony was held to formalize an alliance between the Han Dynasty and the State of Dayuan. Then the Han troops withdrew back to the Han Dynasty.

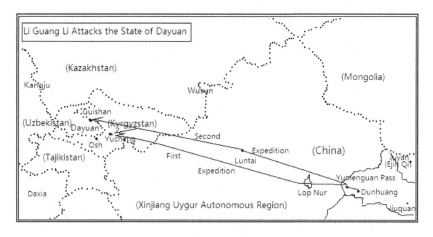

Li Guang Li Attacks the State of Dayuan

When General Li Guang Li was setting out to attack the State of Dayuan from western Dunhuang area, he put Wang Shen Sheng, a high ranking officer, and Hu Chong Guo, the official in charge of ceremonies, in command of a thousand men and sent them to attack the city of Yucheng. The King there, seeing a relatively small force, sent out three thousand men in the morning to push back the Han troops. The Yucheng defenders killed Wang Shen Sheng. Only several Han solders escaped. They ran to General Li Guang Li and reported their defeat to him. General Li Guang Li sent Shangguan Jie to lead some more troops to Yucheng. Shangguan Jie and his troops attacked fiercely and broke into the city. The King of Yucheng ran away to Kangju. Shangguan Jie pursued him all the way there. The King of Kangju got word that the Han army had conquered the State Dayuan, so he arrested the King of Yucheng and presented him to Shangguan Jie. Shangguan Jie haordered four cavalrymen to escort the King of Yucheng back to General Li Guang Li. The four cavalrymen thought their assignment was dangerous; one of them said, "The Han people hate the King of Yucheng very much. Now we are escorting the King of Yucheng. If he escapes on the way, we will be responsible for it." So Zhao Di, one of the four cavalrymen, drew out his sword and killed the King of Yucheng. Then Shangguan Jie commanded his troops to catch up with the Han army under General Li Guang Li.

In spring 100 BC, General Li Guang Li and his troops returned to Chang'an, the capital of the Han Dynasty. The kings of all the small states along the way sent their sons or brothers to follow the Han army to pay tribute to Emperor Liu Che. And they stayed on with the Han Dynasty as hostages. When General Li Guang Li and his army reached Yumen Guan Pass, there were more than ten thousand men in the army with more than one thousand horses. Emperor Liu Che made Li Guang Li Marquis of Haixi, and granted him the tax of eight thousand peasant households. He made Zhao Di, who had killed the King of Yucheng, Marquis of Xinzhi. He appointed Shangguan Jie as Minister of Treasury. More than one thousand officers of the army under Li Guang Li were appointed as chiefs of prefectures and premiers of the states. Emperor Liu Che granted every soldier handsome rewards.

When General Li Guang Li was waging a campaign against the State of Dayuan, the Huns learned about his expedition and planned an attack. But when they saw that the Han army was very strong, so they gave up their plan. The King of the Huns sent an envoy to the State of Loulan (Xinjiang Uygur Autonomous Region, China) to instigate the King of the State of Loulan to block the envoys of the Han Dynasty from passing through the State of Loulan. At that time General Zheng Ren Wen had stationed his troops in Yumen Guan Pass. The troops caught an officer from the State of Loulan and learned that the King had been colluding with the Huns. Zheng Ren Wen reported this to the Emperor. An imperial edict was issued, ordering Zheng Ren Wen to take his troops to Loulan to capture the King. Zhen Ren Wen carried out the order and seized the King, who was escorted to Chang'an and brought before Emperor Liu Che. The Emperor accused the King of the State of Loulan of collusion with the Huns. The King of the State of Loulan replied, "Mine is a small state which is situated between two big states. My state cannot exist if I don't please the two big states. I would like to move all my people to the territory of the Han Dynasty so that they can live peacefully there." Emperor Liu Che agreed with him and sent him back to the State of Loulan. From then on the Huns did not trust the King of Loulan anymore.

After the Han army conquered the State of Dayuan, the other states in the Western Region were scared. The envoys of the Han Dynasty sent to the states of the Western Region were able to fulfill their tasks without impediment. Han troops built pavilions along the way from Dunhuang (wester Gansu Province) Yanze (Salt Lake) (now Lop Nur). Several hundred soldiers were put to work reclaiming wasteland for cultivating grain to provide food for Han envoys on their missions to foreign countries. Officers were sent to these remote places to manage these soldiers.

Several years later, it seemed to the nobles of the State of Dayuan that Mocai, King of the State of Dayuan, had become too friendly with the Han Dynasty. They killed Mocai and put Wugua's younger brother Chanfeng on the throne. Chanfeng sent his son to Chang'an to be an attendant to Emperor Liu Che. Emperor Liu Che sent envoys to convey gifts to King Chanfeng, and King Chanfeng promised to present two precious horses to Emperor Liu Che every year.

89. The Relationship between the Han Dynasty and the Huns

King Yizhixie of the Huns was on the throne for thirteen years. In 114 BC, he died and his son Wuwei succeeded him. At that time, Emperor Liu Che was making an inspection to the prefectures and counties in the Han Dynasty. Then he sent armies to pacify the State of Nanyue and the State of Dongyue. He did not send any troops to attack the Huns. And the Huns did not invade the border areas of the Han Dynasty.

Three years after Wuwei had become King of the Huns, the Han Dynasty had pacified the State of Nanyue and the State of Dongyue. Emperor Liu Che sent General Gongsun He with fifteen thousand cavalrymen to set out from Jiuyuan (by the Great Bend of the Yellow River) north a thousand kilometers to Fujujing (now Darhan Muminggan Lianhe Qi, Inner Mongolia). But he did not see any Huns there. Emperor Liu Che sent Zhao Po Nu, the Marquis of Congpiao, to march out of Lingju (now Yongdeng, Gansu Province) about two thousand kilometers north to the Xiongnu River (now the Baydrag River, in Bayanhongor, Mongolia). But he did not see any Huns in this area, either. They turned back to the Han Dynasty.

Emperor Liu Che was on an inspection to the border areas. He personally went to Shuofang (now Hanggin Qi, Inner Mongolia). He traveled at the head of one hundred and eighty thousand men to show his great military power to the Huns. He sent Guo Ji as his envoy to see King Wuwei. When he reached the area where the Huns were, the official in charge of receiving guests asked him, "What have you come for?" Guo Ji said politely, "I have something to tell your king." Then King Wuwei held a reception with Guo Ji. Guo Ji said to King Wuwei, "The State of Nanyue has been conquered and the King of Nanyue has been killed. If you have the power to fight against the army of the Han Dynasty, our emperor is waiting for you in the border area. If you cannot fight against the Han army, you'd do better to submit and became a vassal. Why should you run away, north of the desert, when it's so cold here and there is no water or grass in this area?" When King Wuwei heard Guo Ji's words, he was very angry. He immediately killed the official in charge of receiving guests; he ordered his men to detain Guo Ji and would not let him go back to the Han Dynasty. King Wuwei sent some soldiers to escort Guo Ji to Beihai Sea (now Lake Baikal, in southern Siberia). The Huns refrained from crossing the Hans' border. He let his people and soldiers have a good rest. He trained his soldiers in hunting. He sent envoys to the Han Dynasty to make peace.

Emperor Liu Chen sent Wang Wu and some others on a mission to see the King of the Huns. According to the laws of the Huns, before an envoy went to meet the King, he had to leave the flag marking him as an envoy of the Han Dynasty outside the tent and tattoo his face. Wang Wu had lived in the north part of China. He knew the customs of the Huns well. So he left the envoy flag outside and tattooed his face. He went in and met King Wuwei of the Huns. King Wuwei seemed to like Wang Wu. He even told him he would send his son to the Han capital as a hostage so as to make peace.

Next, Emperor Liu Che sent Yang Xin as his envoy on a mission to the Huns. At that time, the Han Dynasty had conquered Gojoseon and divided it into four prefectures. Emperor Liu Che established Jiuquan Prefecture (now in Gansu Province) to cut off contact between the Huns and the local tribes in the northwest part of China. He sent envoys to the State of Greater Yuezhi (in now Afghanistan) and the State of Daxia (in now Afghanistan). He married princesses of the imperial clan to the King of the State of Wusun. This way, the Huns would not be able to gang together with the states in the Western Region.

The Emperor expanded the territory northward to Xianlei (now Alxa Zuoqi, southwestern Inner Mongolia) and had a fortress built there. The Huns did not dare to say anything about it.

In that year, Zhao Xin, who was the advisor of the King of the Huns, died. The high officials of the Han Dynasty calculated that the Huns had been weakened and suggested to Emperor Liu Che that now he should make the King of the Huns submit.

The current envoy Yang Xin was an upright man, but he was not a favorite of the Emperor. Neither did the King of the Huns like him. He wanted to summon Yang Xin into his tent, but Yang Xin would not leave his envoy flag outside the tent. So he sat outside the tent to receive Yang Xin. Yang Xin said to King Wuwei of the Huns, "If you want to make peace with the Han Dynasty, you should send your crown prince to the Han Dynasty as a hostage." King Wuwei said, "This does not agree with the original agreement. According to the original agreement, the Emperor of the Han Dynasty should send princesses of the imperial clan to marry the King of the Huns. He should provide cloth, silk, food and other materials to us. In this way, the Emperor of the Han Dynasty and the King of the Huns will become close relatives. Then we will not invade the border areas of the Han Dynasty. Now you are trying to talk me into going against the original agreement, and send my crown prince to the Han Dynasty as a hostage. I will not do that." At that time, the Huns would take measures to retaliate against every step taken by the Han Dynasty. If the Han army entered the area of the Huns, the Huns would make raids inside the territory of the Han Dynasty. If the Han Dynasty detained the Huns' envoys, the Huns would detain the same number of the envoys sent by the Han Dynasty.

After Yang Xin came back, Emperor Liu Che sent Wang Wu and others on a mission to the Huns. The King of the Huns was greedy and wanted to get more treasure from the Han Dynasty. He pretended to be very friendly to Wang Wu. He toild him, "I intend to go to Chang'an to have an interview with your emperor personally. He and I will become sworn brothers." Wang Wu came back to Chang'an and reported the intention of the King of the Huns to Emperor Liu Che. The Emperor ordered to have a residence built in Chang'an for the King of the Huns. Then the King of the Huns said, "The envoy of the Han Dynasty must be a nobleman. Otherwise I will not have an interview with him." And the King of the Huns sent a nobleman as his next envoy to the Han Dynasty.

The noble envoy fell ill while he was in the Han imperial lands. He took some medicine hoping that he could recover. But unfortunately he died. Then Emperor Liu Che granted Lu Chong Guo the seal of an official at the level of one hundred and twenty thousand kilograms of rice to escort thenobleman's corpse back to the Huns to be buried. Emperor Liu Che ordered Lu Chong Guo to take five hundred kilograms of gold to the King of the Huns. Nonetheless, the King of the Huns thought that the Han officials had killed his envoy. Therefore he detained Lu Chong Guo and did not let him go.

When the King of the Huns said to Wang Wu that he would send the crown prince to the Han Dynasty, he was deceiving Wang Wu.

He actually did not have any intention to send the crown prince to the Han Dynasty as a hostage. Instead, he sent troops to invade the border area of the Han Dynasty. Emperor Liu Che appointed Guo Chang as General of Bahu (Bahu means defeating the Huns). He sent Guo Chang and Zhao Po Nu, Marquis of Zhouye, to command the troops under them to station in Shuofang Prefecture (now Hanggin Qi, Inner Mongolia) to prepare to fight against the invasion by the Huns.

King Wuwei of the Huns was on the throne for ten years. In 105 BC, King Wuwei died. His son Zhanshilu became the King of the Huns, but he was very young. So he was called Child King. The Child King of the Huns moved his troops further northwest. The left wing reached Yunzhong (now Togtoh, Inner Mongolia) while the right wing reached the areas of Jiuquan (in western Gansu Province) and Dunhuang (near Jinquan).

After Zhanshilu was made King, Emperor Liu Che sent two batches of envoys to the area of the Huns. One batch of the envoys was sent to mourn the death of King Wuwei. One batch of envoys was sent to mourn for the death of the King of the Right Wing of the Huns. The purpose was to drive a wedge between the two parts of the Huns. When the envoys entered the area of the Huns, they were all escorted to the King of the Huns, who was very angry. He detained all the envoys, more than ten batches of them. Then the envoys sent by the King of the Huns were detained in the Han Dynasty.

In winter that year, there was a heavy snowfall in the area of the Huns. Much of their livestock died of hunger and cold. The King was young and liked to fight; is noblemen were worried. The Left Commander of the army of the Huns decided to kill the King. He sent a man to tell Emperor Liu Che, "I intend to kill the King of the Huns. Then I will surrender to the Han Dynasty. The Han Dynasty is far away from us. I hope Your Majesty will send some troops closer; then I will begin my action." Then Emperor Liu Che ordered General Gongsun Ao to build a city for accepting surrender in Gaojue Guan Pass, in Shuofang Prefecture (Inner Mongolia). The city was called Shouxiang City (meaning "city for accepting surrender").

In spring 104 BC Emperor Liu Che sent Zhao Po Nu, Marquis of Zhouye, to command twenty thousand cavalrymen to go out from Shuofang Prefecture. They marched northward for more than a thousand kilometers. They reached the Junji Mountains (now the Altay Mountains). Zhao Po Nu planned to turn back after they had reached the mountains. When Zhao Po Nu's troops reached the Junji Mountains, the Left Commander of the army of the Huns was ready to carry out his plan to kill the King of the Huns. But his plan was found out, and the King of the Huns killed the Left Commander. Then he sent troops to attack the troops commanded by Zhao Po Nu.

Zhao Po Nu defeated the Huns. The Han troops killed and captured several thousand Hun officers and soldiers; then they turned back. When they reached a place two hundred kilometers away from Shouxiang City, eighty thousand Hun cavalrymen surrounded them. Zhao Po Nu went outside the camp to get water at night, and he was captured. Then the Hun troops started a fierce attack. The Han troops were defeated.

No one ran back to the Han Dynasty to report on this, because according to the military laws of the Han Dynasty, if the troops lost their commanding general and escaped back, they should be executed. Thus, all of the officers and soldiers under Zhao Po Nu surrendered to the Huns. The King of the Huns was extremely glad. He sent troops to attack Shouxiang City. But they could not take it. He sent troops to cross the border of the Han Dynasty. Then the Huns turned back.

In 103 BC King Zhanshilu of the Huns decided to personally lead troops to attack Shouxiang City. But he died of illness before he reached the city.

King Zhanshilu of the Huns was on the throne for only three years. He died in 102 BC. When he died, his son was very young. So the Huns made Julihu, King of the Right Wing of the Huns, King of the Huns. Julihu was the uncle of Zhanshilu.

After Julihu became King of the Huns, Emperor Liu Che sent Xu Zi Wei, a high ranking advisor for the emperor, with troops to build strongholds and fortresses outside Wuyuan Prefecture (Baotou, central Inner Mongolia) as far as to Luqu Mountain (now Yin Shan Mountains). He also sent Han Yue, General of Guerrilla, and Wei Kang, Marquis of Changping, to station their troops by these strongholds and fortresses. He sent General Lu Bo De to build a city by Juyan Lake (now Gaxun Nur, in northwestern Inner Mongolia).

In autumn 102 BC, the Huns invaded the areas of Yunzhong Prefecture (now Togtoh, in the south central part of 1), Dingxiang Prefecture (now Heringer, in the south central part of Inner Mongolia), Wuyuan Prefecture (now Baotou, in the south central part of Inner Mongolia) and Shuofang Prefecture (now Hanggin Qi, in the south central part of Inner Mongolia). They killed several thousand people of the Han Dynasty. Then they went back. They destroyed the strongholds and fortresses built by the Han troops. The King of the Huns sent his King of the Right Wing to invade Jiuquan (in the west part of Gansu Province) and Zhangye (in the northwest part of Gansu Province). The troops under the King of the Right Wing of the Huns killed and captured more than a thousand people. Ren Wen, a Han general, attacked the Huns and defeated them. He got back all the people and property taken by the Huns. When King Julihu of the Huns heard that General Li Guang Li was on his way back after conquering the State of Dayuan and killeing the King, he made plans to attack the Han troops on their way back. But at last he did not dare to do it. In winter that year he died of illness.

King Julihu was on the throne for only one year. After he died, he was succeeded by his younger brother Qietihou.

All the states in the Western Region were shocked by the great victory of the Han army under General Li Guang Li over the State of Dayuan. Emperor Liu Che wanted to carry on the momentum of the victory to attack the Huns. In 101 BC he issued an imperial edict which read, "Emperor Gaozu was once surrounded in Pingcheng by the Huns. The King of the Huns once wrote a letter to insult Empress Dowager Lü Zhi. In the past King Xiang of the State of Qi revenged for the hatred nine generations ago. The Book of Spring and Autumn praised what he had done."

When Qietihou was made King of the Huns, he was afraid that the Han troops would attack the Huns. He let all the envoys detained in the area of the Huns including Lu Chong Guo returned to the Han Dynasty. Emperor Liu Che sent Su Wu, the Commander of the Imperial Guards, to take a lot of treasures to King Qietihou of the Huns. So King Qietihou became very proud of himself and very impolite.

In 100 BC Zhao Po Nu, Marquis of Zhouye, who had been captured by the Huns in 103 BC, escaped back to the Han Dynasty.

In 99 BC Emperor Liu Che sent General Li Guang Li to march west from Jiuquan (in the west part of Gansu Province) with thirty thousand cavalrymen to attack the King of the Right Wing of the Huns in Tian Shan Mountains (situated in Xinjiang Uygur Autonomous Region, China, and Central Asia). They killed and captured more than ten thousand officers and soldiers of the Huns. When they were about to return to the area of the Han Dynasty, the Huns surrounded them. They fought very hard to make a breakthrough, but more than twenty thousand officers and soldiers of the Han army were killed. General Gongsun Ao was sent northward from Xihe Prefecture (now Jungar Qi, Inner Mongolia) to join forces with General Lu Bo De in

Zhuoxie Mountain (in Mandal Govi, Mongolia). They did not find any Huns. Then they turned back.

90. Su Wu Is on a Mission to the Huns

Su Wu was the son of Su Jian, the Commander of the Palace Guards. He became a Palace Guard when he was young. His two brothers were also Palace Guards. He was promoted to be the officer in charge of the horse stables for the emperor. At that time, the Han Dynasty was carrying out expeditions against the Huns. Emperor Liu Che often sent envoys to spy on the situation of the Huns. The King of the Huns detained the envoys sent by the Han Dynasty. Guo Ji, Lu Chong Guo, and the others, more than ten batches of the envoys sent by the Han Dynasty, were detained. The Han Dynasty detained the same number of envoys sent by the King of the Huns.

In 100 BC, Qietihou was made King of the Huns. He was afraid that Emperor Liu Che would send troops to attack his people. However, as he noted, the Emperor of the Han Dynasty was his father-in-law. On that reasoning, he released all the Envoys of the Han Dynasty including Guo Ji and Lu Chong Guo and let them go back. Emperor Liu Che was pleased with what he had done. Therefore he sent Su Wu as his envoy to escort the envoys of the Huns back home. Su Wu also brought a lot of money and precious goods to the King of the Huns to repay for his goodwill. Su Wu, Zhang Sheng, the deputy envoy, and Chang Hui, went to the area of the Huns with a hundred soldiers. They presented all the valuables to the King of the Huns. The King of the Huns became very proud of himself; that wasdiappointing for the Emperor.

When the King of the Huns planned to send representatives of his own to escort Su Wu and the other envoys back to the Han Dynasty, Gouwang and Yuchang were conspiring to revolt against him. Gouwang was the son of the elder sister of King Hunxie. Gouwang and King Hunxie had surrendered to the Han Dynasty in 120 BC. In 103 BC Gouwang and Zhao Po Nu had been captured by the Huns. Wei Lü was originally an envoy sent by the Han Dynasty to the Huns. He surrendered to the Huns and became a high ranking advisor to the King. Gouwang intended to collude with followers of Wei Lü to kidnap the mother of the King of the Huns and take her to the Han Dynasty. When the Han envoy and the deputy envoy arrived, Yuchang let them know, "I hear that the Emperor of the Han Dynasty hates Wei Lü very much. I can give the signal and my archers will kill him. My mother and younger brother are in the Han Dynasty. I hope the Emperor will grant me handsome rewards." Zhang Sheng gave his consent. And he rewarded Yuchang with valuable goods. A month later the King of the Huns went out on a hunting trip. His mother, his sons and his brothers stayed behind. Yuchang led seventy men to carry out his plan.

But one of the men ran out at night and revealed Yuchang's plan to the King's sons and brothers; then supporters of the King of the Huns led troops to fight against the rebels. Gouwang was killed. Yuchang was captured.

The King of the Huns ordered Wei Lü to investigate the rebellion. Zhang Sheng was afraid that his involvement would be revealed. So he told everything to Su Wu. Su Wu said, "Your conspiracy will certainly put me in great danger. Anyone involved in this rebellion will be put to death. It will bring great damage to the Han Dynasty." Su Wu intended to commit suicide. But Zhang Sheng and Chang Hui stopped him.

Yuchang told the King of the Huns that Zhang Sheng had taken part in the conspiracy. The King was certainly very angry. He summoned all the nobles together to discuss the matter. They wanted to kill the envoys of the Han Dynasty. One of the noble said, "They intend to murder our King. They have committed the most serious crime. We'd better make them surrender." The King of the Huns ordered Wei Lü to summon the envoys before him and forced them to surrender. Su Wu said to Chang Hui and the other envoys, "I have failed to carry out my mission and have forfeited my honor. I am too ashamed to go back to the Han Dynasty." Then he drew out his sword and stabbed himself.

Wei Lü was shocked. He held Su Wu and asked his subordinates to call for the doctor. They dug a pit. They set fire in the pit. Then they put Su Wu on the floor of the pit and stepped on his back till the blood came out. Su Wu stopped breathing for half a day. Then he began breathing again. Chang Hui and the other envoys cried bitterly. Then they carried Su Wu back to their camp. The King of the Huns respected Su Wu's moral integrity. He sent officials to visit Su Wu every day. He arrested Zhang Sheng and put him in jail.

When Su Wu recovered from his wound, the King of the Huns sent officials to ask Su Wu to attend the trial of Yuchang. The King of the Huns discussed with Su Wu what punishment should be given to Yuchang. He intended to take this chance to persuade Su Wu to surrender. The King of the Huns killed Yuchang with his sword. Wei Lü said to Zhang Sheng, "You conspired to murder the close officials of the King of the Huns. You should be executed. If you surrender, the King of the Huns will pardon you." Then Wei Lü raised his sword and was about to kill Zhang Sheng. Then Zhang Sheng said that he would surrender.

Wei Lü turned to Su Wu and said, "Your deputy has committed a crime. You should be punished too." Su Wu said, "I did not conspire with Zhang Sheng. And I am not his relative. Why should I be punished for being related to him?" Wei Lü raised his sword to threaten him. Su Wu stood firm.

Wei Lü said, "I betrayed the Han Dynasty and surrendered to the Huns. The King of the Huns has been very kind to me. He granted me the title of a king. Now I have tens of thousands of people under me. My horses and other livestock spread all around the hills. I enjoy wealth and rank. If you surrender today, you will also enjoy wealth and rank tomorrow. If you die here, you will fertilize the grass. Who will know anything about you?" Su Wu did not give any reply.

Wei Lü continued, "If you follow my advice and surrender, you and I will become brothers. If you don't follow my advice now, there will be no chance for you to see me anymore even if you want to."

Su Wu scolded Wei Lü, saying, "You are an official of the Emperor of the Han Dynasty. Now you ignore all the kindness the Emperor has granted to you. You have betrayed your master. You have surrendered to the Huns. Why should I see you anymore? The King of the Huns has given you the power to decide the life and death of other people. You don't uphold righteousness. Instead, you induce the two masters to fight against each other. You stand by and watch the result.

"The King of the State of Nanyue killed the envoys sent by the Han Dynasty. Then the State of Nanyue was conquered by the Han Dynasty and was divided into nine prefectures. The King of the State of Dayuan killed the envoys of the Han Dynasty. His head was cut off and was hung on the north gate of Chang'an. The King of Gojoseon killed the envoys of the Han Dynasty. Gojoseon was conquered by the Han Dynasty. Now only the Huns have not been conquered. If you know clearly that I will not surrender, and you use this to provoke fighting between the Han Dynasty and the Huns, disaster will fall upon the Huns because of me."

Now Wei Lü was really certain that Su Wu would not surrender, and he told this to the King of the Huns. The King wanted all the more to make Su Wu surrender. He had him locked up in a dungeon without any food or water. It was snowing heavily at that time, and some of it drifted into the dungeon cellar through an air shaft. Su Wu lay on the floor. He put snow and the felt of his coat into his mouth and dhewed until he could swallow them. He survived this way.

Several days later the King of the Huns found that Su Wu was still alive. He was greatly surprised. He thought that Su Wu must be a god. Then he sent soldiers to escort Su Wu to Beihai Sea (now Lake Baikal) where no people lived, and he was set to tending the rams there. The King of the Huns said that he would allow Su Wu come back when the male sheep could produce milk.

When Su Wu got to Beihai Sea, he was not provided any food. He dug into rat holes to catch rats and picked fruits from the trees for food. He still held the envoy's emblematic yak tail flag while tending the sheep. He even kept it in hand while he was sleeping. He stayed there for six years.

King Yuqian, the younger brother of the King of the Huns, went hunting by the Beihai Sea. Su Wu made him nets for hunting animals. And he could repair and improved his bows. King Yuqian liked him. He gave Su Wu with food, clothes and a decent tents. He also provided him with horses and livestock. But three years later, King Yuqian fell ill and died; and his people moved away. In winter that year, all the livestock were stolen by thieves. Su Wu again lived in great difficulty.

91. Li Ling Fights against the Huns

Li Ling was Li Guang's grandson. He became an imperial guard when he was young. He was the commander of the guards of Jianzhang Palace. He was good at riding horse and shooting arrows. He was kind to people and courteous to scholars. He was highly praised by the court officials. Emperor Liu Che said that Li Ling had the demeanor of Li Guang.

He put Li Ling at the head of eight hundred cavalrymen and sent them to go deep into the area of the Huns for a thousand kilometers. Li Ling and his cavalrymen went past Juyan Lake (now Gaxun Nur, in western Inner Mongolia). But they did not find any Huns there, so they turned back.

Emperor Liu Che made him Commander of the Cavalrymen and sent him with five thousand brave soldiers to station in Jiuquan and north of Zhangye (Gansu Province) to prevent raids by the Huns. Several years later, the Emperor sent General Li Guang Li to attack the State of Dayuan in the Western Region, and he had Li Ling take his troops to go after General Li Guang Li. When Li Ling reached the Great Wall, General Li Guang Li had his troops turn around. Emperor Liu Che granted a letter to Li Ling ordering him to leave the main force behind and lead five hundred cavalrymen to go out from Dunhuang (in western Gansu Province) to Yanze (Salt Lake) (now Lop Nur), to welcome the returning General Li Guang Li. After that Li Ling and his troops were stationed in Zhangye.

In 99 BC, General Li Guang Li took thirty thousand cavalrymen from Jiuquan (Gansu Province) to attack the King of the Right Wing of the Huns in the Tian Shan Mountains. Emperor Liu Che summoned Li Ling to the court and ordered him to take his troops to transport provisions for the army under General Li Guang Li.

Li Ling touched his head to the ground and said, "My soldiers are all brave fighters. They are good at using swords and shooting arrows. I hope I may take my troops to the south side of Langan Mountains to attack the Huns. In this way the troops of the Huns can be divided so that the King of the Huns cannot send all his troops to harass the troops under General Li Guang Li." Emperor Liu Che said, "You don't want to be a subordinate to General Li Guang Li! I have sent out many troops. I have no cavalrymen to give you."

Li Ling said, "If Your Majesty cannot send me any cavalrymen, I may defeat the enemy troops with a force inferior in number. I will command five thousand foot soldiers to attack the Court of the King of the Huns." Emperor Liu Che admired his courage and gave his consent.

So he issued an imperial edict to General Lu Bo De ordering him to command his troops to meet Li Ling's troops on their way back. But General Lu Bo De did not want to be the backup force for Li Ling. He presented a memorial to the Emperor which read, "It is now autumn time. The Huns' horses are very strong. It is not the right time to fight them. I hope Your Majesty may let me stay here till next spring. By that time I will command five thousand men in Jiuquan and five thousand men in Zhangye to attack the Huns in the East Junji Mountain and the West Junji Mountain. The King of the Huns will be surely captured." After Emperor Liu Che had read the memorial, he was very angry. He suspected that Li Ling had regretted offering to go to attack the Court of the King of the Huns and had instigated Lu Bo De to present the memorial.

He issued an imperial edict to Lu Bo De which read, "I want to send cavalrymen to be put under General Li Ling. He said that he would defeat the Hun troops with a force inferior in number. Now the Huns have come into the area of Xihe. Now I order you to command your troops to Xihe to block the strategic point along the Hunss' route." He issued an imperial edict to Li Ling which read, "You should command your troops in September to march out of the Great Wall to the Le River in the south of East Junji Mountain. Look for the Huns there. If you do not find any, you may go along the way from which General Zhao Po Nu defeated the Huns. Then you may reach Shouxiang City and let your troops to have a good rest. When you get there, send a cavalryman to report to me."

Then Li Ling commanded five thousand foot soldiers to march from Juyan Lake (now Gaxun Nur) to the north. They marched for thirty days and reached Junji Mountains (Altay Mountains). They established camps there. Li Ling drew maps of the mountains and rivers they had passed. Then Li Ling sent Chen Bu Le, a cavalryman under him, to take the maps to Emperor Liu Che. The Emperor summoned Chen Bu Le to have an interview, during which Chen Bu Le said that the officers and soldiers under Li Ling would serve Li Ling heart and soul. Emperor Liu Che was very glad to hear that.

When Li Ling and his troops reached Junji Mountains, the King of the Huns and his troops were there. The King of the Huns sent thirty thousand cavalrymen to surround Li Ling. Li Ling's troops were camped between two mountains. They put all the carts up to form a wall around the camp. Li Ling commanded his troops to march forth, and he arranged them in battle formation. The soldiers at the front of the battle formation held spears and shields. Behind them were soldiers carrying bows and arrows. Li Ling ordered, "When you hear the sound of the drums, you should charge at the enemy. When you hear the sound of the gongs, you should retreat."

The King of the Huns saw that there were only a few Han troops. He commanded his troops to the Han encampment. Li Ling ordered his archers to shoot, and arrows rained down at the Huns. Many Hun soldiers were kille. The Huns retreated to the mountain. The Han troops gave hot pursuit. They killed several thousand Huns soldiers.

The King of the Huns was shocked. He transferred eighty thousand cavalrymen from the left wing and the right wing to attack Li Ling's troops. The out-numbered Han carried on the fight while beating a retreat. They went southward for several days until they reached a valley. Many soldiers under Li Ling were wounded by arrows. Those soldiers wounded by three arrows were put on carts. Those soldiers who were wounded by two arrows took care of the carts. Those who were wounded by one arrow continued to fight. Li Ling asked out loud why the morale of his troops was so low, that the soldiers would not go forward to fight when they heard the beating of the drums. "Are there women in my army?" he asked. As a matter of fact, when the army under Li Ling started out, the wives of the robbers in Northeast China went to the border area and the soldiers took them as their wives. They hid the women in carriages. Li Ling searched the women out and killed all of them.

The next day Li Ling commanded his troops to attack the Huns and they killed three thousand Hun officers and soldiers. Then he commanded his troops to go southeast. They went along the road leading to Longcheng (situated on the right bank of the upper reach of Orkhon River, in the central part of Mongolia) for five days. They reached a swamp with reeds growing in it. The Huns set fire to the reeds. Li Ling also ordered his soldiers to set fire to the reeds so as to protect themselves.

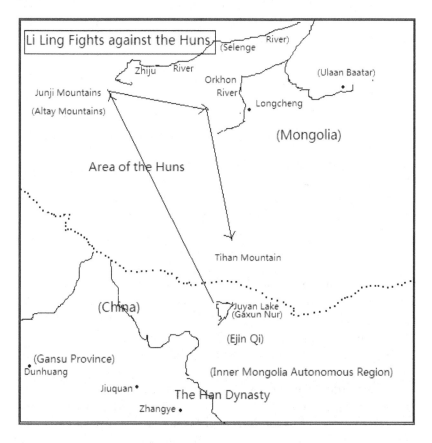

Li Ling Fights against the Huns

The troops under Li Ling went to the foot of a mountain. The Huns were on the top of the mountain. The King of the Huns sent his son to command a cavalry attack on Li Ling. The foot soldiers under Li Ling fought with the Huns in the forest. They killed several thousand Huns. Then Li Ling ordered his archers to aim at the King of the Huns. The King of the Huns climbed down the mountain and made his escape. On that day, the Han troops caught a Hun soldier. He said, "The King of the Huns told us, 'These are the elite troops of the Han army. We cannot defeat them. They retreated southward and got close to the Great Wall. Is there an ambush there?' The heads of the sub tribes said, 'With Your Highness personally at the command, more than thirty thousand cavalrymen attacked several thousand Han troops, but we cannot wipe them out. We cannot make the people of the border areas submit to us anymore. The Han Dynasty will look down upon us.'" Then they fought with the Han troops under Li Ling in the valley. But they could not defeat the Han army and Li Ling. So the King of the Huns planned to lead his troops in retreat.

At that time the troops under Li Ling were in fact in danger. There were many Hun cavalrymen. They had to fight many battles with the Huns in one day. They killed or wounded two thousand Hun soldiers again. The King of the Huns found that the situation was unfavorable for them and he planned to retreat. It happened that Hou Guan Gan, a soldier in the army under Li Ling, was insulted by his officer and he escaped and surrendered to the Huns. He told the King of the Huns, "Li Ling's troops have reinforcements. They have only a few arrows left. Li Ling and Han Yan Nian are leading eight hundred men under each of them as vanguards. They use yellow flags and white flags. You may defeat them with your best cavalry troops."

That information perked up the King of the Huns, who sent his cavalrymen to attack the troops under Li Ling. The Huns shouted loudly, "Li Ling and Han Yan Nian, surrender now!" The Huns attacked Li Ling and Han Yan Nian fiercely. Li Ling's troops were in the valley. The Hun troops were on the mountains, shooting arrows at the Han soldiers in the valley. The Han troops moved southward. Before they reached Tihan Mountain, they had run out of arrows, five hundred thousand in all.

Li Ling ordered his troops to give up all the carts and carriages. He still had three thousand troops. He ordered his soldiers to break the wheels of the carts and carriages and to take the axles of the carts and carriages as weapons. The officers used their swords to fight their way into the valley. The King of the Huns commanded his troops to pursue them. The Huns threw down stones from the mountain to the valley and killed many Han soldiers. The Han troops could not get out of the valley. At night, Li Ling put on the clothes of an ordinary man and planned to go out of the camp. Many officers and soldiers wanted to follow him. Li Ling stopped them, saying, "Don't follow me. I intend to go out to kill the King of the Huns single-handedly." Li Ling was out for some time. Then he returned. He said with a long sigh, "I have been defeated. I will have to die." The officers under him said, "The Huns are awed by your might. But it is the will of the Heaven that you have lost the battles. Now you are looking for a way to return. Zhao Po Nu was captured by the Huns. Later he escaped and came back. The Emperor treated him kindly. You have established much greater military contributions than that of Zhao Po Nu. The Emperor will surely treat you better than Zhao Po Nu." Li Ling said, "Say no more! If I don't die in battle, I will not be regarded as a warrior." Then he ordered the soldiers to cut all the flags down and bury all the precious things in the ground. Li Ling exclaimed, "If I had ten more arrows, I could fight my way out. Now I have no arrows to fight with. I will be captured tomorrow! You may find your way to escape. When you are lucky enough to make your escape, you should report what has happened to the Emperor." He distributed dry food to all the officers and soldiers. At midnight, he beat the drum to urge the soldiers to get up. Li Ling and Han Yan Nian got on their horses and rode out of the camp. Only ten brave men followed them. Several thousand Hun soldiers pursued them. Han Yan Nian was killed in the battle. Li Ling said, "I am too ashamed to see the Emperor!" and he surrendered to the Huns. His troops dispersed. About four hundred men made their escape to the Great Wall.

The place in which Li Ling was defeated was just about fifty kilometers away from the Great Wall. The officer on the Great Wall reported the situation to Emperor Liu Che. Emperor Liu Che wanted Li Ling to fight till he was killed. He summoned Li Ling's mother and wife to the court. He sent a fortune-teller to read their faces. The fortune-teller could not see any sign of sadness for the death of Li Ling.

Later when Emperor Liu Che got word that Li Ling had surrendered to the Huns, and he was very angry. He scolded Chen Bu Le, who committed suicide. All the court officials said that Li Ling had committed a grave crime. Emperor Liu Che asked Sima Qian, the Grand Historian, what he thought about Li Ling. Sima Qian praised Li Ling, saying, "Li Ling is dutiful to his father and mother. He is kind to his subordinates. He is daring regardless of personal danger. He would fight to defend the country to his death. He always put his determination into practice. He is a man of strong character. But once he made a mistake in action, all the officials who have never experienced any danger blame him. This is unjust! Li Ling commanded only five thousand men and went deep into the area of the Huns. He fought with the strong Hun army of more than 30,000 men. His troops have caused great casualties to the Hun army. The King of the Huns sent all his troops to attack Li Ling, but Li Ling commanded his troops to fight for more than five hundred kilometers. His troops used up all their arrows. They were blocked on their way back. His soldiers fought bare-handedly with Huns holding swords and knives. All the soldiers under Li Ling were determined to fight till they died. He has fought as well as the most famous generals in ancient times. Although he was defeated and surrendered, he caused great casualties to the enemy. He did not die in battle and he did not kill himself because he wanted to have a chance to come back alive to serve the Han Dynasty."

At first, when General Li Guang Li commanded a great army to march out, Emperor Liu Che had ordered Li Ling to lead his troops as the reinforcements for Li Guang Li's army. When Li Ling met with the King of the Huns, he won a great victory. But General Li Guang Li did not make much contribution this time. So Emperor Liu Che got the idea that Sima Qian wanted to downplay General Li Guang Li and praise Li Ling. Emperor Liu Che was so angry that he ordered to have Sima Qian castrated.

The King of the Huns as inpressed by Li Ling. He married his daughter to him, and made him King of Youxiao. He made Wei Lü King of Dingling. Both Li Ling and Wei Lü enjoyed high rank and wealth.

92. Li Ling Tries to Persuade Su Wu to Surrender to the Huns

In the past Su Wu and Li Ling had both been Palace Guards. Later, Su Wu was sent on a mission to the Huns, in 100 BC. The next year, 99 BC, Li Ling surrendered to the Huns. At that time he did not dare to see Su Wu.

Later, the King of the Huns sent Li Ling to Beihai Sea (now Lake Baikal) to persuade Su Wu to surrender. When Li Ling got to the place where Su Wu was, Li Ling said to Su Wu, "The King of the Huns knows that you and I are good friends. So he has sent me to persuade you to surrender. You are very devoted to the Emperor. But you cannot go back to the Han Dynasty. You have to stay in this wild place where no people live. Who will know your devotion and good faith?

"And is it worth it? In the past, your eldest brother Su Jian was the commander of the palace guards in charge of the Emperor's carriage. He accompanied the Emperor to Yu Palace in Yong. When he was helping the carriage of the Emperor get down the steps in front of the palace, the carriage hit a post and the carriage axle broke. He was accused of committing a crime violating the Emperpr's majesty. At this, he drew out his sword and killed himself. The Emperor only granted two million coins to bury him.

"Your younger brother Su Yu Qing accompanied the Emperor to Houtu, east of the Yellow River, to offer sacrifices to the Goddess of Earth. A eunuch on horseback and the Emperor's son-in-law were scrambling to get onboard a ship. The eunuch pushed the son-in-law into the waterand he was drowned. The eunuch on horseback escaped. The Emperor ordered Su Yu Qing to catch the eunuch, and he rode after him but could not catch him. He was afraid that the Emperor would punish him for his failure, so he committed suicide by taking poison.

"Before I came here, your mother died. I escorted her coffin to Yang Mausoleum to be buried there. Your wife was still young. She remarried. Your two younger sisters and your two daughters and one son still survived. Now more than ten years have past. I don't know whether they are still alive or not. Life is short. You should not torture yourself like that. When I surrendered, I felt so ashamed of myself that I nearly went mad. I felt ashamed to have betrayed the Han Dynasty. My mother was put into jail because I surrendered.

"You don't want to surrender. Neither do I! His Majesty is old now. The laws are changed frequently. More than thirty families of officials have been exterminated. If you go back, I can't predict whether you will be killed or not. For whom are you working? I hope you may take my advice and surrender."

Su Wu replied, "My father and I have not established great contributions. But the Emperor made us generals and granted us the titles of marquis. My brothers and I are willing to die for the Emperor. If I may sacrifice my life to preserve my virtue, I will willingly die. Serving the Emperor is like the son serving his father. A son is willing to die for his father. Now, say no more!"

Li Ling stayed there for several more days. Then he said to Su Wu, "I hope you will take my advice and surrender." Su Wu stopped him by saying, "I consider that I died long ago. If you really want me to surrender, I will die right in front of you today." Li Ling saw that Su Wu was really a devoted man. He said with a long sigh, "Su Wu is really a righteous man! Wei Lü and I have committed a serious crime!" He wept bitterly. Then he bid farewell to Su Wu and left.

Li Ling wanted to give some livestock to Su Wu, but he was ashamed to send the animals himself. He let his Hun wife give tens of cows and sheep to Su Wu. Later Li Ling went to Beihai Sea again. He said to Su Wu, "The soldiers on the Yunzhong border captured a Han soldier. He said that all the officials and people have put on white clothes. They said that the Emperor of the Han Dynasty had died." When Su Wu heard this, he faced southward and cried bitterly. He cried so bitterly that he spat blood.

Several years after Emperor Liu Fu Ling had ascended the throne of the Han Dynasty, the Han Dynasty implemented the policy of pacification through marriage towards the Huns. The Emperor sent envoys to look for Su Wu. They told the envoys that Su Wu had already died. Chang Hui went to see the envoys at night. He confessed to the envoys all the errors he had made. Then he asked the envoys to tell the King of the Huns that the Emperor of the Han Dynasty had shot down a wild goose in a hunting trip in Shanglin Hunting Ground; he found a piece of white silk tied on the goose's leg, and on it a letter was written saying that Su Wu was still alive, in the wilderness. The envoy was very glad. He told the King of the Huns what Chang Hui had taught him to say. The King was surprised and admitted to the Han envoys, "Yes, Su Wu really is alive."

Then Li Ling held a wine party for Su Wu. He said to Su Wu, "Now you will go back to the Han Dynasty. You are now very famous in the area of the Huns. You have established great contributions to the Han Dynasty. You will be regarded as the most devoted man in history. I am incompetent and timid. If the Emperor had overlooked my crimes and spared my mother, I would do my best to realize my wish created in disgrace. But now all the members of my clan have been exterminated. Now I have nothing to worry about. It's all over. I say all this because I want you to know what I am thinking about. You and I are persons of two different countries. Now, let's part forever." Li Ling rose up from his seat and danced, while singing, "I have gone for a thousand kilometers walking across the great desert. I fought bravely against the Huns for the Emperor. We used up all the arrows and all the weapons were broken. All the soldiers were killed and I have become infamous. My mother has already died. I cannot go back even if I want to pay the debt of gratitude." Then Li Ling shed tears. He said farewell to Su Wu. The King of the Huns let Su Wu go back to the Han Dynasty.

In 81 BC Su Wu went back to Chang'an, the capital of the Han Dynasty. The Emperor made him minister in charge of minority nationality affairs enjoying 120,000 kg of rice yearly as salary. Su Wu had stayed in the area of the Huns for nineteen years. When he was sent on a mission to the Huns, he was in the prime of life. By the time he came back, he had become a white-haired old man.

93. The Birth of Prince Liu Fu Ling

When Emperor Liu Che was on a hunting trip, he went past Hejian (central Hebei Province). A fortune-teller told the Emperor that there was a very special woman in that place. Emperor Liu Che sent an envoy to summon that woman before him. When she came, her fists were always clenched. Emperor Liu Che touched her fists, and her fists opened up. Emperor Liu Che bestowed favor on her. He granted her the concubine rank of Jieyu (the second rank), and she was put in Gouyi Palace. So she was named Lady Gouyi. She conceived a child and was pregnant for fourteen months. In 93 BC she gave birth to a baby boy.

The boy was named Liu Fu Ling. Emperor Liu Che noted, "In the past, Emperor Yao's mother was pregnant for fourteen months and then gave birth to Emperor Yao. Lady Gouyi was also pregnant for fourteen months." So the gate of Gouyi Palace where Lady Gouyi had given birth to Prince Liu Fu Ling was named "The Gate of the Mother of Emperor Yao". When Liu Fu Ling was six years old, he was already tall and strong. He was a clever boy. Emperor Liu Che often said that Liu Fu Ling took after him. He liked the boy very much. He wanted to make Liu Fu Ling the successor to the throne, but Liu Fu Ling was still very young and Lady Gouyi was in the prime of her life. Emperor Liu Che was afraid that if Lady Gouyi gained power, she would ruin the Han Dynasty. So he hesitated for a long time.

94. Jiang Chong Wins the Favor of Emperor Liu Che

Jiang Chong was from Handan (in southern Hebei Province). He had a younger sister who was good at playing musical instrument and dancing. She was married to Liu Dan, the crown prince of the State of Zhao. Jiang Chong won the favor of King Liu Peng Zu of the State of Zhao (southern Hebei Province) and was regarded as the most respected guest by the King of the State of Zhao. Later Crown Prince Liu Dan came to suspect that Jiang Chong had told all his secrets and shameful acts to his father. So Crown Prince Liu Dan hated Jiang Chong very much. He sent officials to arrest Jiang Chong, but they could not get him. They arrested Jiang Chong's father and brothers. They were interrogated and then executed. Jiang Chong ran away from the State of Zhao. He went westward to Chang'an, the capital of the Han Dynasty. He went to the court to present a report to the Emperor that Crown Prince Liu Dan of the State of Zhao had committed adultery with his own sister and the concubines of the King of the State of Zhao, and that Liu Dan had colluded with the local despots to engage in illegal activities. When Emperor Liu Che read the report, he was very angry. He sent envoys to summon the troops in different prefectures to surround the palace of the King of the State of Zhao to arrest Crown Prince Liu Dan. The Crown Prince was arrested and was thrown into the jail in Wei Prefecture. After trial he was sentenced to death.

King Liu Peng Zu of the State of Zhao was Emperor Liu Che's elder half-brother. He wrote a memorial to Emperor Liu Che to defend his son Liu Dan which read, "Jiang Chong is a low ranking official in charge of catching fugitives. He has made false accusation against my son. His purpose is to induce the anger of Your Majesty. He is determined to get Your Majesty's consent to take revenge for his private grudge. He will not recant even if he were put into a big pot and boiled to death or chopped to pieces. I will choose brave men from my state and lead them to fight against the Huns. I will do my best to atone for the crime committed by my son." Emperor Liu Che did not allow him to do that, but he deprived Liu Dan of the title of the crown prince of the State of Zhao.

When Emperor Liu Che summoned Jiang Chong to Quantai Palace in Shanglin Garden (west of Si'an, Shaanxi Province), Zhang Chong asked permission see the Emperor in plain clothes and hat. Emperor Liu Che gave his permission. Jiang Chong put on a light overcoat made of silk, and the back of the coat was like a swallow tail. There was a long bird's feather on the top of his hat. When he walked, his light silk coat fluttered and the feather on his hat waved. Jiang Chong was a tall handsome man. When Emperor Liu Che saw him, he was surprised and said to the officials standing by him, "There are many magnificent persons in the State of Yan and the State of Zhao." When Jiang Chong went before Emperor Liu Che, he answered all the questions raised by the Emperor. Emperor Liu Che liked him very much.

Jiang Chong offered to go to the Huns as an envoy. Emperor Liu Che asked him how he would complete his mission. Jiang Chong answered, "I will act according to the changes of the situation. I will make my plan depending on the plan of the enemy. I will not make my plan before hand." Then Emperor Liu Che appointed him as an envoy and sent him on a mission to the Huns. When he came bac, Emperor Liu Che appointed him the Imperial Councilor in charge of catching thieves in the capital area and prohibiting over extravagance.

Many relatives of the Emperor and the high ranking officials lived an over-luxurious life. Jiang Chong presented a memorial to Emperor Liu Che accusing all of them. He suggested the Emperor confiscate their properties and send them to serve in the north army against the Huns. Emperor Liu Che accepted his suggestion and granted him a reply letter. Jiang Chong took the letter and went to see the commander of the imperial guards. He sent the imperial guards to arrest the high ranking officials who led an over luxurious life. He ordered the palace guards to prohibit anyone to go into or out of the palace without permission from him. All the relatives of the Emperor were panic-stricken. They went into the palace and knelt down before Emperor Liu Che and touched their heads on the ground, begging the Emperor to spare them. They said that they would pay money to atone for the crimes they had committed. Emperor Liu Che gave his consent. He ordered them to give money to the north army. The north army got tens of millions of coins. Emperor Liu Che thought that Jiang Chong was a faithful, law-abiding and devoted man. So Jiang Chong won the favor of the Emperor.

One day when Jiang Chong went out, he saw that Princess Liu Piao, Emperor Liu Che's aunt, and his followers were driving carriages and riding horses on the road set aside for the Emperor. Jiang Chong stopped them and asked loudly why they were so bold as to use the road reserved for the Emperor. Princess Liu Piao said, "I got permission from Empress Dowager." Jiang Chong said, "Only you can walk on this road. Others are not allowed to go on this road." He confiscated all of Princess Liu Piao carriages and horses.

Jiang Chong accompanied Emperor Liu Che to Ganquan (Shaanxi Province). At that time some persons sent by Crown Prince Liu Jü were driving carriages and riding horses along the road reserved for the Emperor. Jiang Chong arrested all of them and sent them to be interrogated. He confiscated all the Crown Prince's carriages and horses. When Crown Prince Liu Jü heard about this, he sent a person to convey his words to Jiang Chong: "I don't care about my carriages and horses. But I really don't want His Majesty to know about this. I hope you will spare the individuals involved. I will scold them seriously." Jiang Chong refused to do that. He presented a memorial to the Emperor to accuse the Crown Prince. Emperor Liu Che praised him, saying, "Jiang Chong is a good example for all the officials." So he won great favor from the Emperor. He became the most powerful man in the capital area.

Jiang Chong was promoted to the position of Minister of the Treasury, in charge of the treasuries of the imperial house. But not long later he was caught committing some crimes and was dismissed from the position.

95. THE CASE OF WITCHCRAFT

Premier Gongsun He's wife was Wei Jun Ru, the elder sister of Empress Wei Zi Fu. So Gongsun He won the favor of Emperor Liu Che. Gongsun He's son Gongsun Jing Sheng took his father's position as the Official in Charge of Emperor's Carriages and Horses. Gongsun Jing Sheng was a conceited and dissolute man. He did not observe the law. He spent nineteen million coins from the north army's budget without permission. His crime was found out. He was arrested and thrown in jail.

At that time Emperor Liu Che issued an imperial order to catch Zhu Shi An, a local tyrant in Yanling (in the east part of Xianyang, Shaaxi Province). Gongsun He asked Emperor Liu Che to let him command some troops to catch Zhu Shi An so as to atone for the crimes committed by his son. Emperor Liu Che gave his permission. After a hard fighting, Gongsun He caught Zhu Shi An. Zhu Shi An laughed and said to him, "You will bring great disaster to your whole clan!" Then Zhu Shi An presented a memorial to Emperor Liu Che from the jail accusing Gongsun Jing Sheng of having committed adultery with Princess Yangshi, Emperor Liu Che's daughter, and of having sent witches to bury little wooden figures on the Emperor's road to curse the Emperor when he rode to Ganquan (Shaanxi Province).

In January 91 BC Gongsun He was arrested and was thrown into jail. Gongsun He and his son Gongsun Jing Sheng were interrogated and then were executed. All the members of Gongsun He's clan were executed. Emperor Liu Che appointed Liu Qu Mao as premier. Liu Qu Mao was the son of King Liu Sheng of the State of Zhongshan. Liu Sheng was the son of Emperor Liu Qi.

When Emperor Liu Che was twenty-nine years old, Empress Wei Zi Fu gave birth to a baby boy. He was given the name of Liu Jü. Emperor Liu Che liked the boy very much. In 122 BC, when the boy was seven years old, the Emperor made Liu Jü Crown Prince. When Liu Jü grew up, he was a benevolent, considerate, kind and cautious man. But Emperor Liu Che thought that Liu Jü was not capable and was not like him. By that time his favorite concubine Lady Wang had given birth to Liu Hong, Concubine Li had given birth to Liu Dan and Liu Xu; Lady Li had given birth to Liu Bo. So Empress Wei Zi Fu and Crown Prince Liu Jü lost favor with the Emperor. They often felt uneasy.

Emperor Liu Che sensed their uneasiness. He said to Grand General Wei Qing, Empress Wei Zi Fu's brother, "The Han Dynasty has just been established. The local tribes around China invade our territory. If I do not make changes to the laws, the later generations will not have appropriate laws to follow. If I don't send troops to carry out expeditions against the invaders, the whole country will be unstable. So I have to shake people up. If my later generations act like me, the Han Dynasty will fall like the Qin Dynasty. The Crown Prince is honest and sincere and likes peace. He will certainly be able to keep the whole country at peace. He will not worry me. Only the Crown Prince may bring peace to the whole country. I hear that the Empress and the Crown Prince feel disturbed. You may go and tell them not to worry about anything." Grand General Wei Qing bowed to the Emperor to express his thanks.

When Empress Wei Zi Fu heard this, she took off all the decorations and asked Emperor Liu Che to pardon her. When the Crown Prince tried to persuade Emperor Liu Che to stop the expeditions against the local tribes, Emperor Liu Che smiled and said, "I will take the trouble and let you have the leisure. Is it a good idea?" Every time when Emperor Liu Che carried out an inspection outside of the capital, he asked the Crown Prince to handle state affairs and let Empress Wei Zi Fu be in charge of palace of the imperial concubines. When Emperor Liu Che came back from his inspection, the Crown Prince and the Empress reported the most important things that had happened in the palace and the state to the Emperor. He was satisfied with their work.

The Emperor applied the laws strictly. He appointed many cruel officials. The Crown Prince was honest and kind. He often redressed misjudged cases. He won the support of the people. But the officials who applied strict laws disliked him. Empress Wei Zi Fu was afraid that the Crown Prince would act against the will of the Emperor. So she persuaded the Crown Prince to pay attention to the Emperor's intention and not do anything at his own will. When Emperor Liu Che heard about this, he said that the Crown Prince was right — and the Empress had taken the wrong view. The officials who were honest and kind were on the side of the Crown Prince. But the cruel officials who applied strict laws were against him. So very few officials praised the Crown Prince but many officials said bad words about the Crown Prince before Emperor Liu Che.

After Wei Qing died, Empress Wei Zi Fu and the Crown Prince had nobody to depend on. The officials who were against the Crown Prince tried to get rid of him. The Emperor was not very close to his sons, and Empress Wei Zi Fu had very few chances to meet the Emperor. One day Crown Prince Liu Jü went to visit Empress Wei Zi Fu. He stayed in her palace for a long time. Su Wen, a eunuch, told the Emperor that the Crown Prince had been playing with the maids in the palace of the Empress. Emperor Liu Che increased the number of maids in the Crown Prince's palace to two hundred girls. When the Crown Prince found out, he hated Su Wen very much.

Su Wen and the other two eunuchs Chang Rong and Wang Bi secretly observed every error made by the Crown Prince and reported them to Emperor Liu Che. Empress Wei Zi Fu hated these eunuchs very much. She wanted to send the Crown Prince to ask Emperor Liu Che to kill them. The Crown Prince said to his mother, "We have not done anything wrong. Why should we be afraid of them? My father is a wise Emperor. He would not believe such slanderous words. There is nothing to worry about."

Then one day Emperor Liu Che fell ill. He sent Chang Rong to summon the Crown Prince before him. When Chang Rong came back, he told the Emperor that the Crown Prince seemed to be glad when to know that the Emperor had fallen ill. When the Crown Prince came, Emperor Liu Che saw that there were tears on his face; but the Crown Prince forced a smile. Emperor Liu Che felt strange and asked the Crown Prince why there were tears on his face. He said that he was very sad when he had heard that his father had fallen ill. Now the Emperor saw that Chang Rong had told a lie. So he ordered to have Chang Rong executed. Empress Wei Zi Fu was very cautious. She avoided doing anything that might arouse suspicion. Although she had lost favor with the Emperor, she still was respected.

At that time many sorcerers and witches gathered in Chang'an, the capital. They practiced unorthodox ways and spread fallacies to deceive people. They did all kinds of wicked things. The sorceress went into the palace of the imperial concubines. They taught the women how to avoid danger. They buried small wooden figures in the ground of the palace and offered sacrifices to them. The imperial concubines were jealous of each other. So they reported each other's wrong doings to the Emperor. They told him that the other concubines had buried small wooden figures to curse the Emperor. Emperor Liu Che was very angry. He ordered that the concubines and the officials should be killed. Several hundred of them were executed.

Emperor Liu Che was often suspicious. One day when he was sleeping, he dreamed that several thousand wooden figures were beating him with rods. He woke up with a start. From then on he was often absent-minded and forgetful.

Jiang Chong pondered his situation. He already had a grudge with Crown Prince Liu Jü and Empress Wei Zi Fu. He saw that Emperor Liu Che was already old. He was afraid that after the Emperor died, the Crown Prince and the Empress would kill him; so he decided to get rid of the Crown Prince and the Empress. He said to the Emperor that his illness was caused by witchcraft. Then Emperor Liu Che appointed Jiang Chong as his envoy in charge of the case of witchcraft. Jiang Chong led some Hun sorcerers into the palace to dig into the ground to look for wooden figures. They arrested the sorcerers and witches. They watched for those who came out at night to offer sacrifices and say curses and those who came out at night to look for supernatural beings. They put distillers' grains on the place where the witches had offered sacrifices and said curses. They tortured the witches with burned iron and clamps to force them to admit that they had cursed the Emperor. From then on, people began to accuse each other of witchcraft and placing curses on the Emperor. Several tens of thousands of people in the capital and the other prefectures and states were involved and executed. Emperor Liu Che was already sixty-six years old. He suspected that the court officials around him were practicing witchcraft and making curses against him. He put them in jail. The officials did not dare to defend themselves against the charges.

Jiang Chong knew the intention of the Emperor. He sent Tanhe, a Hun sorcerer, to say to Emperor Liu Che, "There is a stream of witchcraft in the palace. If it is not got rid of, Your Majesty may not recover from the illness." Then the Emperor sent Jiang Chong into the palace. He went into the hall for the Emperor and destroyed the throne. He ordered his followers to dig into the ground to look for the wooden figures. The Emperor sent Han Yue, Marquis of Andao, Zhang Gan, the Imperial Councilor, and Su Wen, a eunuch, to assist Jiang Chong. Jiang Chong first searched the palaces of the imperial concubines who had lost favor of the Emperor, then the palace of the Empress and the palace of the Crown Prince. They dug the ground of the palaces all over. The palaces were in such a mess that the Crown Prince and the Empress could not set up their beds. Jiang Chong reported to Emperor Liu Che, "We found many small wooden figures in the palace of the Crown Prince. We also found a piece of silk on which cursing words were written. This is an act of treason and heresy. So we have to report this to Your Majesty."

The Crown Prince was very afraid. He asked his teacher Shi De what he should do. Shi De was afraid that he would be accused together with the Crown Prince. So he said to the Crown Prince, "Some time ago Premier Gongsun He and his son Gongsun Jing Sheng, two princesses and the members of the family of Wei, were involved in this case. Now the Hun sorcerers and Jiang Chong have found wooden figures in the palace. We do not know whether these figures were buried in the ground by the Hun sorcerers or they really existed in the ground. We cannot prove that we are innocent. We may pretend that we have received an imperial edict to arrest Jiang Chong and the Hun sorcerers and throw them into jail. They should be punished severely for their treacherous acts. Now His Majesty has fallen ill and he is in Ganquan. You and the Empress have sent officials to convey your greetings to His Majesty. But they were not allowed to see him. We do not know whether His Majesty is still alive or has already passed away. Now the treacherous court officials act as if he were already gone. Do you remember how Ying Fu Su, the eldest son of the First Emperor of the Qin Dynasty, was forced to commit suicide by the treacherous court officials Li Si and Zhao Gao with a false imperial order?" The Crown Prince said, "I am the son of His Majesty. How can I kill a court official at my own will without an imperial edict? It would be better for me to go before His Majesty and beg him to pardon me." The Crown Prince intended to go to Ganquan to see his father. But Jiang Chong was about to arrest the Crown Prince. The Crown Prince did not know what he should do. So he took Shi De's advice.

One day in July 91 BC the Crown Prince sent some men pretending to be envoys sent by the Emperor to arrest Jiang Chong and his followers. Han Yue, the Marquis of Andao, suspected that they were not sent by the Emperor. He would not accept the false imperial edict. So the false envoys killed Han Yue. After Jiang Chong had been arrested, he was brought before the Crown Prince. The Crown Prince drew out his sword and killed Jiang Chong. He said angrily, "You treacherous thief from the State of Zhao. You have ruined the King of the State of Zhao and his son. Now you are going to ruin my father and me!" The Crown Prince arrested all the Hun sorcerers and burned them to death in Shanlin Garden. He sent an envoy to go into the palace of the Empress to tell the her what had happened. Then he ordered his followers to take all the carriages and horses in the palace. They took out the weapons from the armories. He mobilized the guards of the Changle Palace.

Chang'an, the capital of the Han Dynasty, was in great chaos. The people said that the Crown Prince had held a rebellion. Su Wen escaped. He went to Ganquan to tell the Emperor that the Crown Prince had rebelled. The Emperor said, "The Crown Prince has done this because he is afraid and he is angry with Jiang Chong and his followers." Emperor Liu Che sent an envoy to summon the Crown Prince to Ganquan. The envoy did not dare to meet the Crown Prince. He turned back and said to Emperor Liu Che, "The Crown Prince has rebelled. He intended to kill me. So I have run back." Emperor Liu Che was very angry. When Premier Liu Qu Mao got the information that the Crown Prince had held a rebellion, he immediately ran away. He lost his official seals. He sent an officer to take a horse-drawn carriage to report to Emperor Liu Che that the Crown Prince had held a rebellion. The Emperor asked the officer, "What does the premier plan to do?" The officer said, "The premier has kept the rebellion a secret. He did not dare to send troops to suppress it."

Emperor Liu Che was very angry and said, "It is very clear that the Crown Prince has held a rebellion. Why should he keep it a secret! The premier does not have the spirit of the Duke of Zhou who put down the rebellion held by his two younger brothers Guanshu and Caishu and had them executed." Emperor Liu Che granted an imperial edict to Premier Liu Qu Mao which read, "Now I order you to capture and kill the rebels. If you are successful in doing so, I will grant you handsome rewards. You should erect carts as shields. You should not fight face to face with the rebels. You may shut all the gates of the city and you should not let the rebels escape from the city."

Meanwhile the Crown Prince issued a declaration accusing the court officials which read, "The Emperor is now in Ganquan. He is ill. He suspects there is a rebellion. The treacherous court officials are planning to stage an armed rebellion."

Emperor Liu Che came to Chang'an from Ganquan. He stayed in Jianzhang Palace on the outskirts of Chang'an. He mobilized the troops stationed in the nearby counties. He let the high ranking officials and the premier command these troops. The Crown Prince counterfeited an imperial edict to pardon all the prisoners and give them weapons. He let Shi De, his teacher, and Zhang Guang, one of his guests, command them. He sent Qiu Ru Hou, an official in Chang'an, to Changshui and Xuanqu (now in Huxian, west of Chang'an) with the flag with red yak's tail, the symbol of the envoy of the Emperor, to transfer the Hun cavalrymen stationed there to Chang'an. Ma Tong, an officer of the Imperial Guards, ran after Qiu Ru Hou and arrested him. He told the commander of the Hun cavalrymen that Qiu Ru Hou had carried a false envoy's symbol, so the Huns should not listen to him.

He had Qiu Ru Hou executed. Then he commanded the cavalrymen to Chang'an. He also mobilized the naval troops. He put the cavalrymen and the naval troops under the command of Shang Qiu Cheng, the Minister of Minority Nationality Affairs,

The Crown Prince stood on a cart in front of the gate of the north army's camp. He summoned Ren An, the supervisor, and ordered him to mobilize the arm. Ren An accepted the order and went back to the camp. He ordered the soldiers to shut the gate of the camp and de did not come out anymore. The Crown Prince sent soldiers to drive the people in Chang'an, several tens of thousands in all, to the west gate of Chang'an. At that time Premier Liu Qu Mao was commanding an army to attack the west gate. The two armies met and they fought for five days. Many soldiers were killed. The blood flew like streams into the ditches.

People said that the Crown Prince had held a rebellion. So the people did not side with the Crown Prince. They went to the side of Premier Liu Qu Mao. So the army under Liu Qu Mao became much stronger. The army under the Crown Prince was defeated. The Crown Prince turned back into Chang'an City and then dashed away from the south gate of the city. Tian Ren, the Minister of the Law Department, shut the gate and did not let Premier Liu Qu Mao go after the Crown Prince because, after all, the Crown Prince was the son of the Emperor, and he felt he should not press the Crown Prince so cruelly. This gave the Crown Prince the chance to make his escape.

Premier Liu Qu Mao was so angry that he wanted to kill Tian Ren. Bao Sheng Zhi, the Imperial Councilor, stopped him, saying, , "Tian Ren is a high ranking court official. If you want to kill him, you must get permission from His Majesty. And you should not kill the Crown Prince at your own will." Premier Liu Qu Mao had to set Tian Ren free. When Emperor Liu Che heard about this, he was very angry and order to arrest Bao Sheng Zhi and send him to be interrogated. The official in charge interrogated Bao Sheng Zhi by saying, "Tian Ren let the rebel escape. The Premier intended to kill Tian Ren. It is a lawful act. Why did you stop him from doing so?" Bao Sheng Zhi was very afraid and he committed suicide.

Emperor Liu Che sent Liu Chang, the Director of the Royal Affairs, and Liu Gan, the Capital Garrison Commander, to the Empress's palace to confiscate her seal. Then Empress Wei Zi Fu committed suicide. Emperor Liu Che looked at Ren An and thought that he was an old official, waiting for the outcome of the fight; and that he would join whichever side won. So he ordered to have Ren An executed. He also ordered to have Tian Ren executed. All the friends of the Crown Prince were killed. The entire families of those who followed the Crown Prince in the rebellion were exterminated. The officials who were forced to take part in the rebellion were sent into exile in Dunhuang Prefecture (Gansu Province). Since the Crown Prince had escaped from Chang'an, Emperor Liu Che sent troops to the gates of the city of Chang'an.

Emperor Liu Che was in a violent rage. The court officials were worried and scared. They did not know what they should do. Linghu Mao, an old man in Huguan (Shanxi Province), presented a memorial to the Emperor which read, "I hear that the father is the Heaven, the mother is the Earth and the children are all the things in the world. If the Heaven and the Earth are at peace, everything in the universe will be prosperous. If the father is kind and the mother is loving, the son will be dutiful. Now the Crown Prince is the eldest son of Your Majesty and he is the successor to the throne.

"Jiang Chong is only an ordinary official. He is a commoner, promoted to a high rank from. Your Majesty put him in a high position and trusted him with important tasks. He counterfeited an imperial order to oppress the Crown Prince. He committed all kinds of treacherous acts to block communication between the Crown Prince and Your Majesty. The Crown Prince was not permitted to see Your Majesty. He is also harassed by treacherous court officials. He was wronged, with fabricated charges, but he could not find anyone to tell the truth of the unfair treatment he suffered. He was so angry that he killed Jiang Chong. He ran away because he was afraid that he would be punished for killing him. He rose in armed rebellion because he wanted to protect himself. I think that the Crown Prince did not want to betray Your Majesty. I hope Your Majesty will not believe the false accusations against the Crown Prince.

"These false accusations will bring turmoil to the whole country. In the past Jiang Chong falsely accused the crown prince of the State of Zhao. His false accusation led to the crown prince's death. This is already known by the people of the whole country. Now Your Majesty does not investigate the case against your own Crown Prince but believes that he has committed grave crimes. In a fury Your Majesty raised a great army to catch the Crown Prince. Your Majesty appointed the highest ranking officials to command the troops to pursue him. The wise men in the court did not dare to say anything against the will of Your Majesty. No one dared to persuade Your Majesty to stop the action. I am very sad about this. I hope Your Majesty will be broad minded and have pity on your son. Your Majesty should forgive the mistakes the Crown Prince has made and recall all the troops that are pursuing him. Your Majesty should not leave the Crown Prince outside the capital for a long time. I say all this out of my devotion to Your Majesty. I will await whatever punishment may be granted by Your Majesty outside Jianzhang Palace."

After Emperor Liu Che had read the memorial, he realized that he had treated the Crown Prince wrongly. But he did not say anything to pardon him.

The Crown Prince fled eastward to Huxian (in the southeast part of Shaanxi Province). He hid himself in a house in Quanjiuli. The owner of the house was poor. He provided for the Crown Prince by weaving and selling straw sandals. The Crown Prince had a friend in Huxian and he knew that this friend was rich. He sent somebody to call this friend to Quanjiuli. So the officials found out where the Crown Prince was hiding. One day in August 91 BC, the officials and some troops surrounded the place. The Crown Prince knew that it was impossible for him to escape, so he went into the house, shut the door and committed suicide by hanging himself. Zhang Fu Chang, a soldier, kicked the door open. Li Shou, an official in Xin'an, held the Crown Prince, untied the rope and got the Crown Prince down. The owner of the house was killed in the fighting. Two of the sons of the Crown Prince were also killed. Emperor Liu Che was grieved for the death of the Crown Prince.

Later it was found out that the case of witchcraft was an unjust case. Emperor Liu Che realized that the Crown Prince did not have in mind to rebel against the Emperor but that he was just panic-stricken. Che Qian Qiu, a court official, presented a memorial to tell the Emperor that the Crown Prince had been wronged with fabricated charges. Emperor Liu Che promoted Che Qian Qiu to the position of premier. The entire family of Jiang Chong was exterminated. Su Wen was burned to death on a bridge. The entire family of the commander who led the troops to catch the Crown Prince was exterminated. Emperor Liu Che realized that the Crown Prince was innocent. He was very sad. He had a palace built and named it the Palace of Missing One's Son. He had a platform built in Huxian to wait for the Crown Prince to come back.

96. Li Guang Li Is Defeated and Surrenders to the Huns

In September 91 BC, the Huns invaded Shanggu Prefecture (Huailai, northwest Hebei Province) and Wuyuan Prefecture (Baotou, central Inner Mongolia), killing and looting wherever they went. The next spring, they invaded Wuyuan Prefecture and Jiuquan Prefecture (western Gansu Province). They killed the commanders of the Han army stationed in these two prefectures. In March 90 BC Emperor Liu Che sent General Li Guang Li to command seventy thousand men to march north from Wuyuan, General Shang Qiu Cheng to command twenty thousand men to march north from Xihe (now Jungar Qi, southern Inner Mongolia), and General Ma Tong to command forty thousand cavalrymen to march north from Jiuquan to attack the Huns.

The King of the Huns knew that the Han army was coming. He ordered all the army provisions to be moved northward to Zhiju River (Selenge River, in northern Mongolia). The King of the Right Wing of the Huns forced his people to cross Yuwu River (Tuul River, central Mongolia) and move three hundred kilometers north. He let the people stay on the mountain there. He himself commanded elite cavalrymen to cross the Guju River (now an upper reach of the Orkhon River, central Mongolia). Shang Qiu Cheng led his troops to penetrate deep into the Hun area; but he could not find any Huns. So he and his troops turned back. The King of the Huns sent his grand general and Li Ling with thirty thousand cavalrymen to pursue the Han troops. They fought for nine days by the Punu River (now Ongiyn River, south central Mongolia). The Huns found that the situation was not favorable for them and they withdrew. General Ma Tong led his troops to the Tian Shan Mountains (Xinjiang Uygur Autonomous Region, China).

The King of the Huns sent General Yanqu in command of twenty thousand cavalrymen to fight the Han army. General Yanqu saw that the Han army was very strong. He commanded his troops to turn back, so General Ma Tong did not have a chance to fight them. At that time Emperor Liu Che was afraid that the King of the State of Jushi would send troops to attack the Han army under General Ma

Tong, and he sent General Cheng Mian to lead the troops of six states to surround the State of Jushi. They captured the King there.

General Li Guang Li commanded his troops to march out of the Great Wall. The King of the Huns sent his Right Grand Commander and Wei Lü to command five thousand cavalrymen to attack the Han Army commanded by Li Guang Li in the West Mountain of Fuyang (Mongolia). Li Guang Li and his troops fought the Huns and defeated them; they carried on the momentum of this victory to pursue Huns to the City of Fanfuren (or City of Lady Fan; now Dalandzadgad, Mongolia). The Huns fled to the north.

When General Li Guang Li marched out with his army, heading north, Premier Liu Qu Mao accompanied him to the border of Chang'an at the bridge over the Wei River. Li Guang Li said to Liu Qu Mao, "I hope you will ask His Majesty to make the King of Changyi the crown prince. If the King of Changyi becomes emperor, you will be able to enjoy your life." Liu Qu Mao gave his promise readily. Liu Bo, King of Changyi, was the son of Lady Li, a concubine of Emperor Liu Che. Lady Li was Li Guang Li's younger sister, and Li Guang Li's daughter was the wife of Liu Qu Mao's son. This is the reason why they united together to plan to put the King of Changyi on the throne.

Guo Rang, the Chief of the Imperial Attendants, accused Premier Liu Qu Mao's wife of having cursed the Emperor. He also accused her and Li Guang Li of having cursed the Emperor together and of intending to make the King of Changyi emperor. Emperor Liu Che gave orders to arrest them and interrogate them. They were found to have committed the crime of treason and heresy.

In June 90 BC Liu Qu Mao was executed by being cut in two at the waist. Liu Qu Mao's wife was executed by hanging to death. Li Guang Li's wife was arrested and put in jail. When Li Guang Li heard all this, he was struck with fear. Hu Ye Fu, one of his officers, said to Li Guang Li, "Your wife's family members are all put in jail. If you go back and the Emperor is not satisfied with you, you will be also put in jail. By that time it will not be possible for you to surrender to the Huns even if you want to." Li Guang Li hesitated. He wanted to penetrate deep into the area of the Huns to attack them and establish great contributions to for his Emperor. So he commanded his troops to advance to Zhiju River (Selenga River, northern Mongolia). But by the tie they reached the river, the Huns had gone away.

Li Guang Li sent the Supervisor of the Army in command of twenty thousand cavalrymen to cross Zhiju River. It happened that the Left Grand General of the King of the Left Wing of the Huns had come with twenty thousand cavalrymen. The two armies joined in battle and fought for a day, The Han troops killed the Left Grand General of the Huns and many Hun officers and soldiers. The Chief Staff of the Army said to Commander Ye Peng Zi, "General Li Guang Li is disloyal to the Emperor. He wants to establish great contributions to please the Emperor at the sacrifice of our lives. I am afraid that he will be defeated. Perhaps we should arrest General Li Guang Li and report his intention to the emperor." General Li Guang Li got word of their conspiracy and killed them. Then he led his army back to Yanran Mountain (Hangayn Mountain, western Mongolia). The King of the Huns, knowing that the Han troops were already very tired, personally led fifty thousand cavalrymen to attack Li Guang Li. Many Han soldiers were killed. At night the Huns dug a ditch leading to the Han troops and then launched a sudden attack. The Han troops were in a great confusion. Li Guang Li could not escape. He surrendered to the Huns.

King Hulugu of the Huns knew that Li Guang Li was the Grand General of the Han Dynasty. So he married his daughter to Li Guang Li. Since Li Guang Li had surrendered to the Huns, Emperor Liu Che ordered the whole clan of Li Guang Li exterminated.

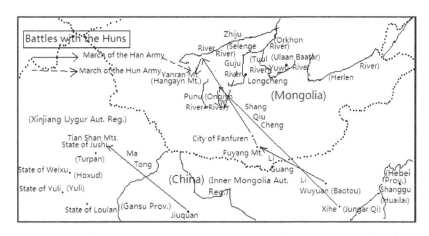

Battles with the Huns

The King of the Huns conferred greater favor on Li Guang Li than on Wei Lü, so Wei Lü was jealous. In August 89 BC, the mother of the King of the Huns fell ill. Wei Lü sent a sorcerer to tell the King of the Huns, "The late king once said angrily that he would use Li Guang Li's head to offer sacrifices to Heaven before the army marched out. Now

Li Guang Li is here. Why shouldn't we use his head to offer sacrifice to Heaven?" Then the King of the Huns arrested Li Guang Li and used him to offer sacrifice to the Heaven. Before Li Guang Li was executed, he cursed angrily: "After I die, I will surely annihilate the Huns."

97. JINMIDI PROTECTS EMPEROR LIU CHE

Xiuchu, King of the Huns in Xiuchu (now Wuwei, central Gansu Province), and King Hunxie had decided to surrender to the Han Dynasty back in 120 BC. But King Xiuchu had gone back on his promise, so King Hunxie had killed him. Then King Hunxie led all his officers and men and all those of King Xiuchu to surrender to the Han Dynasty. Jinmidi, the son of the now departed King Xiuchu, was also arrested and brought to Chang'an at that time, long with his mother and his younger brother. Jinmidi was sent to tend horses in the Emperor's stable. One day Emperor Liu Che held a wine party in a hall in the palace. He wanted to show off his horses to the guests. He stood by the gate of the hall with many beautiful concubines and maids standing by him. When the men led the horses past the hall, they peeped at the concubines and maids standing by Emperor Liu Che. But when Jinmidi was leading his horse by, he looked straight forward and walked sternly past the hall. Jinmidi was a tall man. The horse he was leading was very strong. Emperor Liu Che took an interest in him and asked him several questions. Jinmidi answered all the questions properly. Then Emperor Liu Che granted him the clothes and hat of an official and appointed him as the supervisor of the imperial stables. Soon after that, Emperor Liu Che appointed him chief commander of the imperial guards. Jinmidi performed his job very carefully. He never made any mistakes. Emperor Liu Che liked him and trusted him. He granted Jinmidi considerable rewards in gold. When Emperor Liu Che went out in a carriage, he had Jinmidi as the carriage driver. When Emperor Liu Che was in the court, Jinmidi would stand by him to guard him.

Ma He Luo, an imperial attendant, was a good friend of Jiang Chong. When Crown Prince Liu Ju rose in arms, Ma He Tong, Ma He Luo's younger brother, had fought bravely against the Crown Prince. Emperor Liu Che made Ma He Tong Marquis of He. Later Emperor Liu Che realized that the Crown Prince had been wronged with fabricated charges. He ordered to have all of Jiang Chong's clan and all of those who were in Jiang Chong's party executed. Ma He Luo and Ma He Tong were afraid. So they conspired to hold a rebellion.

Jinmidi noticed that they were upoto something, and he found out about their plans. He secretly watched their actions. Ma He Luo knew that Jinmidi was watching him, so he did not dare to carry out his conspiracy. At that time Emperor Liu Che was staying in Linguang Palace (beside Ganquan Palace west of Si'an). Jinmidi was ill and was lying in bed in a room in the palace. Ma He Luo, Ma He Tong and Ma An Cheng went out with a false imperial order. They killed the commander of the imperial guards and forced the troops to join in their rebellion. At dawn Emperor Liu Che was still in bed. Ma He Luo and his two younger brothers dashed into the palace from outside. At that time Jinmidi was just getting u. He suddenly sensed some danger.

He immediately ran to the hall where the Emperor was sleeping. He sat in front of the door of the hall. Very soon Ma He Luo came from the room on the east side with a sharp dagger in his hand. When he saw Jinmidi sitting in front of the door, he felt a start. He dashed into the hall, but he ran into the zither and fell on the floor. Jinmidi dashed forward and grabbed him. He shouted loudly, "Ma He Luo has rebelled!" Emperor Liu Che woke up with a start. The guards immediately drew out their swords and wanted to kill Ma He Luo. Emperor Liu Che stopped them because he was afraid that the guards might also kill Jimidi. Jinmidi pressed Ma He Luo's head to the ground and ordered the guards to tie him up. Ma He Luo was interrogated by the officials. He admitted his crime of conspiracy to murder the Emperor. From then on Jinmidi was famous for his devotion to the Emperor.

98. Emperor Liu Che Entrusts His Son Liu Fu Ling to Huo Guang's Care

Huo Guang was General Huo Qu Bing's younger brother. With the help of Huo Qu Bing, Huo Guang became a guard of Emperor Liu Che. Later he was promoted to the position of the chief of imperial attendants. After Huo Qu Bing died, Emperor Liu Che appointed Huo Guang as the commander in charge of the carriages and as the imperial advisor. He accompanied the Emperor when he went out of the palace by carriage. When Emperor Liu Che stayed in the palace, Huo Guang would stand on guard by the side of the Emperor. He served Emperor Liu Che for more than twenty years. He worked very carefully and never made mistakes on his job. Emperor Liu Che trusted him very much.

Crown Prince Liu Jü was oppressed to death by Jiang Chong in 91 BC. Thinking that he was the eldest of the Emperor's remaining sons,

Liu Dan, King of the State of Yan, sent a memorial asking the Emperor to let him go to Chang'an to be his guard. Emperor Liu Che knew that Liu Dan had every intention of becoming the crown prince, and this seemed like a devious move. He ordered to have the envoy sent by Liu Dan killed. He took three counties away from the State of Yan. From then on Emperor Liu Che disliked Liu Dan.

Liu Xu, King of the State of Guangling, was Liu Dan's younger brother. He was a powerful man. But he acted at his own will and often against the law. So Emperor Liu Che did not make either Liu Dan or Liu Xu the crown prince. In 88 BC Liu Fu Ling, the son of Lady Gouyi, was six years old. He was already tall and strong. He was wise and a good scholar. Emperor Liu Che would have liked to make Liu Fu Ling the crown Prince, but he and his mother were still young. Finally, he decided to appoint an official to assist Liu Fu Ling. He found Huo Guang honest and kindhearted, and could be entrusted with important tasks. He ordered an artist to draw a picture of the Duke of Zhou carrying King Cheng of the Zhou Dynasty on his back meeting the marquises and high officials in court. He gave this picture to Huo Guang. Several days later Emperor Liu Che scolded Lady Gouyi angrily. Lady Gouyi took off her hairpin and earrings and touched her head on the ground. Emperor Liu Che ordered, "Take her to the palace jail!" When the guards were forcing her out of the hall, she turned her face back and looked at the Emperor with a mournful eye. Emperor Liu Che said, "Go quickly. You must die." Lady Gouyi was soon executed. Several days later, Emperor Liu Che asked the court officials standing around him, "What do the people say about the death of Lady Gouyi?" The court officials said, "The people wonder why Your Majesty has made Lady Gouyi's son the crown prince but has Lady Gouyi executed." Emperor Liu Che said, "You are too foolish to understand this. In the past, many states were in chaos because the kings were young and their mothers were in the prime of their life. The young ladies lived alone and became very proud. They held the power in their own hands. They acted at their own will. Nobody could stop them. Have you ever heard about Empress Dowager Lü Zhi? This is the reason why I had to get rid of Lady Gouyi."

99. Emperor Liu Che Passes Away

In March, 87 BC, Emperor Liu Che was staying in Wuzuo Palace (Shaanxi Province) when he fell seriously ill. Huo Guang wept and asked him, "If anything happens to Your Majesty, who will succeed to the throne?" Emperor Liu Che said, "Don't you understand the picture

I granted to you? I have made my youngest son the Crown Prince. You will act like the Duke of Zhou to assist the young emperor." Huo Guang touched his head to the ground and said, "I am not as good as Jinmidi." Jinmidi said, "I am a foreigner. I am not as good as Huo Guang. If Your Majesty appoints me, the Huns will look down upon the Han Dynasty."

On March 27, Emperor Liu Che issued an imperial edict making Liu Fu Ling the Crown Prince. At that time Liu Fu Ling was eight years old. On March 28, the Emperor appointed Huo Guang commander-in-chief of the army and Grand General; Jinmidi as General of Chariots and Cavalry; Shangguan Jie as Left General. They were entrusted with the task of assisting the Crown Prince. Emperor Liu Che appointed Sang Hong Yang as the Imperial Councilor. On March 29, Emperor Liu Che passed away in Wuzuo Palace at the age of seventy. He had reigned for fifty-four years — longer than any but the Kangxi Emperor of the Qing Dynasty, some 1800 years later.

On March 30, Crown Prince Liu Fu Ling ascended the throne of the Han Dynasty. On April 15 the remains of the Emperor were buried in Mao Mausoleum.

Emperor Liu Che was the seventh emperor of China's Han dynasty. Under his reign, the territory of the empire was greatly expanded. Important water projects were undertaken and agricultural performance was enhanced. Emperor Liu Che took care to organize legal and economic standards across the realm, improved the empire's administration system, and fought corruption, all of which increased prosperity.

Emperor Liu Che was given the posthumous title of Emperor Wu. According to the rules governing such things, the designation "Wu" (Chinese character: 武), indicates that he was powerful, valiant, intelligent and far-sighted.

BIBLIOGRAPHY

Most of the material in this work was taken from the "Records of the Great Historian" (Chinese: 史記 or Shiji) by Sima Qian (145 BC–85 BC) of the Former Han Dynasty. Additional material was taken from "History of the Former Han Dynasty" (Chinese: 前漢書 or qianhanshu) by Ban Gu (32–92) of the Later Han Dynasty.

"A Comprehensive Mirror for the Aid of Government" (Chinese: 資治通鑒 or zizhitongjian) by Sima Guang (1019–1086) of the Song Dynasty is a chronicle, which I have used as a thread to link together materials pulled from different sources.

Chapter One: Liu Bang Founds the Han Dynasty

1. Ying Zheng, King of the State of Qin, Unifies China and Becomes the First Emperor of the Qin Dynasty
    Annals of the First Emperor of the Qin Dynasty, Part Six of Annals, Volume Six of Records of the Grand Historian
    Part One of the First Emperor of the Qin Dynasty, Part One of the Period of the Qin Dynasty, Volume Six of A Comprehensive Mirror for the Aid of Government
    Part Two of the First Emperor of the Qin Dynasty, Part Two of the Period of the Qin Dynasty, Volume Seven of A Comprehensive Mirror for the Aid of Government
2. Liu Bang Rises Up in Rebellion
    Annals of Gaozu of the Han Dynasty, Part Eight of Annals, Volume Eight of Records of the Grand Historian
    Annals of Gaozu, the First Part of Part One of Annals, the First Part of Volume One of History of the Former Han Dynasty

3. The Uprising Led by Chen Sheng and Wu Guang, and the Reinstatement of the Former Five States
Biography of Chen Sheng, Part Eighteen of Biography of Kings and Marquises, Volume Forty-Eight of Records of the Grand Historian
Annals of the First Emperor of the Qin Dynasty, Part Six of Annals, Volume Six of Records of the Grand Historian
Biographies of Chen Sheng, Xiang Yu, Part One of Biography, Volume Thirty-One of History of the Former Han Dynasty
Part One of the Second Emperor of the Qin Dynasty, Part Two of the Period of the Qin Dynasty, Volume Seven of A Comprehensive Mirror for the Aid of Government

4. Liu Bang Revolts in Pei County
Annals of Gaozu of the Han Dynasty, Part Eight of Annals, Volume Eight of Records of the Grand Historian
Annals of Gaozu, the First Part of Part One of Annals, the First Part of Volume One of History of the Former Han Dynasty
Biography of Premier Xiao He, Part Twenty-Three of Biography of Kings and Marquises, Volume Forty-Three of Records of the Grand Historian
Biography of Premier Chao Shen, Part Twenty-Four of Biography of Kings and Marquises, Volume Forty-Four of Records of the Grand Historian
Biographies of Fan Kuai, Li Shang, Xiahou Ying, Guan Yin, Part Thirty-Five of Biography, Volume Ninety-Five of Records of the Grand Historian
Biographies of Zhang Cang, Zhou Chang, Ren Ao, Shen Tu Jia (including Wei Xian, Wei Xiang, Bing Ji, Huang Ba, Wei Xuan Cheng, Kuang Heng), Part Thirty-Six of Biography, Volume Ninety-Six of Records of the Grand Historian
Biographies of Xiao He, Chao Shen, Part Nine of Biography, Volume Thirty-Nine of History of the Former Han Dynasty
Biographies of Zhang Liang, Chen Ping, Wang Ling, Zhou Bo (including his son Zhou Ya Fu), Part Ten of Biography, Volume Forty of History of the Former Han Dynasty
Biographies of Fan Kuai, Li Shang, Xiahou Ying, Guan Ying, Fu Kuan, Jin She, Zhou Xie, Part Eleven of Biography, Volume Forty-One of History of the Former Han Dynasty
Biographies of Zhang Cang, Zhou Chang, Zhao Yao, Ren Ao, Shen Tu Jia, Part Twelf of Biography, Volume Forty-Two of History of the Former Han Dynasty
Part One of the Second Emperor of the Qin Dynasty, Part Two of the Period of the Qin Dynasty, Volume Seven of A Comprehensive Mirror for the Aid of Government

5. Xiang Liang and Xiang Yu Rebel in the Area to the East of the Yangtze River

Annals of Xiang Yu, Part Seven of Annals, Volume Seven of Records of the Grand Historian

Biographies of Chen Sheng, Xiang Yu, Part One of Biography, Volume Thirty-One of History of the Former Han Dynasty

Part One of the Second Emperor of the Qin Dynasty, Part Two of the Period of the Qin Dynasty, Volume Seven of A Comprehensive Mirror for the Aid of Government

6. The Great Changes in the State of Zhao

Part Two of the Second Emperor of the Qin Dynasty, Part Three of the Period of the Qin Dynasty, Volume Eight of A Comprehensive Mirror for the Aid of Government

7. Liu Bang's Military Operations

Annals of Gaozu of the Han Dynasty, Part Eight of Annals, Volume Eight of Records of the Grand Historian

Annals of Gaozu, the First Part of Part One of Annals, the First Part of Volume One of History of the Former Han Dynasty

Part Two of the Second Emperor of the Qin Dynasty, Part Three of the Period of the Qin Dynasty, Volume Eight of A Comprehensive Mirror for the Aid of Government

8. The Death of Chen Sheng, King of Zhang Chu

Biography of Chen Sheng, Part Eighteen of Biography of Kings and Marquises, Volume Forty-Eight of Records of the Grand Historian

Biographies of Chen Sheng, Xiang Yu, Part One of Biography, Volume Thirty-One of History of the Former Han Dynasty

Part Two of the Second Emperor of the Qin Dynasty, Part Three of the Period of the Qin Dynasty, Volume Eight of A Comprehensive Mirror for the Aid of Government

9. Qin Jia Makes Jing Ju King of the State of Chu

Annals of Gaozu of the Han Dynasty, Part Eight of Annals, Volume Eight of Records of the Grand Historian

Annals of Gaozu, the First Part of Part One of Annals, the First Part of Volume One of History of the Former Han Dynasty

Biography of Marquis of Liu, Part Twenty-Five of Biography of Kings and Marquises, Volume Fifty-Five of Records of the Grand Historian

Biographies of Zhang Liang, Chen Ping, Wang Ling, Zhou Bo (including his son Zhou Ya Fu), Part Ten of Biography, Volume Forty of History of the Former Han Dynasty

Part Two of the Second Emperor of the Qin Dynasty, Part Three of the Period of the Qin Dynasty, Volume Eight of A Comprehensive Mirror for the Aid of Government

10. Xiang Liang and Xiang Yu Lead Their Army to the Area to the West of the Yangtze River and Liu Bang Joins Forces with Xiang Liang and Xiang Yu

Annals of Gaozu of the Han Dynasty, Part Eight of Annals, Volume

Eight of Records of the Grand Historian

Annals of Gaozu, the First Part of Part One of Annals, the First Part of Volume One of History of the Former Han Dynasty

Annals of Xiang Yu, Part Seven of Annals, Volume Seven of Records of the Grand Historian

Biographies of Chen Sheng, Xiang Yu, Part One of Biography, Volume Thirty-One of History of the Former Han Dynasty

Part Two of the Second Emperor of the Qin Dynasty, Part Three of the Period of the Qin Dynasty, Volume Eight of A Comprehensive Mirror for the Aid of Government

11. The Promise Made by King Huai of the State of Chu

Annals of Gaozu of the Han Dynasty, Part Eight of Annals, Volume Eight of Records of the Grand Historian

Annals of Gaozu, the First Part of Part One of Annals, the First Part of Volume One of History of the Former Han Dynasty

Annals of Xiang Yu, Part Seven of Annals, Volume Seven of Records of the Grand Historian

Biographies of Chen Sheng, Xiang Yu, Part One of Biography, Volume Thirty-One of History of the Former Han Dynasty

Part Two of the Second Emperor of the Qin Dynasty, Part Three of the Period of the Qin Dynasty, Volume Eight of A Comprehensive Mirror for the Aid of Government

12. The Battle of Julu

Annals of Xiang Yu, Part Seven of Annals, Volume Seven of Records of the Grand Historian

Biographies of Chen Sheng, Xiang Yu, Part One of Biography, Volume Thirty-One of History of the Former Han Dynasty

Part Two of the Second Emperor of the Qin Dynasty, Part Three of the Period of the Qin Dynasty, Volume Eight of A Comprehensive Mirror for the Aid of Government

13. Liu Bang's March to the Area of Guanzhong

Annals of Gaozu of the Han Dynasty, Part Eight of Annals, Volume Eight of Records of the Grand Historian

Annals of Gaozu, the First Part of Part One of Annals, the First Part of Volume One of History of the Former Han Dynasty

Biography of Marquis of Liu, Part Twenty-Five of Biography of Kings and Marquises, Volume Fifty-Five of Records of the Grand Historian

Biographies of Zhang Liang, Chen Ping, Wang Ling, Zhou Bo (including his son Zhou Ya Fu), Part Ten of Biography, Volume Forty of History of the Former Han Dynasty

Part Two of the Second Emperor of the Qin Dynasty, Part Three of the Period of the Qin Dynasty, Volume Eight of A Comprehensive Mirror for the Aid of Government

14. Zhang Han Surrenders to Xiang Yu

Annals of Xiang Yu, Part Seven of Annals, Volume Seven of Records of the Grand Historian

Biographies of Chen Sheng, Xiang Yu, Part One of Biography, Volume Thirty-One of History of the Former Han Dynasty

Part Two of the Second Emperor of the Qin Dynasty, Part Three of the Period of the Qin Dynasty, Volume Eight of A Comprehensive Mirror for the Aid of Government

15. Zhao Gao Kills the Second Emperor of the Qin Dynasty and Puts Ying Zi Ying on the Throne of the State of Qin

Annals of the First Emperor of the Qin Dynasty, Part Six of Annals, Volume Six of Records of the Grand Historian

Part Two of the Second Emperor of the Qin Dynasty, Part Three of the Period of the Qin Dynasty, Volume Eight of A Comprehensive Mirror for the Aid of Government

16. Liu Bang Takes the Area of Qin, and Ying Zi Ying, King of the State of Qin, Surrenders to Liu Bang

Annals of Gaozu of the Han Dynasty, Part Eight of Annals, Volume Eight of Records of the Grand Historian

Annals of Gaozu, the First Part of Part One of Annals, the First Part of Volume One of History of the Former Han Dynasty

Biography of Marquis of Liu, Part Twenty-Five of Biography of Kings and Marquises, Volume Fifty-Five of Records of the Grand Historian

Biographies of Zhang Liang, Chen Ping, Wang Ling, Zhou Bo (including his son Zhou Ya Fu), Part Ten of Biography, Volume Forty of History of the Former Han Dynasty

Part Two of the Second Emperor of the Qin Dynasty, Part Three of the Period of the Qin Dynasty, Volume Eight of A Comprehensive Mirror for the Aid of Government

First Part of Part One of Emperor Gaozu of the Han Dynasty, Part One of the Period of the Han Dynasty, Volume Nine of A Comprehensive Mirror for the Aid of Government

17. Xiang Yu's March to the Area of Guanzhong

Annals of Gaozu of the Han Dynasty, Part Eight of Annals, Volume Eight of Records of the Grand Historian

Annals of Gaozu, the First Part of Part One of Annals, the First Part of Volume One of History of the Former Han Dynasty

Biography of Marquis of Liu, Part Twenty-Five of Biography of Kings and Marquises, Volume Fifty-Five of Records of the Grand Historian

Annals of Xiang Yu, Part Seven of Annals, Volume Seven of Records of the Grand Historian

Biographies of Chen Sheng, Xiang Yu, Part One of Biography, Volume Thirty-One of History of the Former Han Dynasty

First Part of Part One of Emperor Gaozu of the Han Dynasty,

Part One of the Period of the Han Dynasty, Volume Nine of A Comprehensive Mirror for the Aid of Government

18. The Banquet in Hongmen

Annals of Gaozu of the Han Dynasty, Part Eight of Annals, Volume Eight of Records of the Grand Historian

Annals of Gaozu, the First Part of Part One of Annals, the First Part of Volume One of History of the Former Han Dynasty

Biography of Marquis of Liu, Part Twenty-Five of Biography of Kings and Marquises, Volume Fifty-Five of Records of the Grand Historian

Annals of Xiang Yu, Part Seven of Annals, Volume Seven of Records of the Grand Historian

Biographies of Chen Sheng, Xiang Yu, Part One of Biography, Volume Thirty-One of History of the Former Han Dynasty

First Part of Part One of Emperor Gaozu of the Han Dynasty, Part One of the Period of the Han Dynasty, Volume Nine of A Comprehensive Mirror for the Aid of Government

19. The Making of Kings

Annals of Gaozu of the Han Dynasty, Part Eight of Annals, Volume Eight of Records of the Grand Historian

Annals of Gaozu, the First Part of Part One of Annals, the First Part of Volume One of History of the Former Han Dynasty

Biography of Marquis of Liu, Part Twenty-Five of Biography of Kings and Marquises, Volume Fifty-Five of Records of the Grand Historian

Annals of Xiang Yu, Part Seven of Annals, Volume Seven of Records of the Grand Historian

Biographies of Chen Sheng, Xiang Yu, Part One of Biography, Volume Thirty-One of History of the Former Han Dynasty

First Part of Part One of Emperor Gaozu of the Han Dynasty, Part One of the Period of the Han Dynasty, Volume Nine of A Comprehensive Mirror for the Aid of Government

20. Liu Bang's March into Hanzhong

Annals of Gaozu of the Han Dynasty, Part Eight of Annals, Volume Eight of Records of the Grand Historian

Annals of Gaozu, the First Part of Part One of Annals, the First Part of Volume One of History of the Former Han Dynasty

Biography of Marquis of Liu, Part Twenty-Five of Biography of Kings and Marquises, Volume Fifty-Five of Records of the Grand Historian

First Part of Part One of Emperor Gaozu of the Han Dynasty, Part One of the Period of the Han Dynasty, Volume Nine of A Comprehensive Mirror for the Aid of Government

21. The Rebellions of the State of Qi and the State of Zhao against Xiang Yu

Biography of Tian Dan, Part Thirty-Four of Biography, Volume Ninety-four of Records of the Grand Historian

Biographies of Zhang Er, Chen Yu, Part Twenty-Nine of Biography, Volume Eighty-Nine of Records of the Grand Historian

Biography of Tian Dan, Part Thirty-Four of Biography, Volume Ninety-four of Records of the Grand Historian

Biographies of Wei Bao, Peng Yue, Part Thirty of Biography, Volume Ninety of Records of the Grand Historian

Biographies of Wei Bao, Tian Dan, Haan Xin, King of the State of Haan, Part Three of Biography, Volume Thirty-Three, History of the Former Han Dynasty

Biographies of Zhang Er, Chen Yu, Part Two of Biography, Volume Thirty-Two, History of the Former Han Dynasty

First Part of Part One of Emperor Gaozu of the Han Dynasty, Part One of the Period of the Han Dynasty, Volume Nine of A Comprehensive Mirror for the Aid of Government

22. Han Xin Is Appointed Commander-in-chief of the Army of Han

Annals of Gaozu of the Han Dynasty, Part Eight of Annals, Volume Eight of Records of the Grand Historian

Annals of Gaozu, the First Part of Part One of Annals, the First Part of Volume One of History of the Former Han Dynasty

Biography of Marquis of Huaiyin, Part Thirty-Four of Biography, Volume Ninety-Two of Records of the Grand Historian

Biographies of Han Xin, Peng Yue, Ying Bu, Lu Wan, Wu Rui, Part Four of Biography, Volume Thirty-Four, History of the Former Han Dynasty

First Part of Part One of Emperor Gaozu of the Han Dynasty, Part One of the Period of the Han Dynasty, Volume Nine of A Comprehensive Mirror for the Aid of Government

23. Liu Bang's Action to Pacify the Area of Guanzhong

Annals of Gaozu of the Han Dynasty, Part Eight of Annals, Volume Eight of Records of the Grand Historian

Annals of Gaozu, the First Part of Part One of Annals, the First Part of Volume One of History of the Former Han Dynasty

Biography of Marquis of Huaiyin, Part Thirty-Four of Biography, Volume Ninety-Two of Records of the Grand Historian

Biographies of Han Xin, Peng Yue, Ying Bu, Lu Wan, Wu Rui, Part Four of Biography, Volume Thirty-Four, History of the Former Han Dynasty

First Part of Part One of Emperor Gaozu of the Han Dynasty, Part One of the Period of the Han Dynasty, Volume Nine of A Comprehensive Mirror for the Aid of Government

24. Xiang Yu's Decision to Attack the State of Qi

Annals of Gaozu of the Han Dynasty, Part Eight of Annals, Volume Eight of Records of the Grand Historian

Annals of Gaozu, the First Part of Part One of Annals, the First Part of Volume One of History of the Former Han Dynasty

Biography of Tian Dan, Part Thirty-Four of Biography, Volume Ninety-four of Records of the Grand Historian

Biographies of Zhang Er, Chen Yu, Part Twenty-Nine of Biography, Volume Eighty-Nine of Records of the Grand Historian

Biography of Tian Dan, Part Thirty-Four of Biography, Volume Ninety-four of Records of the Grand Historian

Biography of Marquis of Liu, Part Twenty-Five of Biography of Kings and Marquises, Volume Fifty-Five of Records of the Grand Historian

Annals of Xiang Yu, Part Seven of Annals, Volume Seven of Records of the Grand Historian

Biographies of Chen Sheng, Xiang Yu, Part One of Biography, Volume Thirty-One of History of the Former Han Dynasty

First Part of Part One of Emperor Gaozu of the Han Dynasty, Part One of the Period of the Han Dynasty, Volume Nine of A Comprehensive Mirror for the Aid of Government

25. Liu Bang's Action to Conquer the Areas around the Yellow River

Annals of Gaozu of the Han Dynasty, Part Eight of Annals, Volume Eight of Records of the Grand Historian

Annals of Gaozu, the First Part of Part One of Annals, the First Part of Volume One of History of the Former Han Dynasty

First Part of Part One of Emperor Gaozu of the Han Dynasty, Part One of the Period of the Han Dynasty, Volume Nine of A Comprehensive Mirror for the Aid of Government

26. The Battle of Pengcheng

Annals of Gaozu of the Han Dynasty, Part Eight of Annals, Volume Eight of Records of the Grand Historian

Annals of Gaozu, the First Part of Part One of Annals, the First Part of Volume One of History of the Former Han Dynasty

Annals of Xiang Yu, Part Seven of Annals, Volume Seven of Records of the Grand Historian

Biographies of Chen Sheng, Xiang Yu, Part One of Biography, Volume Thirty-One of History of the Former Han Dynasty

First Part of Part One of Emperor Gaozu of the Han Dynasty, Part One of the Period of the Han Dynasty, Volume Nine of A Comprehensive Mirror for the Aid of Government

27. Wei Bao's Betrayal of Liu Bang

Annals of Gaozu of the Han Dynasty, Part Eight of Annals, Volume Eight of Records of the Grand Historian

Annals of Gaozu, the First Part of Part One of Annals, the First Part of Volume One of History of the Former Han Dynasty

Biographies of Wei Bao, Peng Yue, Part Thirty of Biography, Volume Ninety of Records of the Grand Historian

Biographies of Wei Bao, Tian Dan, Haan Xin, King of the State of Haan, Part Three of Biography, Volume Thirty-Three, History of the Former Han Dynasty

Biographies of Empresses and Concubines, First Part of Part Sixty-Seven of Biography, First Part of Volume Ninety-Seven, History of the Former Han Dynasty

First Part of Part One of Emperor Gaozu of the Han Dynasty, Part One of the Period of the Han Dynasty, Volume Nine of A Comprehensive Mirror for the Aid of Government

28. The Battle to Defeat the King of the State of Wei

Annals of Gaozu of the Han Dynasty, Part Eight of Annals, Volume Eight of Records of the Grand Historian

Annals of Gaozu, the First Part of Part One of Annals, the First Part of Volume One of History of the Former Han Dynasty

Biographies of Han Xin, Peng Yue, Ying Bu, Lu Wan, Wu Rui, Part Four of Biography, Volume Thirty-Four, History of the Former Han Dynasty

Biographies of Wei Bao, Peng Yue, Part Thirty of Biography, Volume Ninety of Records of the Grand Historian

Biographies of Wei Bao, Tian Dan, Haan Xin, King of the State of Haan, Part Three of Biography, Volume Thirty-Three, History of the Former Han Dynasty

First Part of Part One of Emperor Gaozu of the Han Dynasty, Part One of the Period of the Han Dynasty, Volume Nine of A Comprehensive Mirror for the Aid of Government

29. Pacification of the State of Dai, the State of Zhao and the State of Yan

Annals of Gaozu of the Han Dynasty, Part Eight of Annals, Volume Eight of Records of the Grand Historian

Annals of Gaozu, the First Part of Part One of Annals, the First Part of Volume One of History of the Former Han Dynasty

Biographies of Han Xin, Peng Yue, Ying Bu, Lu Wan, Wu Rui, Part Four of Biography, Volume Thirty-Four, History of the Former Han Dynasty

Second Part of Part One of Emperor Gaozu of the Han Dynasty, Part Two of the Period of the Han Dynasty, Volume Ten of A Comprehensive Mirror for the Aid of Government

30. The Fall of Xingyang

Annals of Gaozu of the Han Dynasty, Part Eight of Annals, Volume Eight of Records of the Grand Historian

Annals of Gaozu, the First Part of Part One of Annals, the First Part of Volume One of History of the Former Han Dynasty

Biographies of Han Xin, Peng Yue, Ying Bu, Lu Wan, Wu Rui, Part Four of Biography, Volume Thirty-Four, History of the Former Han Dynasty

Annals of Xiang Yu, Part Seven of Annals, Volume Seven of Records of the Grand Historian

Biographies of Chen Sheng, Xiang Yu, Part One of Biography, Volume Thirty-One of History of the Former Han Dynasty

Second Part of Part One of Emperor Gaozu of the Han Dynasty, Part Two of the Period of the Han Dynasty, Volume Ten of A Comprehensive Mirror for the Aid of Government

31. Han Xin Defeats the State of Qi

Annals of Gaozu of the Han Dynasty, Part Eight of Annals, Volume Eight of Records of the Grand Historian

Annals of Gaozu, the First Part of Part One of Annals, the First Part of Volume One of History of the Former Han Dynasty

Biographies of Han Xin, Peng Yue, Ying Bu, Lu Wan, Wu Rui, Part Four of Biography, Volume Thirty-Four, History of the Former Han Dynasty

Second Part of Part One of Emperor Gaozu of the Han Dynasty, Part Two of the Period of the Han Dynasty, Volume Ten of A Comprehensive Mirror for the Aid of Government

32. The Battle of Chenggao

Annals of Gaozu of the Han Dynasty, Part Eight of Annals, Volume Eight of Records of the Grand Historian

Annals of Gaozu, the First Part of Part One of Annals, the First Part of Volume One of History of the Former Han Dynasty

Second Part of Part One of Emperor Gaozu of the Han Dynasty, Part Two of the Period of the Han Dynasty, Volume Ten of A Comprehensive Mirror for the Aid of Government

33. Bo Ji Becomes Liu Bang's Concubine and Liu Heng Is Born

Biographies of Empresses and Concubines, First Part of Part Sixty-Seven of Biography, First Part of Volume Ninety-Seven, History of the Former Han Dynasty

34. The Confrontation between Liu Bang and Xiang Yu in Guangwu Mountain Area

Annals of Gaozu of the Han Dynasty, Part Eight of Annals, Volume Eight of Records of the Grand Historian

Annals of Gaozu, the First Part of Part One of Annals, the First Part of Volume One of History of the Former Han Dynasty

Annals of Xiang Yu, Part Seven of Annals, Volume Seven of Records of the Grand Historian

Biographies of Chen Sheng, Xiang Yu, Part One of Biography, Volume Thirty-One of History of the Former Han Dynasty

Second Part of Part One of Emperor Gaozu of the Han Dynasty, Part Two of the Period of the Han Dynasty, Volume Ten of A Comprehensive Mirror for the Aid of Government

35. Han Xin Pacifies the State of Qi

Annals of Gaozu of the Han Dynasty, Part Eight of Annals, Volume

Eight of Records of the Grand Historian

Annals of Gaozu, the First Part of Part One of Annals, the First Part of Volume One of History of the Former Han Dynasty

Biographies of Han Xin, Peng Yue, Ying Bu, Lu Wan, Wu Rui, Part Four of Biography, Volume Thirty-Four, History of the Former Han Dynasty

Second Part of Part One of Emperor Gaozu of the Han Dynasty, Part Two of the Period of the Han Dynasty, Volume Ten of A Comprehensive Mirror for the Aid of Government

36. The Decisive Battle in Gaixia

Annals of Gaozu of the Han Dynasty, Part Eight of Annals, Volume Eight of Records of the Grand Historian

Annals of Gaozu, the First Part of Part One of Annals, the First Part of Volume One of History of the Former Han Dynasty

Annals of Xiang Yu, Part Seven of Annals, Volume Seven of Records of the Grand Historian

Second Part of Part One of Emperor Gaozu of the Han Dynasty, Part Two of the Period of the Han Dynasty, Volume Ten of A Comprehensive Mirror for the Aid of Government

37. Liu Bang Becomes Emperor of the Han Dynasty

Annals of Gaozu of the Han Dynasty, Part Eight of Annals, Volume Eight of Records of the Grand Historian

Annals of Gaozu, the First Part of Part One of Annals, the First Part of Volume One of History of the Former Han Dynasty

Second Part of Part One of Emperor Gaozu of the Han Dynasty, Part Two of the Period of the Han Dynasty, Volume Ten of A Comprehensive Mirror for the Aid of Government

Part Two of Emperor Gaozu of the Han Dynasty, Part Three of the Period of the Han Dynasty, Volume Eleven of A Comprehensive Mirror for the Aid of Government

38. Under the Rule of Emperor Liu Bang

Annals of Gaozu of the Han Dynasty, Part Eight of Annals, Volume Eight of Records of the Grand Historian

Annals of Gaozu, the First Part of Part One of Annals, the First Part of Volume One of History of the Former Han Dynasty

Part Two of Emperor Gaozu of the Han Dynasty, Part Three of the Period of Han Dynasty, Volume Eleven of A Comprehensive Mirror for the Aid of Government

39. The Rise of the Huns

Bibliography of the Huns, Part Fifty of Biography, Volume One Hundred and Ten of Records of the Grand Historian

Bibliography of the Huns, First Part of Part Sixty-four of Biography, First part of Volume Ninety-four of History of the Former Han Dynasty

Part Two of Emperor Gaozu of the Han Dynasty, Part Three of the

Period of Han Dynasty, Volume Eleven of A Comprehensive Mirror for the Aid of Government

40. Haan Xin, the King of the State of Haan, Betrays the Han Dynasty and Defects to the Huns
Annals of Gaozu of the Han Dynasty, Part Eight of Annals, Volume Eight of Records of the Grand Historian
Annals of Gaozu, the First Part of Part One of Annals, the First Part of Volume One of History of the Former Han Dynasty
Biographies of Haan Xin, King of the State of Haan, Lu Wan, Part Thirty-Two of Biography, Volume Ninety-Three of Records of the Grand Historian
Biographies of Wei Bao, Tian Dan, Haan Xin, King of the State of Haan, Part Three of Biography, Volume Thirty-Three of History of the Former Han Dynasty
Part Two of Emperor Gaozu of the Han Dynasty, Part Three of the Period of Han Dynasty, Volume Eleven of A Comprehensive Mirror for the Aid of Government

41. Liu Jing's Advice to Improve Relations with the Huns
Annals of Gaozu of the Han Dynasty, Part Eight of Annals, Volume Eight of Records of the Grand Historian
Annals of Gaozu, the First Part of Part One of Annals, the First Part of Volume One of History of the Former Han Dynasty
Bibliographies of Liu Jing, Susun Tong, Part Thirty-Nine of Biography, Volume Ninety-Nine of Records of the Grand Historian
Part Three of Emperor Gaozu of the Han Dynasty, Part Four of the Period of Han Dynasty, Volume Twelve of A Comprehensive Mirror for the Aid of Government

42. The Emperor's Intension to Replace the Crown Prince
Annals of Empress Dowager Lü, Part Nine of Annals, Volume Nine of Records of the Grant Historian
Annals of Empress Dowager Lü, Part Three of Annals, Volume Three of History of the Former Han Dynasty
Part Three of Emperor Gaozu of the Han Dynasty, Part Four of the Period of Han Dynasty, Volume Twelve of A Comprehensive Mirror for the Aid of Government

43. Chen Xi's Rebellion and the End of Han Xin
Annals of Gaozu of the Han Dynasty, Part Eight of Annals, Volume Eight of Records of the Grand Historian
Annals of Gaozu, the First Part of Part One of Annals, the First Part of Volume One of History of the Former Han Dynasty
Bibliography of Marquis of Huaiyin, Part Thirty-Two of Biography, Volume Ninety-Two of Records of the Grand Historian
Biographies of Han Xin, Peng Yue, Ying Bu, Lu Wan, Wu Rui, Part Four of Biography, Volume Thirty-Four of History of the Former Han Dynasty

Part Three of Emperor Gaozu of the Han Dynasty, Part Four of the Period of Han Dynasty, Volume Twelve of A Comprehensive Mirror for the Aid of Government

44. The End of Haan Xin, the Former King of the State of Haan
Annals of Gaozu of the Han Dynasty, Part Eight of Annals, Volume Eight of Records of the Grand Historian
Annals of Gaozu, the First Part of Part One of Annals, the First Part of Volume One of History of the Former Han Dynasty
Biographies of Haan Xin, King of the State of Haan, Lu Wan, Part Thirty-Two of Biography, Volume Ninety-Three of Records of the Grand Historian
Biographies of Wei Bao, Tian Dan, Haan Xin, King of the State of Haan, Part Three of Biography, Volume Thirty-Three of History of the Former Han Dynasty
Part Three of Emperor Gaozu of the Han Dynasty, Part Four of the Period of Han Dynasty, Volume Twelve of A Comprehensive Mirror for the Aid of Government

45. The Death of Peng Yue, the King of the State of Liang
Biographies of Wei Bao, Peng Yue, Part Thirty of Biography, Volume Ninety of Records of the Grand Historian
Biographies of Han Xin, Peng Yue, Ying Bu, Lu Wan, Wu Rui, Part Four of Biography, Volume Thirty-Four, History of the Former Han Dynasty
Part Three of Emperor Gaozu of the Han Dynasty, Part Four of the Period of Han Dynasty, Volume Twelve of A Comprehensive Mirror for the Aid of Government

46. The Rebellion of Ying Bu, the King of the State of Huainan
Annals of Gaozu of the Han Dynasty, Part Eight of Annals, Volume Eight of Records of the Grand Historian
Annals of Gaozu, the First Part of Part One of Annals, the First Part of Volume One of History of the Former Han Dynasty
Biography of Jing Bu, Part Thirty-One of Biography, Volume Ninety-One of Records of the Grand Historian
Biographies of Han Xin, Peng Yue, Ying Bu, Lu Wan, Wu Rui, Part Four of Biography, Volume Thirty-Four, History of the Former Han Dynasty

47. Lu Wan's Rebellion
Annals of Gaozu of the Han Dynasty, Part Eight of Annals, Volume Eight of Records of the Grand Historian
Annals of Gaozu, the First Part of Part One of Annals, the First Part of Volume One of History of the Former Han Dynasty
Part Three of Emperor Gaozu of the Han Dynasty, Part Four of the Period of Han Dynasty, Volume Twelve of A Comprehensive Mirror for the Aid of Government

48. The Death of Liu Bang, the Emperor of the Han Dynasty

Annals of Gaozu of the Han Dynasty, Part Eight of Annals, Volume
Eight of Records of the Grand Historian
Annals of Gaozu, the First Part of Part One of Annals, the First Part
of Volume One of History of the Former Han Dynasty
Part Three of Emperor Gaozu of the Han Dynasty, Part Four of the
Period of Han Dynasty, Volume Twelve of A Comprehensive Mirror
for the Aid of Government

Chapter Two: Emperor Liu Ying and Empress Dowager Lü Zhi

1. The Troubles in the Palace after Liu Bang's Death
    Annals of Empress Dowager Lü Zhi, Part Nine of Annals, Volume
    Nine of Records of the Grand Historian
    Annals of Empress Dowager Lü Zhi, Part Three of Part One of
    Annals, Volume Three of History of the Former Han Dynasty
    Emperor Xiao Hui of the Han Dynasty, Part Four of the Period of
    Han Dynasty, Volume Twelve of A Comprehensive Mirror for the
    Aid of Government
2. Empress Dowager Lü Zhi Takes Power
    Annals of Empress Dowager Lü Zhi, Part Nine of Annals, Volume
    Nine of Records of the Grand Historian
    Annals of Empress Dowager Lü Zhi, Part Three of Part One of
    Annals, Volume Three of History of the Former Han Dynasty
    Emperor Xiao Hui of the Han Dynasty, Part Four of the Period of
    Han Dynasty, Volume Twelve of A Comprehensive Mirror for the
    Aid of Government
    Emperor Xiao Hui of the Han Dynasty, Part Four of the Period of Han
    Dynasty,   Volume Twelve of A Comprehensive Mirror for the
    Aid of Government
    Empress Dowager Lü Zhi. Part Five of the Period of the Han Dynasty,
    Volume Thirteen of A Comprehensive Mirror for the Aid of
    Government
3. The Death of Empress Dowager Lü Zhi
    Annals of Empress Dowager Lü Zhi, Part Nine of Annals, Volume
    Nine of Records of the Grand Historian
    Annals of Empress Dowager Lü Zhi, Part Three of Part One of
    Annals, Volume Three of History of the Former Han Dynasty
    Empress Dowager Lü Zhi. Part Five of the Period of the Han
    Dynasty, Volume Thirteen of A Comprehensive Mirror for the Aid
    of Government
4. The Lü Family Is Exterminated
    Annals of Empress Dowager Lü Zhi, Part Nine of Annals, Volume
    Nine of Records of the Grand Historian
    Annals of Empress Dowager Lü Zhi, Part Three of Part One of
    Annals, Volume Three of History of the Former Han Dynasty

Annals of Emperor Xiao Wen, Part Ten of Annals, Volume Ten of Records of the Grand Historian

Annals of Emperor Wen (Liu Heng), Part Four of Annals, Volume Four of History of the Former Han Dynasty

Biographies of Zhang Liang, Chen Ping, Wang Ling, Zhou Bo (including his son Zhou Ya Fu) , Part Ten of Biography, Volume Forty, History of the Former Han Dynasty

Empress Dowager Lü Zhi. Part Five of the Period of the Han Dynasty, Volume Thirteen of A Comprehensive Mirror for the Aid of Government

Chapter Three: The Reign of Emperor Liu Heng

1. Liu Heng, King of the State of Dai, Ascends the Throne of the Han Dynasty

    Annals of Emperor Xiao Wen, Part Ten of Annals, Volume Ten of Records of the Grand Historian

    Annals of Emperor Wen (Liu Heng), Part Four of Annals, Volume Four of History of the Former Han Dynasty

    Biographies of Zhang Liang, Chen Ping, Wang Ling, Zhou Bo (including his son Zhou Ya Fu) , Part Ten of Biography, Volume Forty, History of the Former Han Dynasty

    Empress Dowager Lü Zhi. Part Five of the Period of the Han Dynasty, Volume Thirteen of A Comprehensive Mirror for the Aid of Government

2. Emperor Liu Heng Grants Awards to the Officials and Generals Who Have Established Great Contributions in Putting Him to the Throne

    Annals of Emperor Xiao Wen, Part Ten of Annals, Volume Ten of Records of the Grand Historian

    Annals of Emperor Wen (Liu Heng), Part Four of Annals, Volume Four of History of the Former Han Dynasty

    Biographies of Zhang Liang, Chen Ping, Wang Ling, Zhou Bo (including his son Zhou Ya Fu) , Part Ten of Biography, Volume Forty, History of the Former Han Dynasty

    Part One of Emperor Xiao Wen, Part Five of the Period of the Han Dynasty, Volume Thirteen of A Comprehensive Mirror for the Aid of Government

3. Emperor Liu Heng Makes His Eldest Son Liu Qi Crown Prince

    Annals of Emperor Xiao Wen, Part Ten of Annals, Volume Ten of Records of the Grand Historian

    Annals of Emperor Wen (Liu Heng), Part Four of Annals, Volume Four of History of the Former Han Dynasty

    Part One of Emperor Xiao Wen, Part Five of the Period of the Han Dynasty, Volume Thirteen of A Comprehensive Mirror for the Aid of Government

4. Emperor Liu Heng Grants Benefits to the People of the Whole Realm

Annals of Emperor Xiao Wen, Part Ten of Annals, Volume Ten of Records of the Grand Historian

Annals of Emperor Wen (Liu Heng), Part Four of Annals, Volume Four of History of the Former Han Dynasty

Part One of Emperor Xiao Wen, Part Five of the Period of the Han Dynasty, Volume Thirteen of A Comprehensive Mirror for the Aid of Government

5. Emperor Liu Heng Suppresses the Rebellion Held by Liu Xing Jü, King of the State of Jibei

Annals of Emperor Xiao Wen, Part Ten of Annals, Volume Ten of Records of the Grand Historian

Annals of Emperor Wen (Liu Heng), Part Four of Annals, Volume Four of History of the Former Han Dynasty

Part One of Emperor Xiao Wen, Part Five of the Period of the Han Dynasty, Volume Thirteen of A Comprehensive Mirror for the Aid of Government

6. Emperor Liu Heng Orders to Arrest Zhou Bo, Marquis of Jiang, and Then Releases Him

Annals of Emperor Xiao Wen, Part Ten of Annals, Volume Ten of Records of the Grand Historian

Annals of Emperor Wen (Liu Heng), Part Four of Annals, Volume Four of History of the Former Han Dynasty

Biography of Zhou Bo, Marquis of Jiang, Part Twenty-Seven of Biography of Kings and Marquises, Volume Fifty-Seven of Records of the Grand Historian

Biographies of Zhang Liang, Chen Ping, Wang Ling, Zhou Bo (including his son Zhou Ya Fu), Part Ten of Biography, Volume Forty of History of the Former Han Dynasty

7. Emperor Liu Heng Prevents the Conspiracy of Rebellion Carried Out by Liu Chang, King of the State of Huainan

Annals of Emperor Xiao Wen, Part Ten of Annals, Volume Ten of Records of the Grand Historian

Annals of Emperor Wen (Liu Heng), Part Four of Annals, Volume Four of History of the Former Han Dynasty

Biography of King Li of the State of Huainan, Liu An, King of Huainan, King of the State of Hengshan, Part Fifty-Eight of Biography, Volume One Hundred and Eighteen of Records of the Grand Historian

Biographies of Zhang Cang, Zhou Cang, Ren Ao, Shentu Jia (including Wei Xian, Wei Xiang, Bing Ji, Huang Ba, Wei Xuan Cheng, Kuang Heng), Part Thirty-Six of Biography, Volume Ninety-Six of Records of the Grand Historian

Biographies of Zhang Cang, Zhou Cang, Zhao Yao, Ren Ao, Shentu Jia, Part Twelve of Biography, Volume Forty-Two, History of the Former Han Dynasty

Part Two of Emperor Xiao Wen, Part Six of the Period of the Han Dynasty, Volume Fourteen of A Comprehensive Mirror for the Aid of Government

8. Emperor Liu Heng Implements the Policy of Pacification through Marriage towards the Huns

Annals of Emperor Xiao Wen, Part Ten of Annals, Volume Ten of Records of the Grand Historian

Annals of Emperor Wen (Liu Heng), Part Four of Annals, Volume Four of History of the Former Han Dynasty

Biographies of the Huns, Part Fifty of Biography, Volume One Hundred and One of Records of the Grand Historian

Biographies of the Huns, Part One of Part Sixty-Four of Biography, Part One of Volume Ninety-Four of History of the Former Han Dynasty

Part Three of Emperor Xiao Wen, Part Seven of the Period of the Han Dynasty, Volume Fifteen of A Comprehensive Mirror for the Aid of Government

9. The Pass Away of Emperor Liu Heng

Annals of Emperor Wen (Liu Heng), Part Four of Annals, Volume Four of History of the Former Han Dynasty

Biographies of the Huns, Part Fifty of Biography, Volume One Hundred and One of Records of the Grand Historian

Part Three of Emperor Xiao Wen, Part Seven of the Period of the Han Dynasty, Volume Fifteen of A Comprehensive Mirror for the Aid of Government

Chapter Four: The Reign of Emperor Liu Qi

1. Liu Qi, the Crown Prince, Ascends the Throne of the Han Dynasty

Annals of Emperor Xiao Wen, Part Ten of Annals, Volume Ten of Records of the Grand Historian

Annals of Emperor Wen (Liu Heng), Part Four of Annals, Volume Four of History of the Former Han Dynasty

Annals of Emperor Xiao Jing, Part Eleven of Annals, Volume Eleven of Records of the Grand Historian

Annals of Emperor Jing (Liu Qi), Part Five of Annals, Volume Five of History of the Former Han Dynasty

Part Three of Emperor Xiao Wen, Part Seven of the Period of the Han Dynasty, Volume Fifteen of A Comprehensive Mirror for the Aid of Government

2. Emperor Liu Qi Suppresses the Rebellion of the Seven States

Annals of Emperor Xiao Jing, Part Eleven of Annals, Volume Eleven of Records of the Grand Historian

Annals of Emperor Jing (Liu Qi), Part Five of Annals, Volume Five of History of the Former Han Dynasty

Part Two of Emperor Xiao Jing, Part Eight of the Period of the Han Dynasty, Volume Sixteen of A Comprehensive Mirror for the Aid of Government

3. Emperor Liu Qi Makes His Son Liu Che the Crown Prince

Annals of Emperor Xiao Jing, Part Eleven of Annals, Volume Eleven of Records of the Grand Historian

Annals of Emperor Jing (Liu Qi), Part Five of Annals, Volume Five of History of the Former Han Dynasty

Part Two of Emperor Xiao Jing, Part Eight of the Period of the Han Dynasty, Volume Sixteen of A Comprehensive Mirror for the Aid of Government

4. Emperor Liu Qi Carries Out the Policy of Pacification through Marriage towards the Huns

Annals of Emperor Xiao Jing, Part Eleven of Annals, Volume Eleven of Records of the Grand Historian

Annals of Emperor Jing (Liu Qi), Part Five of Annals, Volume Five of History of the Former Han Dynasty

Part Two of Emperor Xiao Jing, Part Eight of the Period of the Han Dynasty, Volume Sixteen of A Comprehensive Mirror for the Aid of Government

5. The Pass Away of Emperor Liu Qi

Annals of Emperor Xiao Jing, Part Eleven of Annals, Volume Eleven of Records of the Grand Historian

Annals of Emperor Jing (Liu Qi), Part Five of Annals, Volume Five of History of the Former Han Dynasty

Part Two of Emperor Xiao Jing, Part Eight of the Period of the Han Dynasty, Volume Sixteen of A Comprehensive Mirror for the Aid of Government

Chapter Five: Under the Magnificent Reign of Emperor Liu Che

1. Liu Che, the Crown Prince, Ascends the Throne of the Han Dynasty

Annals of Emperor Xiao Jing, Part Eleven of Annals, Volume Eleven of Records of the Grand Historian

Annals of Emperor Jing (Liu Qi), Part Five of Annals, Volume Five of History of the Former Han Dynasty

Part Two of Emperor Xiao Jing, Part Eight of the Period of the Han Dynasty, Volume Sixteen of A Comprehensive Mirror for the Aid of Government

2. Emperor Liu Che Puts Scholars of Confucianism in Important Positions

Annals of Emperor Xiao Wu, Part Twelve of Annals, Volume

Twelve of Records of the Grand Historian

Annals of Emperor Wu (Liu Che), Part Six of Annals, Volume Six of History of the Former Han Dynasty

Biography of Dong Zhong Shu, Part Twenty-Six of Biography, Volume Twenty-Six, History of the Former Han Dynasty

First Part of Part One of Emperor Xiao Wu, Part Nine of the Period of the Han Dynasty, Volume Seventeen of A Comprehensive Mirror for the Aid of Government

3. Emperor Liu Che's Plan to Beat the Huns

Annals of Emperor Xiao Wu, Part Twelve of Annals, Volume Twelve of Records of the Grand Historian

Annals of Emperor Wu (Liu Che), Part Six of Annals, Volume Six of History of the Former Han Dynasty

Biography of Han An Guo, Part Forty-Eight of Biography, Volume One Hundred and Eight of Records of the Grand Historian

Biography of Li Guang, Part Forty-Nine of Biography, Volume One Hundred and Nine of Records of the Grand Historian

Biographies of Dou Ying, Tian Fen, Guan Fu, Han An Guo, Part Twenty-Two of Biography, Volume Fifty-Two, History of the Former Han Dynasty

First Part of Part One of Emperor Xiao Wu, Part Nine of the Period of the Han Dynasty, Volume Seventeen of A Comprehensive Mirror for the Aid of Government

4. Wei Qing Wins the First Victory over the Huns for the Han Dynasty

Annals of Emperor Xiao Wu, Part Twelve of Annals, Volume Twelve of Records of the Grand Historian

Annals of Emperor Wu (Liu Che), Part Six of Annals, Volume Six of History of the Former Han Dynasty

Biographies of Wei Qing, Huo Qu Bing (including Li Xi, Gongsun Ao, Li Ju, Zhang Ci Gong, Zhao Xin, Zhao Shi Qi, Guo Chang, Lu Bo De, Zhao Po Nu), Part Fifty-One of Biography, Volume One Hundred and Ten of Records of the Grand Historian

Biographies of Wei Qing, Huo Qu Bing (including Li Xi, Gongsun Ao, Li Ju, Zhang Ci Gong, Zhao Xin, Zhao Shi Qi, Guo Chang, Lu Bo De, Zhao Po Nu), Part Twenty-Five of Biography, Volume Fifty-Five, History of the Former Han Dynasty

Second Part of Part One of Emperor Xiao Wu, Part Ten of the Period of the Han Dynasty, Volume Eighteen of A Comprehensive Mirror for the Aid of Government

5. Emperor Liu Che Makes Wei Zi Fu Empress

Annals of Emperor Wu (Liu Che), Part Six of Annals, Volume Six of History of the Former Han Dynasty

First Part of Part One of Emperor Xiao Wu, Part Nine of the Period of the Han Dynasty, Volume Seventeen of A Comprehensive

Mirror for the Aid of Government

6.   Zhufu Yan's Advice to Emperor Liu Che to Be Moderate in the War against the Huns

Annals of Emperor Xiao Wu, Part Twelve of Annals, Volume Twelve of Records of the Grand Historian

Annals of Emperor Wu (Liu Che), Part Six of Annals, Volume Six of History of the Former Han Dynasty

Biographies of Yan Zhu, Zhu Mai Chen, Wuqiu Shou Wang, Zhu Fu Yan, Xu Yue, First Part of Part Thirty-Four of Biography, First Part of Volume Sixty-Four, History of the Former Han Dynasty

Second Part of Part One of Emperor Xiao Wu, Part Ten of the Period of the Han Dynasty, Volume Eighteen of A Comprehensive Mirror for the Aid of Government

7.   Emperor Liu Che Carries Out the Order of Expending Favors Suggested by Zhufu Yan

Biographies of Yan Zhu, Zhu Mai Chen, Wuqiu Shou Wang, Zhu Fu Yan, Xu Yue, First Part of Part Tirty-Four of Biography, First Part of Volume Sixty-Four, History of the Former Han Dynasty

Second Part of Part One of Emperor Xiao Wu, Part Ten of the Period of the Han Dynasty, Volume Eighteen of A Comprehensive Mirror for the Aid of Government

8.   Wei Qing Wins More Victories over the Huns

Biographies of Wei Qing, Huo Qu Bing (including Li Xi, Gongsun Ao, Li Ju, Zhang Ci Gong, Zhao Xin, Zhao Shi Qi, Guo Chang, Lu Bo De, Zhao Po Nu), Part Fifty-One of Biography, Volume One Hundred and Ten of Records of the Grand Historian

Biographies of Wei Qing, Huo Qu Bing (including Li Xi, Gongsun Ao, Li Ju, Zhang Ci Gong, Zhao Xin, Zhao Shi Qi, Guo Chang, Lu Bo De, Zhao Po Nu), Part Twenty-Five of Biography, Volume Fifty-Five, History of the Former Han Dynasty

Second Part of Part One of Emperor Xiao Wu, Part Ten of the Period of the Han Dynasty, Volume Eighteen of A Comprehensive Mirror for the Aid of Government

9.   Zhang Qian's Mission to the Western Regions and the Open Up of the Silk Road

Biographies of Zhang Qian, Li Guang Li, Part Thirty-One of Biography, Volume Sixty-One, History of the Former Han Dynasty

Part One of Biographies of the Western Region, Part One of Part Sixty-six of Biography, Part One of Volume Ninety-Six, History of the Former Han Dynasty

Part One of Biographies of the Western Region, Part One of Part Sixty-six of Biography, Part One of Volume Ninety-Six, History of the Former Han Dynasty

Second Part of Part One of Emperor Xiao Wu, Part Ten of the

Period of the Han Dynasty, Volume Eighteen of A Comprehensive
Mirror for the Aid of Government

10. Liu An, King of the State of Huainan, Secretly Plans to Rebel
Biography of King Li of the State of Huainan, Liu An, King of
Huainan, King of the State of Hengshan, Part Fifty-Eight of
Biography, Volume One Hundred and Eighteen of Records of the
Grand Historian
Biographies of King Li of the State of Huainan (Liu Chang), King
of the State of Hengshan (Liu Ci), King of the State of Jibei (Liu
Bo), Part Fourteen of Biography, Volume Forty-Four, History of
the Former Han Dynasty
First Part of Part Two of Emperor Xiao Wu, Part Eleven of the
Period of the Han Dynasty, Volume Nineteen of A Comprehensive
Mirror for the Aid of Government

11. Wei Qing Wins Still More Victories over the Huns
Annals of Emperor Wu (Liu Che), Part Six of Annals, Volume Six
of History of the Former Han Dynasty
Biographies of Wei Qing, Huo Qu Bing (including Li Xi, Gongsun
Ao, Li Ju, Zhang Ci Gong, Zhao Xin, Zhao Shi Qi, Guo Chang, Lu
Bo De, Zhao Po Nu), Part Fifty-One of Biography, Volume One
Hundred and Ten of Records of the Grand Historian
Biographies of Wei Qing, Huo Qu Bing (including Li Xi, Gongsun
Ao, Li Ju, Zhang Ci Gong, Zhao Xin, Zhao Shi Qi, Guo Chang,
Lu Bo De, Zhao Po Nu), Part Twenty-Five of Biography, Volume
Fifty-Five, History of the Former Han Dynasty
First Part of Part Two of Emperor Xiao Wu, Part Eleven of the
Period of the Han Dynasty, Volume Nineteen of A Comprehensive
Mirror for the Aid of Government

12. Huo Qu Bing Establishes Great Contributions in the Fighting
against the Huns
Biographies of Wei Qing, Huo Qu Bing (including Li Xi, Gongsun
Ao, Li Ju, Zhang Ci Gong, Zhao Xin, Zhao Shi Qi, Guo Chang, Lu
Bo De, Zhao Po Nu), Part Fifty-One of Biography, Volume One
Hundred and Ten of Records of the Grand Historian
Biographies of Wei Qing, Huo Qu Bing (including Li Xi, Gongsun
Ao, Li Ju, Zhang Ci Gong, Zhao Xin, Zhao Shi Qi, Guo Chang,
Lu Bo De, Zhao Po Nu), Part Twenty-Five of Biography, Volume
Fifty-Five, History of the Former Han Dynasty
First Part of Part Two of Emperor Xiao Wu, Part Eleven of the
Period of the Han Dynasty, Volume Nineteen of A Comprehensive
Mirror for the Aid of Government

13. Wei Qing and Huo Qu Bing Fight with the King of the Huns in
the Area to the North of Gobi Desert
Biographies of Wei Qing, Huo Qu Bing (including Li Xi, Gongsun
Ao, Li Ju, Zhang Ci Gong, Zhao Xin, Zhao Shi Qi, Guo Chang, Lu

Bo De, Zhao Po Nu), Part Fifty-One of Biography, Volume One
Hundred and Ten of Records of the Grand Historian

Biographies of Wei Qing, Huo Qu Bing (including Li Xi, Gongsun
Ao, Li Ju, Zhang Ci Gong, Zhao Xin, Zhao Shi Qi, Guo Chang,
Lu Bo De, Zhao Po Nu), Part Twenty-Five of Biography, Volume
Fifty-Five, History of the Former Han Dynasty

First Part of Part Two of Emperor Xiao Wu, Part Eleven of the
Period of the Han Dynasty, Volume Nineteen of A Comprehensive
Mirror for the Aid of Government

14. The Death of Huo Qu Bing

Biographies of Wei Qing, Huo Qu Bing (including Li Xi, Gongsun
Ao, Li Ju, Zhang Ci Gong, Zhao Xin, Zhao Shi Qi, Guo Chang, Lu
Bo De, Zhao Po Nu), Part Fifty-One of Biography, Volume One
Hundred and Ten of Records of the Grand Historian

Biographies of Wei Qing, Huo Qu Bing (including Li Xi, Gongsun
Ao, Li Ju, Zhang Ci Gong, Zhao Xin, Zhao Shi Qi, Guo Chang,
Lu Bo De, Zhao Po Nu), Part Twenty-Five of Biography, Volume
Fifty-Five, History of the Former Han Dynasty

Second Part of Part Two of Emperor Xiao Wu, Part Twelve of the
Period of the Han Dynasty, Volume Twenty of A Comprehensive
Mirror for the Aid of Government

15. Zhang Qian's Second Mission to the Western Region

Biographies of Zhang Qian, Li Guang Li, Part Thirty-One of
Biography, Volume Sixty-One, History of the Former Han
Dynasty

Second Part of Part Two of Emperor Xiao Wu, Part Twelve of the
Period of the Han Dynasty, Volume Twenty of A Comprehensive
Mirror for the Aid of Government

16. Emperor Liu Che and the Necromancers

Annals of Emperor Xiao Wu, Part Twelve of Annals, Volume
Twelve of Records of the Grand Historian

Annals of Emperor Wu (Liu Che), Part Six of Annals, Volume Six
of History of the Former Han Dynasty

First Part of Part Two of Emperor Xiao Wu, Part Eleven of the
Period of the Han Dynasty, Volume Nineteen of A Comprehensive
Mirror for the Aid of Government

Second Part of Part Two of Emperor Xiao Wu, Part Twelve of the
Period of the Han Dynasty, Volume Twenty of A Comprehensive
Mirror for the Aid of Government

17. The Pacification of the State of Nanyue

Biographies of Minority Nationalities in the Southwest Part
of China, the Kings of the State of Nanyue, Kings of Minyue,
Cojoseon, Part Sixty-Five of Biography, Volume Ninety-Five, the
Former Han Dynasty

Biographies of King Yu Tuo, King of the State of Nanyue, Part

Fifty-Three of Biography, Volume One Hundred and Thirteen of Records of the Grand Historian

Second Part of Part Two of Emperor Xiao Wu, Part Twelve of the Period of the Han Dynasty, Volume Twenty of A Comprehensive Mirror for the Aid of Government

18. The Rebellion Held by Zou Yu Shan, King of the State of Dongyue

Biographies of Kings of the State of Dongyue, Part Fifty-Four of Biography, Volume One Hundred and Fourteen of Records of the Grand Historian

Biographies of Minority Nationalities in the Southwest Part of China, the Kings of the State of Nanyue, Kings of Minyue, Cojoseon, Part Sixty-Five of Biography, Volume Ninety-Five, the Former Han Dynasty

Second Part of Part Two of Emperor Xiao Wu, Part Twelve of the Period of the Han Dynasty, Volume Twenty of A Comprehensive Mirror for the Aid of Government

19. Emperor Liu Che Worships Heaven and Earth on Mount Tai

Annals of Emperor Xiao Wu, Part Twelve of Annals, Volume Twelve of Records of the Grand Historian

Annals of Emperor Wu (Liu Che), Part Six of Annals, Volume Six of History of the Former Han Dynasty

Book of Offering Sacrifices to Heaven and Earth, Part Six of Eight Books, Volume Twenty-Eight of Records of the Grand Historian

Second Part of Part Two of Emperor Xiao Wu, Part Twelve of the Period of the Han Dynasty, Volume Twenty of A Comprehensive Mirror for the Aid of Government

20. The Expedition against Gojoseon

Biographies of Kings of Cojoseon, Part Fifty-Five of Biography, Volume One Hundred and Fifteen of Records of the Grand Historian

Biographies of Minority Nationalities in the Southwest Part of China, the Kings of the State of Nanyue, Kings of Minyue, Cojoseon, Part Sixty-Five of Biography, Volume Ninety-Five, the Former Han Dynasty

First Part of Part Three of Emperor Xiao Wu, Part Thirteen of the Period of the Han Dynasty, Volume Twenty-One of A Comprehensive Mirror for the Aid of Government

21. Princess Liu Xi Jun and Princess Liu Jie You Are Married to the Kings of the State of Wusun

Part Two of Biographies of the Western Region, Part Two of Part Sixty-Six of Biography, Part Two of Volume Ninety-Six, History of the Former Han Dynasty

First Part of Part Three of Emperor Xiao Wu, Part Thirteen of the Period of the Han Dynasty, Volume Twenty-One of A Comprehensive Mirror for the Aid of Government

Fifteen of Biography, Volume Forty-Five, History of the Former Han Dynasty

Second Part of Part Three of Emperor Xiao Wu, Part Fourteen of the Period of the Han Dynasty, Volume Twenty-Two of A Comprehensive Mirror for the Aid of Government

29. The Case of Witch craft

Annals of Emperor Wu (Liu Che), Part Six of Annals, Volume Six of History of the Former Han Dynasty

Biographies of Crown Prince Lei (Liu Ju), King Huai of State of Qi, King Ci of State of Yan (Liu Qie), King Li of State of Guangling (Liu Xu), King Ai of State of Changyi (Liu Bo), Part Thirty-Three of Biography (Biographies of the Five Sons of Emperor Wu) Volume Sixty-Three, History of the Former Han Dynasty

Biographies of Tong, Wu Pi, Jiang Chong, Xi Fu Gong, Part Fifteen of Biography, Volume Forty-Five, History of the Former Han Dynasty

Biographies of Gongsun He (including his son Gongsun Jing Sheng), Liu Qu Mao, Che Qian Qiu, Wang Xin, Yang Cang (including his son Yang Yun), Cai Yi, Chen Wan Nian (including his son Chen Cheng), Zheng Hung, Part Thirty-Six of Biography, Volume Sixty-Six, History of the Former Han Dynasty

Second Part of Part Three of Emperor Xiao Wu, Part Fourteen of the Period of the Han Dynasty, Volume Twenty-Two of A Comprehensive Mirror for the Aid of Government

30. Li Guang Li Is Defeated and Surrenders to the Huns

Biographies of Zhang Qian, Li Guang Li, Part Thirty-One of Biography, Volume Sixty-One, History of the Former Han Dynasty

Second Part of Part Three of Emperor Xiao Wu, Part Fourteen of the Period of the Han Dynasty, Volume Twenty-Two of A Comprehensive Mirror for the Aid of Government

31. Jinmidi Protects Emperor Liu Che

Biographies of Huo Guang, Jinmidi, Part Thirty-Eight of Biography, Volume Sixty-Eight, History of the Former Han Dynasty

Second Part of Part Three of Emperor Xiao Wu, Part Fourteen of the Period of the Han Dynasty, Volume Twenty-Two of A Comprehensive Mirror for the Aid of Government

32. Emperor Liu Che Entrusts His Son Liu Fu Ling to Huo Guang's Care

Annals of Emperor Wu (Liu Che), Part Six of Annals, Volume Six of History of the Former Han Dynasty

Biographies of Huo Guang, Jinmidi, Part Thirty-Eight of Biography, Volume Sixty-Eight, History of the Former Han Dynasty

Second Part of Part Three of Emperor Xiao Wu, Part Fourteen of the Period of the Han Dynasty, Volume Twenty-Two of A Comprehensive Mirror for the Aid of Government

33. The Pass-away of Emperor Liu Che
Annals of Emperor Wu (Liu Che), Part Six of Annals, Volume Six of History of the Former Han Dynasty
Second Part of Part Three of Emperor Xiao Wu, Part Fourteen of the Period of the Han Dynasty, Volume Twenty-Two of A Comprehensive Mirror for the Aid of Government

Printed in the United States
By Bookmasters